Date Due

2 69			
OCT 9 70			
DEC - 1 1983			
DEC 1 1 1984			
DEC - 1 1986			

17-1

ALLIED INTERVENTION IN RUSSIA

ALLIED INTERVENTION
IN RUSSIA 1918–1919

And the Part Played by Canada

JOHN SWETTENHAM

THE RYERSON PRESS—TORONTO

PRINTED IN GREAT BRITAIN
in 11-point Granjon type by
BILLING & SONS LTD
GUILDFORD
AND LONDON

PREFACE

The origin of this book lies in three parts of a chapter, 'Outside the Corps', which the author drafted for Colonel G. W. L. Nicholson's *Canadian Expeditionary Force, 1914–1919*, the Official History of the Canadian Army in the First World War. These described very briefly (as was necessary in a one volume history of more than four years of war) the operations of Canadian troops in South Russia, North Russia and Siberia in 1918 and 1919.

It was found, when reviewing the material available, that no official British or American history of the intervention had as yet appeared. There were many published works on the Russian Civil War and on the course of intervention in the individual spheres but very little had been written on Allied intervention in Russia as a whole. This book, then, is primarily about the intervention in the three main theatres. It has been written against the double background of the issues and events of the Russian Civil War and of the international intrigues and rivalries of the erstwhile Allies, so that the moves and counter-moves can be seen in a broad perspective.

The subject matter is both an interesting and an important story. Undoubtedly one of the momentous events of the century has been the victory of Bolshevism in Russia and its subsequent spread into various parts of the world. The Allied intervention, according to Churchill, came near to reversing the results of the Bolshevik Revolution and thereby changing the course of modern history. It did not do so and the reasons for its failure have been described and analysed.

No apology is made for the detailed treatment of Canadian operations. Canadian troops were integrated with British troops in South Russia and with American and British troops in the north; in Siberia the British Empire force was under Canadian command. The Canadian story is thus closely linked with that of the other interventionist powers, and in addition an interesting light is thrown on Canada's growing sovereignty at that time.

A large part of the research has been done at the Dominion Public Archives where the author was given the privilege of examining the papers of Sir Robert Borden—Prime Minister of Canada during the intervention period—and other pertinent documents. The Public Archives Record Centre contained the war diaries; in addition, it housed the papers of General Elmsley who commanded the Empire's Siberian Force. The Elmsley Papers were of especial value as included in them were the Canadian copies of British documents for this period which are not yet open in London.

A number of persons assisted in the writing of the book and to all of them the author is profoundly grateful.

First among them is Professor J. S. Moir, late of Carleton University and now of Scarborough College, who commented in detail on every chapter. It is largely due to Dr Moir's encouragement that the manuscript was completed.

A debt of gratitude is owed to Captain John Hundevad, Editor-in-Chief of the Canadian *Legionary*, who served at Murmansk and who placed his excellent 'Saga of the North' at the author's disposal as well as other material which he has accumulated for many years.

Special thanks are due to the members of the Army Historical Section. Lieutenant-Colonel H. F. Wood, Captain D. P. Morton, and Dr. J. Mackay Hitsman all read parts of the manuscript and offered useful criticism. Captain F. R. McGuire was good enough to edit the completed draft and to work unstintedly on the references; his contribution is particularly acknowledged.

To these names are added those of Mr Henry Logan of the Public Archives Record Centre who was indefatigable in hunting out material; Mr Sidney Wallingford for his accurate typing of the preliminary draft; and Mr Harry Ellwand who drew the maps.

The author alone is responsible for the opinions expressed and for any errors or omissions that the book may contain.

J. A. S.

ACKNOWLEDGEMENTS

The Author and Publishers would like to thank the following for permission to reproduce material quoted in this book.

EDWARD ARNOLD LTD. for permission to quote from *The Adventures of Dunsterforce* by Major-General L. C. Dunsterville, London, 1920

JONATHAN CAPE LTD. for permission to quote from *America's Siberian Adventure* by William S. Graves, London, 1931

CONSTABLE & Co. LTD. for permission to quote from *Archangel, 1918–1919* by Edmund Ironside, London, 1953

HARPER & ROW INC. for permission to quote from *The Ignorant Armies* by E. M. Halliday, London, Weidenfeld & Nicolson, 1961, and *The Russian Revolution* by Alan Moorehead, London, Collins: Hamish Hamilton, 1958

RUPERT HART-DAVIS LTD for permission to quote from *The Fate of Admiral Kolchak* by Peter Fleming, London, 1963

HODDER & STOUGHTON LTD. for permission to quote from *The Murmansk Venture* by Major-General Sir C. Maynard, London, 1928

THE MACMILLAN COMPANY for permission to quote from *The Russian Revolution* by W. H. Chamberlin, New York, 1936, and *The White Armies of Russia* by George Stewart, New York, 1933

PROFESSOR CLARENCE A. MANNING for permission to quote from *The Siberian Fiasco* by Clarence A. Manning, New York, Library Publishers, Inc., 1952

MRS RACHEL BAKER NAPIER for permission to quote from *Woodrow Wilson, Life and Letters* by Ray Stannard Baker, New York, Doubleday; London, Heinemann, 1927–1929

ODHAMS BOOKS LTD. AND CHARLES SCRIBNER'S SONS for permission to quote from *The Aftermath* by Winston S. Churchill, London, 1929

PRINCETON UNIVERSITY PRESS for permission to quote from *Intervention at Archangel* by Leonid I. Strakhovsky, New York, 1944, and *The Siberian Intervention* by John Albert White, New York, 1950

PUTNAM & Co. LTD. for permission to quote from *Memoirs of a British Agent* by Robert Bruce Lockhart, London, 1961

D. VAN NOSTRAND Co. INC. for permission to quote from *Modern Far Eastern International Relations* by MacNair and Lach, Princeton, N.J., 1950

YALE UNIVERSITY PRESS for permission to quote from *The Rise of Russia in Asia* by David J. Dallin, London, Hollis & Carter, 1950

CONTENTS

CONTENTS

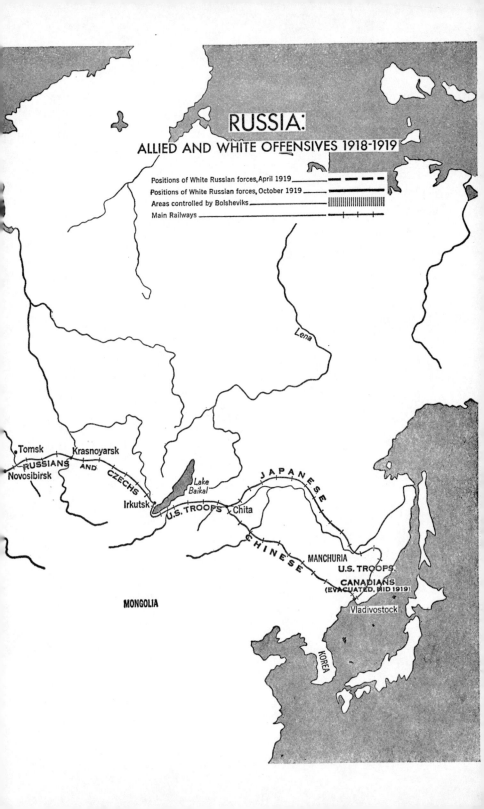

RUSSIA:
ALLIED AND WHITE OFFENSIVES 1918-1919

Positions of White Russian forces, April 1919 _____
Positions of White Russian forces, October 1919 _____
Areas controlled by Bolsheviks _____
Main Railways _____

Lena

•Tomsk   Krasnoyarsk
RUSSIANS AND CZECHS
Novosibirsk

Irkutsk   *Lake Baikal*   U.S. TROOPS   •Chita

JAPANESE

CHINESE   MANCHURIA
U.S. TROOPS.
CANADIANS
(EVACUATED, MID 1919)
Vladivostock•

MONGOLIA

KOREA

CHAPTER I

WHY INTERVENTION
WAS NECESSARY

THE TWO REVOLUTIONS

In 1917 news of the March Revolution in Petrograd and the abdication of the Czar astounded the Allied capitals. Of immediate concern to the Allies was whether the new authority would continue hostilities against the Central Powers.

For two and a half years, Russia had fought loyally and steadfastly in support of France, and had held on her front more than half the total number of enemy divisions; it would be disastrous for the British and French—on whom the concentration of German troops would mainly fall—if the Eastern Front should collapse and permit the Central Powers to achieve overwhelming superiority against them.

The Provisional Government of liberal and radical statesmen which succeeded the Czarist autocracy, however, gave ground for optimism. Continued loyalty to the Allies was assured and the war would be fought to a victorious conclusion. The principal Allied Powers thereupon recognized the new Russian government.

Had the Provisional Government been the sole authority in Russia, it might have been possible to carry out the commitment. But two rival authorities with divergent policies shared the power, one the government and the other the Soviet (Council) of Soldiers' and Workmen's Deputies at Petrograd, better known as the Petrograd Soviet.

The Petrograd Soviet was prominent in the revolution but maintained a separate existence and policy from the Provisional Government. It directly controlled the post offices, the State Bank, the treasury, and the railway stations of Petrograd. The control of the army was, however, the real issue at stake between the government and its rival, and here the Soviet seized the initiative. On the day the Provisional Government was formed, the Soviet broadcast its notorious Order No. 1 placing all servicemen under the command of the

Soviet, through their own committees, in all political matters. The new government, unsure both of itself and of the reaction of the men to any change, accepted the order but hoped that nothing would come of it.

The two groups hammered out their rival programmes, neither really knowing what to do with the newly won liberty. Each was against what the Czar had stood for, and needed the other. The Soviet sought shelter behind a government which was assuming all responsibility; the government tolerated the Soviet because it was representative of a large body of opinion and, more important, exercised real control over the armed forces. Thus, surrounded by the fog of mutual hostility, a partial compromise existed.

The result for the armed forces was, however, fatal. The Soviet, in no way hampered by responsibility, criticized, harangued, and appealed; through Soldiers' and Sailors' Councils it weakened still further a discipline already shaken by the abolition of saluting and the death penalty. Every order became a debating point. Mutinous soldiers, with deserters, crowded trains on the way back from the front, so that armies crumbled away and disorderly elements were added to the overcrowded centres of population. Disruptive movements, confusion and agitation—fed by the Petrograd Soviet through its offshoot 'soviets'—spread throughout the land. Administration at all levels functioned badly or completely broke down. Supplies, whether for the front or for civilians, were scarce.

Meanwhile, like vultures awaiting the demise, Germans, Austrians and Turks were arrayed along the front in readiness to devour the Russian carcass. They were too wary to launch an all-out offensive that might weld the disunited forces of Russia once more into a nation.

In June, against this unlikely background, the Provisional Government determined on an offensive that would, it was hoped, restore discipline and morale amongst the troops. Kerensky, a more moderate member of the Soviet, had thrown in his lot with the government, and in the middle of May had been appointed Minister of War. He attacked his new tasks vigorously. His lightning campaign had effect, not only on the troops, but also in the soviet ranks, sections of which began to wonder if anything but victory in the field could safeguard the revolution.

Thus the Russian armies made their last attempt at a serious offensive. The Commander-in-Chief, Alexeiev, was dismissed early in June, and he was succeeded by Brussilov, who had mounted a successful offensive against the Germans in the summer of 1916. Brussilov personally supervised every detail of the forthcoming operations. Kornilov and Kaledin, both seasoned generals, commanded two of the Russian armies. Kerensky, dressed in the uniform of a private soldier, was with the troops inspiring them with some of his own zeal.

The time was opportune for attack. The Central Powers had made up their minds that for the moment there was no danger of a Russian offensive. Germany, though still maintaining seventy-six divisions in the East, had derived some benefit from the revolution by replacing the fittest units with those in need of recuperation from the West. Austria had already transferred divisions and artillery to the Italian front. As a result of this the whole line from the Baltic to the Carpathians was not held in its former strength.

Brussilov selected Galicia as the scene of operations, and, opposite Lemberg, assembled in three armies the best fighting material at his disposal—the cream of the Finnish, Caucasian and Siberian regiments and the best of the Cossack cavalry. But the Russian commander was fully aware that his first bid must succeed, for he could not hope to find reserves of the same quality.

The Russian blow, aimed at the junction of the German and Austrian groups, fell on 1st July after a two-day artillery preparation. It met with instant success. The Austrian line broke; by the evening of the second day, some 18,000 prisoners were in Russian hands. On 3rd and 4th July the enemy counter-attacked, though feebly, for reserves had not yet arrived. But the Austro-German communications, unlike those of the Russians (which shared in the general domestic confusion), were well organized and capable of reinforcing the front speedily. The impetus of the Russian attack, however, was not yet blunted despite two hastily committed German divisions; the advance continued until the 11th when the high-water mark of success was reached. Lemberg was in danger of being outflanked. A further 10,000 prisoners had fallen to the Russians. But now it was clear that Brussilov's picked troops were exhausted, and he had no reserves on which he could rely. For a week longer his gallant armies struggled on in swaying battles; but on the 16th, in the face of mounting German force, they began to give ground. The example they had given was not the signal for a resurgence of Russian valour —the canker of indiscipline had already eaten far too deeply.

The weight of German reserves made itself felt and the trembling Russian pendulum swung backwards to advance no more. By the evening of 20th July the Russians were no longer wavering; their troops were in full retreat. In a week the Germans had advanced more than thirty miles—Tarnapol fell on Monday the 24th without a struggle—and by the end of the month the Russians had fallen back within their own borders. Although no longer actively pursued, the disorderly flight of their armies was marked by burning, rape, and pillage. All pointed to low morale and a complete absence of discipline.

The Russian failure was not lost upon the Western Allies. But Russia had not capitulated; enemy troops still manned the Eastern Front in strength. Furthermore, the United States had now entered the war and although it would take time to train and ship American troops to the Western Front, the balance of force lay in the Allies' favour—provided Russia could continue to hold out.

In Russia there were two main consequences. Kerensky became Prime Minister on 20th July, retaining the Ministry for War. Eleven days later, Kornilov, whose Eighth Army had done well in this last desperate throw, replaced Brussilov as Commander-in-Chief.

Kerensky himself was not popular. There were many who had supported the revolution in the beginning who by now were completely disillusioned and looked back on the past with regret. They sought a dictator, a strong man who could save the country from the prevailing chaos. Kerensky—too much of a Socialist, too eloquent, too emotional, too lacking in decision—would not do. To many, the new Commander-in-Chief appeared to be the man; and this belief was strengthened with Kornilov's advocacy of the revival of discipline. The folly of the revolutionaries had destroyed the army; only discipline could recreate it. There must be discipline behind the lines as well, for already the output of munitions had been cut by more than half. Without discipline, Russia would perish. These were plain words which made a good deal of sense when the enemy was already massed on Russia's borders.

At the time of his appointment, it is doubtful if Kornilov had any political ambitions whatsoever, but he was naïve and completely inexperienced in politics so that the flattery of public men of conservative sentiments, who urged him forward as the one hope of Russia, was not without effect. An undercurrent of suspicion began to poison Kerensky's mind, strengthened by Kornilov's first overt move on 20th August when he transferred the 3rd Cavalry Corps to within striking distance of Petrograd and Moscow.

By the end of August, Kornilov had indeed worked out plans for a military *coup*. On the pretext of disorders in Petrograd, which it was confidently expected would follow the stricter measures for restoring discipline in the army which the government would soon proclaim, three cavalry divisions were to envelop and seize the capital from the south. Orders to issue hand-grenades to these formations were given on 3rd September. The same day marked the fall of the great city of Riga, for meanwhile the Germans were acting.

The German Commander, Ludendorff, had already made plans for a great offensive in the West with the aid of troops now on the Eastern Front. He wished to test new tactical methods before that time on the moribund Russian forces in the northern sector. The operation was entrusted to von Hutier, an apostle of infiltration, who moved forward in the last week of August to meet with immediate success. By 29th August Hutier was on the river Dvina, ten miles south of the Latvian port of Riga, while German warships entered the Gulf of Riga from the Baltic Sea. Three days later the river had been crossed, and on the following day the Dvinsk railway was cut. The defences of Riga were turned on the south-east; and on 3rd September the Russian Twelfth Army evacuated the city, falling back north-eastward along the coast on the road to Petrograd. Alexeiev, hastily called back to deal with the situation, succeeded in establishing a front some seventy miles from Riga; but the Germans, having secured spacious winter billets and the port and Gulf of Riga for their navy, did not pursue farther. Russia was ripe to fall without outside interference, and there seemed no point in wasting men and munitions, needed in the West, in an eastern winter campaign which might only delay the process of Russia's collapse.

Kerensky feared the reaction of the capital to this new defeat, and in his dilemma stretched out a hand to Kornilov by requesting on 5th September a cavalry corps to enforce martial law in Petrograd, and to defend the Provisional Government. He specified however that General Krimov, the commander of the 3rd Cavalry Corps, should not command the expedition, and that the Savage Division (formed from Circassian tribesmen) should not be included. Kornilov was jubilant. His scheme was being forwarded at the invitation of the government, and in his exuberance he naïvely revealed to an associate of the Prime Minister his conviction that the Commander-in-Chief, whoever he might be, should become President of a Council of National Defence, with Kerensky as Vice-President. He did not change his original dispositions, and retained Krimov and the Savage Division. Indeed, it might be argued that, with the Germans on the road to Petrograd, Kornilov was right to waste no time and to use the troops he had in readiness.

Kerensky was informed of Kornilov's convictions on the 8th. His recent suspicions must have been instantly confirmed, especially when he learned that, despite his specific instructions, the 3rd Cavalry Corps, led by Krimov and including the Savage Division, was already on the march. His vanity piqued, Kerensky decided to crush Kornilov, but in so doing he crushed himself.

At four in the morning of the 9th, Kerensky convoked a Cabinet session, at which he obtained unlimited powers of dealing with what he termed an emergency. Some measure of Kornilov's popularity may be judged from the fact that the liberal members of the cabinet all resigned. A message of dismissal to Kornilov, temporarily appointing General Lukomsky in his place, followed the meeting. Kornilov refused to be dismissed. Lukomsky refused to take over, and the commanders of the four Russian fronts all supported Kornilov, but this was of little significance when troops no longer obeyed orders and where ordinary army discipline did not prevail. In fact, both Kerensky and Kornilov issued orders as if they had great forces ready to do their bidding—orders which in fact disappeared into a void. The real power lay with the Petrograd Soviet and the soldiers themselves, and there Kerensky finally looked for his salvation. Both decided against Kornilov and from that moment on his *coup* was doomed. His every move was sabotaged. Men poured out of factories and barracks to defend the city; railway workers destroyed the tracks on the line of Krimov's advance; and exchange operators blocked Kornilov's messages to formations. On the night of the 9th, the 3rd Cavalry Corps, halfway to Petrograd, abandoned the operation and turned docilely to the Soviet for instructions. The end was now merely a matter of time. On 12th September Krimov, seized by his own soldiers and handed over to the Government, committed suicide. Kerensky himself took over the post of Commander-in-Chief and ordered Alexeiev, his newly appointed Chief of Staff, to arrest Kornilov—which he did next day. Russia was proclaimed a republic, with Kerensky as its head. By the 18th Alexeiev had resigned and other generals who had supported Kornilov were dismissed or imprisoned. It seemed that Kerensky had emerged triumphant, but it was an empty triumph. With Kornilov's failure the hopes of all moderate men in Russia were finally extinguished. The event of most significance in the whole abortive affair was the stretching-out of greedy Bolshevik hands for arms released for the defence of the capital from the Petrograd arsenals. The Bolsheviks armed, the scene was set and the followers of Lenin were almost ready to seize the reins of power.

Lenin, the leader of the Bolsheviks, had gained in authority in Russia since his return from exile in Switzerland in April 1917. Conditions in Russia following the revolution, he instinctively realized, were favourable for the application of his Marxist theories on an unprecedented scale. His programme at least was clear : to attack the Provisional Government savagely and ruthlessly, and to sue for peace with the Central Powers. The Bolshevik party, alone in Russia, offered a firm course of action from which it never wavered. 'Bread, Peace, and Freedom' was a powerful slogan very close to the feelings of the irresponsible masses, who, still in a rebellious mood against authority, were sick of the war and wanted nothing better than freedom to seize the land and to share the wealth of capitalists. Destruction and loot were much more attractive than helping to build up law and order once again.

The fortunes of the Bolsheviks suffered as a result of an abortive, Bolshevik-inspired outbreak which took place on 16th July (the day on which the German counter-attack began at the front) in Petrograd. They were not yet ready and were thus reluctant to stake all on a grab for power. The government was not unseated. Worse for the Bolsheviks, Kerensky released a dossier offering proof that Lenin was a German agent. It seemed to be true. The German onslaught, coinciding so nicely with the Bolshevik outbreak, was redolent of collusion. Lenin's return from Switzerland in a German train was remembered. And, as further proof in the eyes of the masses, Lenin did not wait to face the music when all this burst around his head. Instead, he fled the country leaving his co-worker Trotsky and others to be flung into jail. The government's revelation spelled the doom of the rising. The printing-office of the Bolshevik newspaper *Pravda* was smashed, hostile crowds demanded reprisals, and all across the country Bolsheviks were labelled German agents. A wave of repression followed.

But in September, when armed Bolsheviks supported the Soviet in the defence of Petrograd against Kornilov, the wheel had turned full circle. No longer were they suspect. The real enemies in the eyes of the people were the Czarist generals who, far from wanting peace, were symbols of everything that was reactionary in Russia. Now it was not the Bolsheviks but 'monarchists' and officers who were hunted off the streets.

On 12th September, when the anti-Kornilov feeling was at its height, the swing towards the Bolsheviks suddenly became apparent: by 279 votes to 115 the Petrograd Soviet passed a Bolshevik resolution that Russia should be declared a republic; that the government should be completely socialist; that the land should be given to the peasant soviets; that the workers should control industry; and finally that peace should be concluded immediately. Here was the whole Bolshevik programme in a nutshell. Pressure was exerted on Kerensky to bring this about; the Prime Minister allowed himself to be blown with the wind to the extent of proclaiming a republic. He made other concessions, notably that of the shelving of Kornilov's programme for restoring discipline in the army, and the freeing of Trotsky and the other Bolshevik leaders.

The Bolsheviks were not slow to exploit this upswing in their favour. On 22nd September, five days after his release, Trotsky managed to introduce the issue of new elections for the presidium into the Soviet, a side-issue of which was a vote of confidence in Kerensky who was still formally a member; the latter was anything but popular among the rank-and-file members, whose votes decided the issue. The Bolsheviks won a decisive victory, and from that moment the Petrograd Soviet was in their hands. Trotsky was elected president on 8th October, from which vantage point he was able to bring all the Soviet's influence with the armed forces over to the side of the Bolsheviks. The Soviet's support of Kerensky was withdrawn. At the end of September Bolsheviks also dominated the Moscow Soviet, as they later did other centres in the Urals and as far distant as Siberia.

The time for action had now come. From Finland, Lenin threw the whole weight of his authority on the side of armed insurrection and the seizure of power. On 23rd October and again on the 29th the disguised leader smuggled himself into the Russian capital to meet with the Party Central Committee and to convince the waverers; this he managed to do.

In Petrograd, practically the only armed force on which the

government could rely was provided by the Institute of Military Cadets. Against this Trotsky, who besides being chairman of the Soviet was also chairman of the Military Revolutionary Committee, had forces of workers—the 'Red Guard'—who had been armed at the time of the Kornilov affair and who had drilled and trained ever since. Though a crude and amateurish force, the Red Guard was considered effective enough to overcome the feeble opposition which it might encounter. There were two units of the garrison, however, which caused concern. Cyclists and gunners occupied the Fortress of Peter and Paul, situated strategically on an island in the river Neva. The guns of this place commanded the Winter Palace, and its arsenal would materially affect either side in a struggle for power. These units, unlike the others, had not come over to the side of the Military Revolutionary Committee.

The Bolsheviks contemplated the use of force, but this proved unnecessary. On the afternoon of Monday, 5th November, Trotsky visited the fortress to see what he could do. He made his way to where he could see across the green waters of the Neva river, high above the white walls of the fortress, the pitiless, agonizingly sharp Peter and Paul spire looming in cold detachment against the sky. This place, which seemed so remote, he knew to be the key to Petrograd. When he arrived, a soldiers' meeting was in progress which he addressed. The garrison succumbed to his appeals. Without a struggle a principal stronghold of the Provisional Government fell to the Bolsheviks, and the arsenal yielded up its weapons to the insurrectionists.

On the night of the 6th, the Bolsheviks took the offensive. Trotsky's military *coup* in the capital, as so often is the case when the army co-operates, was accomplished with ease and little bloodshed. Resistance put up by cadets, a few Cossacks, and a women's battalion, was soon overcome. At one o'clock on the morning of the 8th, Red Guards penetrated the inner rooms of the Winter Palace where the Provisional Government was in session, captured the ministers and hustled them off to the dungeons of Peter and Paul.

Kerensky, who had left Petrograd to rally troops, managed to raise a force of Cossacks which reached Tsarskoe Syelo on the 9th. With a few regiments of infantry it could probably have entered the capital. No regiments came forward and the Cossacks declared they could go no farther without infantry. But on the 12th, the Cossacks moved forward to attack the Red Forces which had massed on high ground outside Petrograd. The Reds displayed the will and the capacity to fight, and the Cossacks fell back on Gatchina. There, undermined by Bolshevik propaganda, they were persuaded to abandon hostilities and even to deliver up Kerensky. But Kerensky was gone. Disguised as a Serbian soldier, he fled to Murmansk and was soon to leave Russia.

On 15th November Moscow, too, passed into Bolshevik hands when government forces in the Kremlin surrendered. In a little over a week a few indomitable men, a handful viewed in terms of the immense population of Russia—there were certainly not more than 240,000 members of the Bolshevik party—had by seizure of two cities gained control of an empire.

Peoples' reaction in the rest of Russia, however, could not be immediately established. Ten days after the fall of Moscow elections for the Constituent Assembly began. Lenin had not the slightest shred of legal authority to justify his assumption of power: the country had not elected him. Perhaps he hoped by means of elections to remove this anomaly, or perhaps it was to justify in the eyes of the masses the slogan, 'Long live the Constituent Assembly', with which the Bolsheviks had risen against Kerensky. Whatever his reasons, elections were permitted; and the results were startling. Of the total votes cast throughout Russia, only some 25 per cent were for the Bolsheviks. The Social Revolutionaries, with nearly 60 per cent, were the leading party. Liberals and conservatives polled about 13 per cent, while the Mensheviks had almost disappeared. Suddenly the Bolsheviks discovered that they had no faith in freely elected parliaments after all. The slogan of the day became 'Down with the Constituent Assembly!'

Not until January 18, 1918, was the Assembly allowed to meet, and then it was broken up by armed Bolsheviks. The next day, the Executive Committee of the Congress of Soviets passed a resolution dissolving the assembly; guards were posted to prevent any of the deputies from returning. It never met again. 'The simple, open, brutal breaking-up of the Constituent Assembly', Trotsky wrote later, 'dealt formal democracy a finishing stroke from which it has never recovered.'* Power, after its seizure during November, was firmly grasped by the self-elected Council of People's Commissars, never to be relinquished.

In these early days the position of the Bolsheviks was extremely

---

* Alan Moorehead, *The Russian Revolution* (New York, 1958), 269.

precarious. Haste was necessary to consolidate the new government before the inevitable reaction set in, for Lenin still remembered the ominous results of the November elections. An early step was the re-establishment of secret police so necessary to a tyranny; the old Okhrana had gone with the Czar. Dzerzhinsky, a Polish Bolshevik, was given the job of forming the Cheka whose task would be the extermination of political rivals and the enforcement of Lenin's decrees. These decrees thrust the Marxist code on Russia as the law, uprooting and overturning every accepted social institution. Church lands were confiscated and religious teaching in schools was forbidden; the state religion was now Leninism. Banks and the merchant marine were nationalized. Industries which refused to accept workers' control were taken over by the state; strikes were to be in future an act of treason. The Bolsheviks annulled all debts of the Russian government, and abolished the stock market. As for individual rights, they forbade private ownership of land and inheritance of any property; men and women were declared equal, and could obtain divorce by merely asking. All privately owned gold was declared the property of the state.

In other fields the Soviet Government displayed a further capacity for innovation. It revised the Russian alphabet and westernized the Julian calendar by moving it ahead thirteen days. Petrograd, exposed to attack and seething with unrest, was no longer to be the capital. The move to Moscow took place after the Treaty of Brest-Litovsk, in March 1918.

And what of the attitude of Russia as a whole? Petrograd and Moscow had fallen; but there still remained an area equivalent to one-sixth of the earth's surface, with a population of about 175 million, which might not submit to domination by a quarter of a million Bolsheviks. News of the *coup* had spread through Russia proper and the dependent states, and the Bolshevik leaders waited in a fever of impatience for signs of its reception throughout these lands. Thanks to poor communications and the vast distances involved, a month passed before the issue had resolved itself. In central and northern Russia the Bolshevik seizure of power encountered little serious or sustained resistance. The story was the same in Siberia. In the Caucasus, Baku and Tiflis (the latter being the capital of Georgia where nationalistic Mensheviks predominated) took opposite sides. In the Kiev area of the Ukraine a government hostile to Lenin arose. In Rostov, capital of the Don Cossack Territory, and in Ekaterinodar

and Orenburg (capitals of the Kuban and Orenburg Cossack Territories), independence from Moscow was proclaimed. Indeed, a volunteer army was assembling in the Don area to fight the Bolsheviks.
The Baltic States, Finland, and Poland, then occupied by German
troops, were bent on independence.

In the main, the Bolsheviks could be satisfied. Subsequent events
proved that the new régime had little depth; but Soviet promises of
bread, peace and freedom were sufficient at the time to lull the
masses into acceptance. Famine, internal resentment, and disillusionment had not yet combined with foreign intervention to overthrow
the new masters of Russia in many newly-won areas. But even in
November there were signs of what was to come. The bread ration
was reduced to two ounces a day, and armed gangs were sent out
into the country to forage for food—this even before the Ukraine, the
granary of Russia, was lost to Germany.

In one field alone could the Bolsheviks fulfil their promises—war
or peace. Little time was lost before they sought to end the war.
General Dukhonin, after the flight of Kerensky, was commander of
all the Russian forces. On the night of 20th November, the Soviet
Government ordered Dukhonin to propose an armistice for the purpose of opening up peace negotiations with the Central Powers. He
refused, contending that he could act only on the orders of a central
government. He was promptly replaced by an ensign, the Bolshevik
Krilenko, who had no scruples concerning a truce with Germany.

On 28th November Germany accepted Bolshevik overtures for a
truce. Hostilities ceased on the Eastern Front and fraternization
began four days later.

Thus, at the end of 1917, the heaviest blow yet sustained fell upon
the Allied Powers. No shots sounded over the whole length of the
Eastern Front from the Baltic to the Black Sea. The German nightmare of war on two fronts was for all practical purposes now over,
and the Western Allies nerved themselves to face the ordeal which
would surely follow.

Their hopes for an early and successful end to the war had, with
the loss of Russia, radically changed. Though America had entered
the war in April 1917, the effect of her entry would not become
apparent until well into 1918. The Nivelle offensive early in 1917
had led to mutinies in the French armies which had required time
for recuperation; and the British had exhausted themselves in ceaseless offensives from Arras to Passchendaele throughout the year. In-

deed, without the re-creation of an Eastern Front the war might not be won at all and for that reason the British and French drew up plans for a task which both considered vital to a successful conclusion of the war—armed intervention in Russia.

CIVIL WAR BEGINS

Dukhonin, the new commander of the Russian forces, was murdered on December 4, 1917, at army headquarters. Anti-Bolshevik standards were raised five days later by Kaledin, and shortly afterwards by Kornilov, on the Don. Though the external war was over for the present, Russia was soon to reel under the horrors of a struggle much more terrible—civil war.

The appointment of a mere ensign as Commander-in-Chief, the murder of Dukhonin, and the German truce, marked the end of the old Russian Army. For the former military leaders the writing on the wall was plain, and they had no wish to serve the Bolsheviks under Krilenko. It was vain to stem the torrent of homeward-moving soldiers already pouring back from the fronts. All they could do was to make their individual way to territories not under Bolshevik control: to raise forces there in opposition to the new Bolshevik masters of Russia.

Kaledin, the Ataman of the Don Cossacks, arrived at Rostov early in December 1917, where he became the main hope of propertied and military classes. His territories became a refuge for aristocrats, the well-to-do, businessmen and merchants—as well as officers—who had fled from the proletarian decrees now making themselves felt elsewhere. Kornilov, and Generals Denikin, Lukomsky, Romanovsky and Markov, who had been associated with him, escaped from Bolshevik-held territory and moved south-east to the Don where they joined the veteran Alexeiev who was busy founding the 'Volunteer Army' to fight the Reds.

The Don, then, was a main centre of opposition to the Bolshevik régime. Another was the Ukraine, and a third, Finland.

On December 6, 1917, Finland—in a move for national independence and wishing to escape from barbarism— declared her separateness from Bolshevik Russia. A month later the Soviet Government recognized this proclaimed independence, but then brought down the Finnish Government on 26th January by a general strike combined with unrest provoked by Red Guards in Finland. Two days later, in support of Finnish revolutionaries, the Bolsheviks invaded and captured the capital, Helsingfors. This was the signal for a three-month war, fought out bitterly by Finnish 'Red' and anti-Bolshevik troops. General Mannerheim, the anti-Bolshevik leader, established his headquarters at Vaasa, on the Gulf of Bothnia, while the whole of the industrial south and south-western part of Finland came under Soviet rule. Early success won by Mannerheim was not decisive. In March, following the Treaty of Brest-Litovsk, Russian troops and warships were withdrawn; the Soviet Government kept the struggle alive by supplying munitions and volunteers. The issue was finally decided, however, when on April 3, 1918, a German force under General von der Goltz landed at Hango to support Mannerheim. Helsingfors was reoccupied on 13th April; the last Red stronghold capitulated a month later.

German intervention reduced Finland to the status of a military and economic vassal of Germany; a German prince (Friedrich Karl of Hesse) was elected king but the general armistice forced German withdrawal before he could rule. The presence of German troops in Finland while the war continued, and the fear that they would establish submarine bases in the Barents Sea from which they could attack Atlantic shipping then busily engaged in transporting American troops to France, was a decisive factor in bringing Allied interventionist troops to Murmansk in north Russia.

In the Ukraine, an organized nationalist government existed—the Rada. As early as 10th November fighting had broken out in Kiev between members of the local Soviet and officers who supported the Provisional Government. After three days of street fighting the latter, learning that Bolshevik troops were approaching, evacuated the city. But it was the Rada, not the Bolsheviks, which emerged triumphant at Kiev. Ukrainian troops, who had remained neutral during the earlier struggle, now took over in the name of the Rada the strategic points and more important public buildings in the city. Other Ukrainian troops, brought up by the Rada, succeeded in disarming the Bolshevik forces, so that by 3rd December the government felt sufficiently secure to proclaim itself the sole authority in the Ukraine, now declared to be a People's (not a Soviet) Republic. The power of the Rada was, however, confined to the western part of the Ukraine. In the industrialized east and south-east, where Ukrainian nationalism had fewer roots and where the Russian population was larger, a rival authority grew up, based on Kharkov, in the form of the Ukrainian Soviet Republic; this repudiated the authority of the Rada on 7th December.

In December 1918, with their power secure in northern and central Russia, the Soviet leaders determined to crush the theatres of resistance both in the Don and the Ukraine. A force consisting of about 7,000 ill-disciplined troops was placed under command of the Bolshevik Antonov for the purpose.

Antonov regarded Kaledin as the more dangerous enemy, and planned to cut off the Don from the Ukraine, using Black Sea sailors in diversionary operations against Kaledin's rear. To this end, the first blows were directed against the Don. The rejection of a Soviet ultimatum by the Rada at the end of December, however, led to the dispatch of a small force against the Ukraine. Poltava, the first large town from Bolshevik headquarters at Kharkov on the way to Kiev, fell quickly. The successful Bolshevik drive continued and town after town capitulated: Ekaterinoslav on 10th January; Zhmerinka and Vinnitsa thirteen days later; Odessa on 30th January; Nikolaev on 4th February; and five days later, Kiev itself. But Soviet occupation did not last long. Negotiations at Brest-Litovsk between the Bolsheviks and the Germans paved the way for German occupation of the Ukraine and (after an oppressive rule marked by shootings without trial) the expulsion of the Bolsheviks. On 1st March German troops marched into Kiev; the Rada was nominally reinstated, but the real power lay in the hands of the occupiers. A German puppet, Skoropadski, replaced the Rada, while Field-Marshal von Eichorn, the German commander, really ruled.

Meanwhile, Antonov's main force had been thrown against the Don. At first the Bolsheviks prospered; even the Cossacks fought feebly, if at all, for they had not yet realized the true nature of Bolshevism; Rostov and Taganrog were towns with a working-class population which felt more affinity with the Bolsheviks than the Cossack government of Kaledin. In these circumstances Antonov had little difficulty, on 10th December, in taking Rostov, but five days later Alexeiev and his Volunteer Army came to Kaledin's aid and reoccupied the town.

In Taganrog, at the end of January, a revolt of factory workers against the government led to Bolshevik occupation of the place, and early in February the Bolsheviks won a decisive victory over Alexeiev at Matveev Kurgan. Even in this early phase of the civil war, fighting was extremely bitter. Few prisoners were taken, for the Volun-

teer Army was made up largely of men whose families had suffered
at the hands of the Bolsheviks and who welcomed the chance to even
the score. Their fighting quality was very high, but they lacked
artillery so that their individual superiority was outmatched by Bolshevik numbers and better arms. Rostov was now threatened and on
11th February, Kaledin, who considered the fight hopeless, committed suicide.

On 24th February Rostov fell to the Bolsheviks once more. The
Volunteer Army with 1500 loyal Cossacks withdrew across the Don,
leaving the Bolsheviks to extend their rule to Orenburg and to the
Crimea.

In April the Volunteers joined the Kuban Cossacks in an attempt
to wrest the Kuban capital, Ekaterinodor, from the Reds. The
attack, led by Kornilov, went in on 9th April and continued for four
days despite overwhelming Bolshevik superiority. On 13th April
Kornilov was killed by a shell, and command passed to Denikin
who, considering the cost too great, ordered retreat.

The Bolsheviks, despite these victories, were forced to relinquish
the Don territory. This came about through an uprising of the Cossacks who, disillusioned with the Bolsheviks through the practices of
their occupying detachments, rose against them, and by an invasion
of Germans from the Ukraine. Anti-Bolshevik 'Whites'—whose uniform was motley and who, at about this time, sewed a white strip on
their caps to distinguish themselves from the Reds—turned the
lower and middle Don into a turmoil of guerrilla fighting, while in
the west the Bolsheviks tried vainly to stem the German advance.
Under these pressures, the Reds were forced to quit Taganrog (occupied by the Germans on 1st May) and Rostov one week later. By the
11th, the Don Territory had been completely cleared of Bolsheviks.

The Volunteer Army took no part in these operations. Its preliminary skirmishes and battles against the enemy had not, in the
main, been successful. At this period it was still too early in the civil
war for counter-revolutionaries to swell its ranks with the masses it
later attracted : those who, for one reason or another, had become
disgusted with the Soviet régime. Yet it was not demoralized or discouraged. Under Alexeiev, and with Denikin as its field commander,
it had become a cohesive whole, the nucleus of a White Army which
was to alarm and severely test the Bolsheviks in the future. And there
could be little doubt that the Allies, who in the emotional climate of
the time saw nothing but treachery in Bolshevik defection from their

I
(above left)
Major-General Maynard (left),
Commander of the British Forces at
Murmansk

(above right)
Major-General Graves, the American
Commander in Siberia

Major-General Elmsley, the Canadian
Commander in Siberia

(photo: Imperial
War Museum)

2
(above)
Leon Trotsky, the chief Soviet delegate
at the Russian Peace Conference,
January 1918

Vice-Admiral Kolchak

General Rudolf Gaida

ranks, would sooner or later find themselves supporting the White cause in this theatre.

THE TREATY OF BREST-LITOVSK

The failure of Kerensky's last offensive against the Central Powers in July 1917 had, at the least, been disturbing for the Western Allies. But disturbing news from Russia had been commonplace throughout the war. Though Germany had gone a long way towards eliminating Russia, nevertheless Russia technically was still a belligerent—a nuisance that still remained to be beaten—and German troops were still required on the Eastern Front until Russia should at last acknowledge defeat. Despite apathy in the Russian forces, chaos behind the lines, and feeble resistance, it was still vital to the Allies that Russia should not finally lay down her arms.

The Bolsheviks had changed all that, precipitately, and without consultation with Russia's allies. Cessation of hostilities in December 1917 freed the Germans from the Eastern Front, and, moreover, gave them three months in which to transfer divisions to the Western Front before the 1918 campaigning season. On 21st March of that year the Germans launched a massive offensive which overwhelmed the British Fifth Army. The front caved in, and the Germans swept on until Paris came under the bombardment of their long-range guns.

It was in these days of desperation that the idea of intervention gained strength. The reconstitution of an Eastern Front was a military necessity to France and Britain if the war was to be won at all. And if intervention brought them into conflict with the Bolsheviks, who had done so much damage to the Allied cause by defecting from it, that would be accepted. Thus, as early as December 23, 1917, when the German offensive in France was foreseen, the Allied Supreme War Council recommended that all anti-Bolshevik troops in Russia who were determined to continue the war against Germany should be fully supported. In the same month the British War Cabinet decided to give Kaledin 'financial support up to any figure necessary'; but the transfer of funds presented difficulties which had not been solved when the Cossack leader ended his own life in February.* Little in a material sense had been done in aiding anti-

---

* Peter Fleming, *The Fate of Admiral Kolchak* (London, 1963), 31.

Bolshevik factions when the Treaty of Brest-Litovsk delivered Russia completely to German domination.

Negotiations leading to the treaty had been protracted. A preliminary Bolshevik deputation arrived at the headquarters of Prince Leopold of Bavaria at Brest-Litovsk on 3rd December. The main Russian demands were threefold: that the Germans should retire from the islands in the Gulf of Riga; that there should be no other troop movements while negotiations continued; and, finally, that there should be an armistice on all fronts alike. The Germans refused these demands, and the Bolshevik doctrinaires wasted days in irrelevant debate. Not until the 15th was an armistice agreement signed. This provided for a twenty-eight-day truce on the Eastern Front starting at noon on 17th December. In the meantime, in reply to a Bolshevik request probably made in an attempt to stave off Allied reprisals for taking Russia out of the war, the Germans agreed to transfer no troops to the West, but they continued transporting them to France. As Ludendorff said, 'From the end of November onwards troop-trains were incessantly passing from East to West. It was no longer a case of replacing tired divisions in the West by fresh ones, but of really adding to the number of combatants in the West.'*

The Brest-Litovsk meeting to discuss peace terms opened on 22nd December, but was adjourned without anything definite having been settled. Resuming on 9th January, negotiations dragged out until on the 18th the Germans spread out a map of Eastern Europe and indicated a blue line running north of Brest-Litovsk to the Baltic as the future boundary of Russia. This line exactly coincided with the present German front and separated from Russia most of Poland, all Lithuania, western Latvia (including Riga) and the islands in Moon Sound. That day saw a further adjournment.

In Petrograd, meanwhile, there were two schools of thought. A faction of extremists favoured absolute refusal to sign the 'annexionist' terms proposed by Germany. They would fight rather than sign. Lenin, supported by Stalin, anxious for a breathing space in which to consolidate the Bolshevik position within Russia, stood for signature. In any case, the army could not resist. A compromise proposed by Trotsky, that they should refuse to sign a peace on German terms and at the same time declare that Russia was no longer at war, carried the day and negotiations resumed on 30th January.

---

* Ludendorff, *My War Memories*, II, 511.

Before Trotsky produced this final card, German troops marched into the Ukraine to support the Rada against the Reds, and, as we have seen, soon occupied the new republic. Trotsky's unique proposal was ignored; Germany was tired of evasion. On 18th February German troops resumed military operations in the north, sweeping back without difficulty Krilenko's 'garrulous warriors' on a front of a thousand miles in response to Prince Leopold's order to ward off the 'moral infection' of Bolshevism. On the 19th, the Bolsheviks eagerly offered to sign peace on the terms proposed, but the Germans disregarded them. For three days the offensive continued until German acquisitions had been rounded out as far as the eastern borders of Latvia and Estonia. On the 22nd, new peace conditions, harder than formerly and which had to be accepted within forty-eight hours and ratified within two weeks, reached Petrograd. Lenin reinforced the ultimatum with one of his own : either the terms would be accepted, or he would quit the Soviet Government. The Bolsheviks capitulated, and on 3rd March signed the peace treaties.

Before ratification, Trotsky, smarting from his personal defeat at the hands of Germany, sounded out the Allies; would they, he asked, in the event either of Soviet refusal to ratify the peace, or of a subsequent breach with Germany, support the Soviet Government? President Wilson of the United States was sympathetic, but unhappily 'was not in a position to render . . . direct and effective aid'. The other Allies, alienated by the actions of the Bolsheviks in quitting the war, in repudiating Russia's foreign debts, and in issuing appeals for world revolution, had no intention of collaborating. Nor indeed, in the absence of a Russian army, was it seen how collaboration could in any way be effective. The Allies ignored the appeal, apart from the stationing by the British of a small naval force at the north Russian port of Murmansk at Trotsky's invitation. On 15th March, their last hope gone, the Bolsheviks accepted the Treaty of Brest-Litovsk.

The Central Powers gained heavily by the treaty. Germany's occupation of the Ukraine split Russia and afforded access to the Steppes. Turkey gained Kars, Ardahan, and Batum in the Caucasus. Poland, the Baltic States, and Finland were stripped from Russia. And losses of territory influenced adjoining regions and brought enormous economic benefits to the Central Powers. Germany now had access to the Black Sea, and soon controlled both it and the Caucasus. In the Ukraine, the granary of Russia, the Germans replenished the national larder which enabled them—and Austria—to continue the war :

'The supplies she drew from the Ukraine, combined with our assistance, undoubtedly saved Austria and her Army from starvation. . . . In the summer of 1918 it supplied us with meat, and thus the scanty meat ration we had was made possible without encroaching upon our own livestock reserves and those of the occupied territories. The Army was also able to get horses in great numbers; without them warfare would have been altogether impossible, for if Germany had been obliged to raise these horses our own agriculture would have been hard hit. We also obtained raw materials of all kinds from the Ukraine.'*

Roumania, which had been forced to quit the war through the Russian defection, also suffered. Dobrudja, the Petroseny coal basin, and the Carpathian passes had to be given up, and Austro-German traffic permitted through Moldavia and Bessarabia to Odessa. Her industry and oilfields passed under the control of Austro-German interests.

It was a triumph for the Central Powers, for indirect opportunities were presented as well. Hundreds of thousands of Austro-Hungarian prisoners in Siberia† were now free to push Germany's interests between the Urals and the Pacific. Only the areas of north and central Russia would remain to the Bolsheviks, and these, undermined by the detestation of a starving people towards Bolshevism would soon, it was thought, rot and fall into the victor's hand.

The Treaty of Brest-Litovsk alienated from the Soviet Government those Russians who possessed national pride, for, at a single stroke, it had swept away the conquests both of Peter the Great and Catherine. It threw Russia back from the Black and Baltic Seas. It was the harbinger of famine as the loss of the Ukraine—and later of the Don territory—brought starvation. 'The fight for bread became a fight for the very existence of the Soviet régime.'‡ A bitter class war was fought in every hamlet and village as the peasants rose against their neighbours, perhaps only a little better off than themselves, hunting desperately for hidden grain. And this was the policy

* Ludendorff, *My War Memories*, II, 625.
† One reputable source quoted by Fleming gives the figure of 2,111,146 captured Austrians alone. (*The Fate of Admiral Kolchak*, 58, fn.)
‡ Chamberlin, *The Russian Revolution* (New York, 1952), I, 425.

of the Party. Only if it was able to divide the village into two camps, announced Sverdlov, and to stir up the same class war as in the cities, could the party achieve in the villages what had been accomplished in the urban areas.

That this policy would lead to ferocious and bloody civil war was obvious, but the prospect did not dismay the Bolshevik leaders. Trotsky welcomed it emphatically. 'Our Party is for Civil War,' he said. 'The civil war rages around the question of bread . . . long live civil war in the name of bread for our children and old people, for the workers and the Red Army, in the name of direct and merciless struggle with counter-revolution.'*

In the cities the industrial workers were content to throw out the owners of factories, to seize their homes and property; but they viewed the prospect of work with no enthusiasm. Many, indeed, gripped by famine, were physically incapable of labour. The dissatisfaction of the hungry masses was directed against the new government in riots and fighting. Ironically enough, food surpluses in Siberia could not be brought in, because the railroad system was so chaotic. There was a shortage of fuel, and locomotives rusted in sidings while the people starved.

Unemployment was now widespread. Factories were forced to close through acute shortages of raw material and fuel. The war industries, which had found employment for a large proportion of the city workmen, were all closed down as a part of demobilization. The unemployed drifted back to their native villages to join in the hunt for food. There was a mood of disillusionment among these men on whom the Bolsheviks had always counted for their main support.

The Russian Orthodox Church did not stand idle under the anti-Christian Bolshevik decrees. The Patriarch of Moscow and of All Russia denounced Bolshevism and appealed to the people to oppose it, and the people responded. Through the influence of all these dissatisfactions, political and religious—the disillusionment and hunger of the peasants and the workers—riots broke out all over Russia. The Soviet newspapers in the spring of 1918 were filled with accounts of small but ferocious affrays, often characterized by great brutality, put down with equal ruthlessness by Red soldiers. Human misery was infinitely more widespread than during Kerensky's period of government, but at that time revolt against Kerensky's government had

* Trotsky, cf. Chamberlin, *The Russian Revolution*, I, 426.

been given driving force by a determined revolutionary organization —the Bolshevik Party—and it had succeeded. Now there was no leader, no generally accepted panacea, no unifying force among the many discontented elements to give direction. As Chamberlin said, 'The country sputtered like damp wood, but failed to burst out in a general conflagration of anti-Soviet revolt'.*

The outbreaks of revolt which did occur, though not universal, were symptomatic of the general unrest. The Soviet régime, weak as it was, had sufficient strength to suppress them, but the very fact that they occurred at all, and on such a widespread basis, showed that the Bolshevik power stood on uneasy foundations, and could hardly remain upright if pushed by a strong hostile force.

For the Allies, Brest-Litovsk provided a double reason for intervention in Russia. The always valid reason of somehow reconstructing an Eastern front against Germany still, of course, applied; both the German hands were now free to fight the Western Allies; perhaps one could be, at least, partially tied. The second reason, now painfully obvious when the terms of the treaty became known, was the urgent necessity for the withholding of Russian supplies from the Central Powers. Germany had Russia in an iron grip. The resources of the old Russian Empire could be drawn upon to defeat the stranglehold of naval blockade. Nourished by supplies from occupied or dominated territories, the enemy could prolong the war indefinitely. If the war was to be won by the Allies at all something had to be done about Russia. France and Britain, accordingly, pushed forward plans for intervention.

* Chamberlin, *The Russian Revolution*, I, 420.

CHAPTER II

INTERVENTION BEGINS

THE BRITISH ENTER SOUTH RUSSIA

From the Allies' point of view, the Russian Revolution, which they had hailed as the overthrow of a pro-German court and a reactionary régime, was now recognized as a major disaster. The Bolsheviks had come to power and made truce with Germany, thus depriving the Allies of twelve million men and permitting the release of more than seventy enemy divisions from the East.

As early as December 23, 1917, military representatives of the Supreme War Council, in an attempt to reconstitute the Eastern Front, had recommended that all possible support should be given to Russians who were resolved to continue the war against Germany.

An Anglo-French convention of that month apportioned certain 'spheres of influence' between the two countries. Britain took as her share of responsibility the Cossack territories, Armenia, the Caucasus, and the territory east of the Caspian Sea; North Russia was later added tacitly. France was to be responsible for Bessarabia, the Ukraine, and the Crimea.[1] But these territories, apart from the Caucasus region from Mesopotamia and the area east of the Caspian from India, were not accessible to the Allies at the end of 1917.

The shape that Allied intervention would eventually take to meet the desperate situation in Russia was foreshadowed in a report on recommended policy submitted early in 1918 to the British War Cabinet by General Alfred Knox, then in London. Knox had been British Military Attaché in Petrograd until the Bolshevik Revolution, and was fully conversant with Russian affairs. In his report he stated that a nucleus of Allied military force must be provided, followed by economic assistance to opponents of Bolshevism. He recommended intervention on three lines—from the North, the South, and in the Far East. In the North, he said, 'the occupation of the northern ports is desirable, but intervention based on these ports . . . can by no means be regarded as an excuse for the continuation of inaction in other Russian theatres'. From the South, Knox advo-

39

cated intervention through Persia towards the Caucasus, Trans-Caspia, and Turkestan—'essential to protect the tranquillity of India'. 'It is not suggested', he went on, 'that armed forces should be sent into Russian territory, but troops must be moved into Northern Persia to prevent the infiltration of German and Turkish agents which has naturally followed the withdrawal of the Russian forces.' But decisive intervention, he emphasized, must come from the Far East, where the main share could be provided by Japan, and, in the event of Japan consenting, the next step would be to approach the President of the United States. Knox could see no useful purpose in 'flirtations with the Bolshevik usurpers in the hope of inducing them to invite or to agree passively to intervention'. Their hope lay 'in gaining time to complete the robbery of the propertied classes in Russia and in the hope of a general communist revolution in the world—they know that the re-establishment of order and the re-crudescence of national feeling in Russia would be fatal to inter-nationalism and to their power, for it would give the majority of the people a chance of once more expressing their will'. Knox firmly believed that Allied intervention, properly applied, would lead to the overthrow of the Bolsheviks and the restoration of order. 'The Allies', he said, 'should not interfere in Russian internal politics, but should leave the decision as to the future form of government to a Constituent Assembly which would be called on the conclusion of peace.'[2]

Though Siberia offered the best approach to the Allies, it was not there that they first intervened. Negotiations with America and Japan dragged on through the spring and early summer of 1918 before a decision was finally made. Britain, never slow to act where her own vital interests are concerned, had taken what steps she could in South Russia to safeguard her position before any seaborne troops reached Siberia. It was the same in North Russia, where Trotsky's invitation to base a British naval squadron at Murmansk (see above, p. 35) gave a foothold in that area which led to Allied intervention later. Canadian troops participated in these early operations, both in South and North Russia.

British intervention in the south preceded that in the north, and will therefore be examined first.

The situation in the Caucasus region of South Russia and in the neighbouring North-west Persian region—east of the Turkish border —was of extreme interest to Britain. Throughout the war, India was

faced by the possibility of danger from the north-west frontier ag-
gravated by the hostility of a considerable section of the Afghan
nation, so much so that the authorities in India found it necessary to
investigate and discuss the extent of representative government
which it was possible to apply to India itself. Any advance by Turkey
across Persia to the borders of India might powerfully affect the
fortunes of the Indian Empire and would be intolerable to the
British. Furthermore, the situation in Persia always affected British
operations in Mesopotamia—an attack by Turkey against the port of
Basrah or the line of communications from there to Baghdad might
have disastrous results on that campaign.

The Anglo-Russian Convention of 1907 entirely dominated the
situation in Persia until the end of 1917. By that convention, Britain
gained military advantages in Persia during the war in that the
Caucasus–Persian front was manned by Russian troops and, despite
some incursions, had been successfully held against the Turks.

By October 1917 it became obvious to the British that while the
Russian troops still retained their positions in the Caucasus and
North-west Persia, lack of discipline rendered them so ineffective
that the best that could be hoped for was that they would not evacuate
Persia and leave the roads into that country open to the enemy. Following the Bolshevik seizure of power, anarchy spread and Russian
troops began to leave the line, while soldiers' committees on the spot
were selling arms, ammunition, clothing and military equipment of
all kinds to the local races—Persians, Kurds, and others. The Persian
Government passed information from enemy sources to the British
that a Turco-German offensive would begin early in 1918 in which
the Turks would occupy Azerbaijan, invade Persia, and then move
on Turkestan in the north and Afghanistan in the south. As a preliminary, the enemy were sending 300,000 rifles to arm certain Persian tribes hostile to the British.[3]

At the beginning of 1918 the British could not spare a sufficiently
large force from any theatre for despatch to this area. As an indication of what an adequate force might be, the Caucasus–Persian front
had been held by between 100,000 and 200,000 Russian troops, but
what remained of this force could no longer be relied upon. Another
barrier to hostile penetration eastwards was desperately required, but
how was it to be formed? The nearest British force was the army in
Mesopotamia and small parties in Persia, but they had enough on
their hands. With the Russian defection, the Mesopotamian force

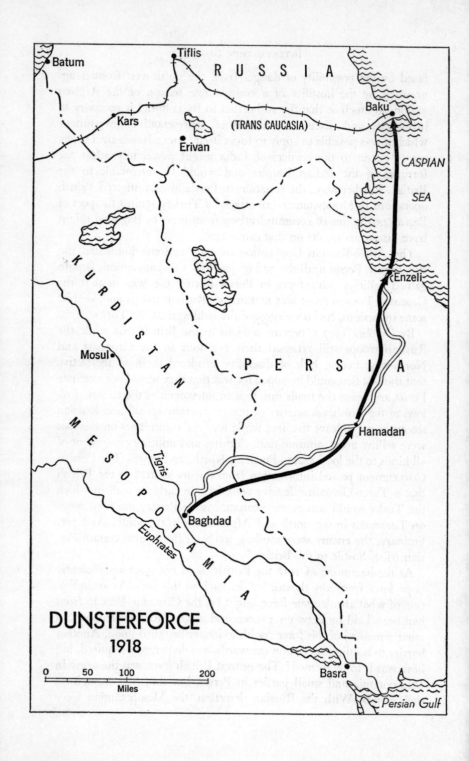

Batum

Tiflis

R U S S I A

Kars

(TRANS CAUCASIA)

Baku

Erivan

CASPIAN

SEA

Enzeli

K U R D I S T A N

Mosul

P E R S I A

Hamadan

Tigris

M E S O P O T A M I A

Baghdad

Euphrates

DUNSTERFORCE
1918

0   50   100   200
Miles

Basra

Persian Gulf

could expect a Turkish offensive aimed at the recapture of northern Mesopotamia and Baghdad; it had to guard the line of communications from Basrah; and in addition, responsibility for keeping open the road from Baghdad to the Caspian against Turkish incursions from the west rested with the British commander in Mesopotamia. That road, about 630 miles long, crossed a devastated area through Khaniquin, Kermanshah, and Hamadan to the Caspian port of Enzeli. It climbed a succession of mountain ranges and was in a bad state of repair, almost impassable in the winter. The task was made more hazardous by the uncertain attitude of the tribes along the route, and of the Persians; one of these tribes, the Jangalis of Gilan, on the south-western shores of the Caspian, was being encouraged by Turco-German agents and by the Bolsheviks, as well as the extreme section of Persian nationalists, to oppose all British action. Indeed, Jangali tribesmen, in co-operation with the Bolsheviks, controlled the approaches to the port of Enzeli and were well armed.[4]

The British, in this predicament, were forced to adopt an expedient —that of trying to organize a local defensive force in the Caucasus region from Georgians, Armenians, Assyrians and Russian volunteers.[5] To this end a British mission to the Caucasus was authorized by the War Office on January 14, 1918, under Major-General L. C. Dunsterville who arrived in Baghdad from India on the 18th with orders to proceed to Tiflis in the Caucasian state of Georgia as British representative to the Trans-Caucasian Government. He would need, it was considered, 150 officers and 300 N.C.O.s—who were the nucleus of a force which became known as 'Dunsterforce'—for the main purpose of 'organizing, training and leading native troops to be raised from the tribes of Asia Minor and Mesopotamia'.[6]

Canada contributed fifteen officers and twenty-six N.C.O.s to Dunsterforce. Sir Edward Kemp, the Canadian Overseas Minister in London, reported to the Prime Minister (Sir Robert Borden) in these terms:

'The Imperial authorities were confronted with a difficult and hazardous situation owing to the demoralization and retirement of the Russian Army in the Caucasus which was operating on the Eastern or right flank of the British Army in Mesopotamia. . . . I was asked to furnish them with 15 level-headed Officers and 26 Non-Commissioned Officers, to co-operate with the British Officers and Officers from other Dominions in organizing a somewhat mixed and irregular army of different tribes and nationalities which inhabit the territory to the North and East of the British Army. The population of this area is of a very mixed character, but to a considerable extent it is antagonistic to the Turk, and included in it is a certain number of Armenians.'[7]

All the Canadians, who had to be of 'strong character, adventurous spirit, especially good stamina',[8] came from the Canadian Corps and left the Western Front for England on 13th January. Officers below the rank of captain were made acting captains, while junior N.C.O.s and men became acting sergeants. The Canadian contingent joined others in England drawn from the British, Australian, New Zealand and South African forces, together with a party of fourteen Russian officers and one Persian. The aim, they were told, was an ambitious one—to protect the Baku oilfields, to operate against the Turks from the east, and to 'hold the Batum–Tiflis–Baku–Krasnovodsk line to Afghanistan'.[9]

The Western Front contingent, including the Canadians, reached Basrah in Mesopotamia on 2nd March. There the long voyage up the river Tigris began, all parties assembling in camps south of Baghdad by the end of March. Some of the Tigris rivercraft carrying them had been manned by Canadians.*[10]

Dunsterville, meanwhile, had left Baghdad with a small party at the end of January, hoping to be in Baku a fortnight later. Prevented by Bolsheviks at Enzeli from embarking for Baku, he returned to Hamadan. A swift onrush of events which followed Brest-Litovsk found him still at Hamadan; and because of chaotic conditions in the Caucasus he was ordered to remain in Persia, where he undertook famine relief and began to organize and train local levies and improve the roads using tribesmen unfit for military service.[11]

The political situation in the Caucasus at this period was exceedingly complicated. Three peoples, the Georgians, the Armenians, and the Azerbaidjan Tartars, constituted the majority of the mixed population living south of the Caucasus range and north of the borders of Turkey and Persia. Following the Bolshevik Revolution

---

* Some five officers and twenty-three other ranks were provided by the Canadian Expeditionary Force for special service in Mesopotamia. They were obtained from pioneers recruited in B.C. (1st Overseas Canadian Pioneer Details, Vancouver) and attached to Inland Water Transport R.E. for work on the Tigris. They served for three years after arrival in July 1916.

a Trans-Caucasian Government came into being through the influence of the Georgians which in November 1917 proclaimed an independent republic to include Georgians, Armenians, and Tartars, despite their Moslem and Christian differences. It was to this government at Tiflis that Dunsterville had been sent, but as we have seen, he was unable to reach it. In March 1918 the Brest-Litovsk treaty ceded Batum, Kars and Ardahan to Turkey, which the new Trans-Caucasian government had at first recognized; but this created such a storm of protest within the country that the decision was reversed. On April 22, 1918, an independent Federated Trans-Caucasian Republic was proclaimed which declared Trans-Caucasia separate and independent of Russia and not bound by the terms of Brest-Litovsk. Thus released from any obligation to abide by the treaty terms, Turkey began to take over the whole of the Caucasian region by means of the Moslem inhabitants. Germany—with designs on Baku and its oilfields—could on no account permit Turkish control of such vital territory. Beset by the opposing designs of Turkey and Germany the Trans-Caucasian republic split into three parts based on racial lines —a Tartar republic (including Baku) and an Armenian republic, both under Turkish protection, while Georgia welcomed a German expeditionary force as a safeguard against Turkish invasion. The Bolsheviks held out at Baku, their only stronghold in the area, and on this the Turks were advancing in defiance of the Germans.[12]

Even in Persia, circumstances were not reassuring, and Dunsterville—still at Hamadan—requested reinforcements. The time was propitious. It was now obvious that a British offensive, brilliantly conducted by General Allenby in the Palestine and Syrian theatre, had forced the Turks to abandon their offensive in Mesopotamia so that General Maude in Baghdad could now spare reinforcements. Persia was in the grip of famine. A large portion of the grain-producing areas was occupied by demoralized Russian troops whose necessities forced them to pillage. Brigands infested the roads, robbing and murdering at will. The Jangalis, Austrian trained and German led, still controlled the road to Enzeli. In the mountains of Kurdistan, only a hundred miles to the west, a Turkish army threatened the line of communications.[13]

Into this turbulence the Canadians plunged by way of Kermanshah, thence to Hamadan through the Asadabad Pass in the Pistokosh mountains. They joined Dunsterville, who had by now received British reinforcements during the early part of July 1918, and were at once dispersed; they found themselves in such unfamiliar tasks as training local levies, gaining the support of distant tribes, supervising road construction, doling out food, and policing the road to Hamadan.[14] Dunsterville was busily engaged in forming a brigade at Hamadan from his regular troops, local tribesmen, and Christian Armenians who had fled from Kurdistan following a massacre by Turks and Kurds which had cost more than 40,000 lives. The British general had hastily improvised a protective rearguard to enable the Armenians to reach Hamadan, and in this seven Canadians played an effective part.[15] One Russian force remained loyal to the Allies—that of General Bicharakoff, who had himself turned Bolshevik a month before as being the only means of retaining a foothold in this region. He accepted the post of Commander of the Red Army in the Caucasus, which did not prevent his continued co-operation with Dunsterville. A Canadian, Major H. K. Newcombe, was ordered to join Bicharakoff as financial adviser, subsequently accompanying him throughout the Caucasus. He is, so far as is known, the only Canadian who ever saw active service with the Red Army.[16]

Meanwhile, towards mid-June, British and Russian troops attacked the Jangalis (who were under German leadership and provided with munitions by the Turks), defeated them, and opened the road to Enzeli. A 500-man British detachment took up position at the town of Resht on the Enzeli road to keep communications open. On 20th July a Jangali force of 2500 attacked this detachment but was beaten off, and thereafter British communications to the Caspian remained undisturbed. Bicharakoff, who had reached Enzeli at the end of June, embarked for Baku on 1st July accompanied by five British officers and four armoured cars from Dunsterforce. At this port, on 26th July, a *coup d'état* succeeded. The Bolshevik members of the government resigned, and the new government, terming itself Centro-Caspian, asked for British aid at Bicharakoff's instigation.[17]

Ever since June the War Office had been pressing Dunsterville to enter Baku. By their occupation of Sevastopol on 1st May and their seizure of a portion of the Russian Black Sea Fleet, the Germans had gained a route to Trans-Caucasia on which they would be quite independent of Turkey—a factor of distinct advantage having regard to the divergent aims of the two countries. The inhabitants of the Caucasus, with the sole exception of the Armenians, were either pro-German or pro-Turkish. In June, the German advance through the Ukraine and the Don basin to the Volga was taking place with in-

credible speed. German troops at Tiflis were only waiting for reinforcements to march on Baku and its essential oil. And in Turkestan
there were 40,000 Austrian and German prisoners of war, a very real
danger to Afghanistan and India should the advancing Germans link
up with them. The War Office foresaw the need of interrupting the
Trans-Caspian railway and this, it was considered, could best be done
by closing the sea route from Baku to Krasnovodsk* on the eastern
shore of the Caspian. There was thus a double reason for the occupation of Baku—to deny its oil to the enemy, and to block the enemy
route to India.[18] Dunsterville, therefore, although he had received by
no means all of the reinforcements requested a month before, accepted the Russian invitation.

Baku, a city surrounded by hills, consisted of three main parts. To
the west was Bibiabat containing docks and an oilfield, while to the
east lay the refinery area. Between these was the old walled city,
together with the business district, and the residential part of the
town. Standing on the oil-rich Apsherom Peninsula, the whole place
was surrounded by wells, derricks, and storage tanks, with pipelines
leading in to the refineries and piers while one major line crossed to
Batum on the Black Sea. The bay on which the city stood was five
miles across, and contained an island which sheltered the port from
the prevailing south winds. The importance of Baku in 1918, apart
from its strategic value, lay in the fact that it supplied most of south
and central Russia with oil and could equally well supply Germany.[19]

By August the Turks, well ahead of the Germans in the race for
Baku, approached the town. The first British soldiers, troops of the
7th North Staffordshire, arrived at Baku from Enzeli on 4th August.
Inspired by their presence, local forces next day repulsed the Turkish
attack, which was not immediately renewed. Taking advantage of
the respite during the middle of August, the British defence force
was increased to two battalions as reinforcements arrived in North
Persia; and with the increment six Canadian officers in all proceeded
to Baku. It was found necessary to divert some troops, intended for
Baku, to meet a Turkish advance from Kurdistan which threatened
to cut the line of communications to Enzeli; other Canadians accom-

---

* The threat to Afghanistan and India was effectively removed by a British
force from North-east Persia under command of Major-General W. Malleson
which occupied Krasnovodsk during August 1918. This operation, although it
had immense political importance for Britain, is not part of our present story,
and will not be further described.

panied this force. Around Baku twenty-two local infantry battalions, mostly Armenian, with a total strength of about 6000, were attempting to hold a twelve-mile line of defence, a difficult task as the local troops were poorly organized, had few officers, and were 'so lacking in discipline that they left their positions whenever they pleased'.[20]

The defences were poorly sited:

'The line of defence, which was very indefinite, lay for the most part along the crest of stony cliffs, from which the fire was plunging and ineffective. There were very few trenches, such rifle pits as existed being badly sited, and there was no wire. The whole line was so close to the town and harbour that the enemy guns . . . could bombard the whole place without difficulty.'[21]

The Turks attacked again on 26th August. Four separate attacks were thrown back by the North Staffordshire but a fifth was successful owing to local troops giving no support, which enabled the Turks to bring enfilading fire to bear causing heavy British losses. Some ground was lost. A further Turkish attack, four days later, again gained ground. On 31st August, Russians and Armenians held their positions for only an hour in the face of another attack, when they retired hurriedly. The 9th Royal Warwickshire, both flanks uncovered, was obliged to fall back, fighting a rearguard action which cost it seventy casualties. So far the British had done all the fighting, the local troops having consistently failed to support them. Captain Robert Harrison, a Canadian commanding the 24th Armenian Battalion, found that his unit ceased to exist on occasions through the predisposition of his men to scamper off at the first appearance of the enemy. Dunsterville was heavily outnumbered. He now had 900 British troops, including a field battery, and about 1000 Russians against a Turkish force made up of 6000 regulars and 8000 irregulars. Baku itself, a predominantly Tartar town, swarmed with enemy sympathizers and agents.[22]

By 12th September the British had in Baku the equivalent of three battalions—the 7th North Staffordshire, 9th Worcestershire, the 9th Royal Warwickshire (less one company) and one platoon of the 1/4 Hampshire. To this force was added 500 of Bicharakoff's men, with ten machine guns. Major Newcombe had already arrived in Baku on 19th August, and was given the job of paymaster, field cashier, and 'Chancellor of the Baku Exchequer'. Of the other Canadians, Major J. W. Van der Berg was given supervision over the entire machine gun situation in and around Baku. A third, Colonel John Warden, became Inspector of Infantry. A fourth, Captain G. S. Hopkins, was assisting in arranging supplies. Harrison, as we have seen, was *de facto* commander of an Armenian battalion. Captain A. H. Gilmour, the sixth Canadian, was dispatched by sea on a mission to the British force under Malleson on the eastern Caspian. Warned that a Turkish attack would take place on the 14th, Dunsterville inspected the line. Preparations were rushed to meet the projected onslaught. By the night of the 13th he was satisfied that the Turks could be held if the troops showed the will to fight, but as to this he had grave doubts.[23]

The offensive began at dawn the next day. Dunsterville's misgivings were amply justified. The Turks broke clean through an Armenian battalion at the most defensible part of the line and the position was soon hopeless. Only a stand by the British battalions, which forced the Turks to go to ground and inflicted heavy losses,* allowed the British to withdraw that night in two armed ships. The withdrawal was extremely hazardous, as the ships had to pass under the guns of the Russian fleet; one transport was fired on, but the force got through to Enzeli without loss of life.[24] The final act in this drama took place at the Persian port. There General Dunsterville received a deputation from the revolutionary sailors of one of the vessels which had been taken over to evacuate the British troops. The deputation presented a written petition which read :

> 'We, the Committee and the crew of the S.S. *Kursk* have witnessed with intense admiration the heroic conduct of your brave British soldiers in the defence of Baku. We have seen them suffering wounds and death bravely in defence of our town, which our own people were too feeble to defend. It is wonderful to us that these fine fellows from that distant island in the North Sea should have come all this way to the Caspian and have given up their lives there in the cause of honour and glory.
>
> 'We are so much impressed by their bearing and valour and by the whole episode of the British endeavours to save Baku from the Turks, that we wish to be at once taken over as a body and granted British nationality.'[25]

Three days later, orders were issued recalling General Dunsterville and disbanding his mission.[26] Canadian members were offered

---

* Estimated at 2000. British casualties were 180.

four choices of employment—with irregulars in the Near East, with Indian infantry in Mesopotamia or elsewhere, in a newly formed North Persian force (Norperforce), or with their original units in France. Two officers and two N.C.O.s joined the irregulars, and the same number Norperforce. Two officers and three N.C.O.s left for the British Military Mission to Siberia. The remainder chose the fourth alternative.[27]

Dunsterforce held a Russian city against the enemy at a crucial time. Though the oil at Baku had not been destroyed, the delay imposed by the short-lived occupation, through readiness to exploit events, served its purpose. The Turks, foreseeing the loss of their Arabian provinces and looking to the occupation of the Caucasus as compensation, controlled the oilfields in defiance of a compact with Germany—but not until September. Then, on October 30, 1918, the armistice with Turkey provided for an Allied occupation of Baku, effected by the British Norperforce on 17th November.[28]

Dunsterforce failed to penetrate to Tiflis and never created Caucasian forces to hold the line between Batum, Tiflis and Baku. But the forces mustered in North Persia, whose numbers were wildly exaggerated by local rumour, were sufficient to hold a Turkish army stationary in Kurdistan, thus protecting the flank of the Mesopotamia Force and discouraging hostile penetration to the east. Dunsterforce, hastily improvised though it was, achieved its purpose. And while it proved inadequate to hold Baku, it did succeed in denying Caspian oil to the enemy at a time when its possession would have been of immense value.[29]

CANADIAN CONTINGENTS FOR NORTH RUSSIA

Further Allied intervention, again preceding that in the Siberian theatre, took place early in 1918 in north Russia. The main reason for landing there was to keep the ice-free ports of Murmansk and Petchenga (Petsamo) out of German hands. There were other reasons which we shall consider later.

A German army of 55,000 men under General von der Goltz was in Finland ostensibly to counteract Russian Bolshevik forces which had invaded that country during January 1918, and in addition some 50,000 'White Finns' were acting under the orders of the German commander. In April strong detachments of these forces were pushing northwards, and it seemed certain that the German aim was to seize one or both of the ports for use as a submarine base, which would have serious results on the British convoy system; naval defences in the Straits of Dover could then be turned. 'Here was the real and pressing danger which brought about the appearance of Allied troops in North Russia.'[30]

Murmansk was the terminal of the railway running north from Petrograd and was free from ice throughout the year. It already possessed many of the conveniences required for a submarine base. Petchenga, on the other hand, had no railway communications, and was in fact difficult of access on the land side. Despite this, and though partially ice-bound during the winter months, it could nevertheless be utilized for submarines during part of the year. Both ports were so situated that submarines operating from them would find the North Sea minefields no barrier to their operations in the Atlantic, and this at a time when the flow of American troops to Europe was in full spate.[31]

The British, apprised of the German approach towards the ports, reacted swiftly. In March, a body of 150 marines was put ashore at Murmansk, followed by 370 more in May. With the co-operation of local Finns who were opposed to the Germans, this small force occupied the barracks close to the town, but was not strong enough to do more.

Meanwhile, on 3rd April, Allied ambassadors and military representatives in Russia recommended an intervention in the north.[32] The Supreme War Council at Versailles considered the matter. There were other reasons for intervention besides that already given. A landing in northern Russia might enable part of a Czech Corps operating in the heart of Russia to strike north to link up with an Allied force if established there; these, combined, would have the effect of re-forming an Eastern Front which could be supplied by sea and the result in France would quickly become apparent. There was a feeling that great support might be expected in the north from the sturdy and independent peasants. Furthermore, vast quantities of munitions and equipment supplied by the Allies, and still believed to be at Archangel, must be saved from the Germans or they would be transported to the Western Front to prolong the fighting. On 3rd June, with this in mind, the War Council sanctioned the dispatch under British command of a military expedition at once to Murmansk, and later (or if possible, simultaneously) to the White Sea port of Archangel, 370 miles to the south-east.[33]

The British had anticipated the War Council decision. The White Finns, aided by the Germans, were rapidly gaining supremacy in Finland and it was obvious that the small party of marines already at Murmansk must be strengthened. A force, known as 'Syren', was to land there under Major-General C. C. M. Maynard. In addition, a British Mission under Major-General F. C. Poole to be known as 'Elope' was intended for Archangel, where it would help muster anti-Bolshevik forces into trained formations. As early as May 16, 1918, a conference was held at the War Office to consider the composition of the 'Elope' party. It was decided that this should not exceed 500 all ranks, none of whom need be fit for general service. A Canadian contribution of five officers and eleven N.C.O.s was suggested.[34] On 27th May, Sir Edward Kemp, the Overseas Minister, agreed to the suggestion, and the officers and men were obtained from units stationed in England.[35] The party sailed for Russia in June.[36]

The 'Syren' force (to which Canada was not at first asked to contribute) numbered originally 600 British infantry, plus a machine-gun company and a half-company of Royal Engineers; in addition some 500 Royal Marines, who had landed at Murmansk during March and May, were to come under Maynard's command on his arrival. On 23rd June this force, together with the 'Elope' party, was off Murmansk as part of an Allied squadron consisting of two British, two White Russian, one American, and one French warship, all under British command. Both forces landed at Murmansk, thus averting the immediate threat to that port, but it was not until 31st July that a naval force, carrying French and Polish infantry and 100 British marines under General Poole, attacked Archangel, and with the help of a local anti-Bolshevik uprising, succeeded in taking over the town. The wharves, captured intact, yielded far less in the way of useful stores than had been expected for the Bolsheviks had had time to ship them south. It was now possible to transfer the 'Elope' party from Murmansk to Archangel during August.

During July the question of reinforcing the 'Syren' force arose; on July 12, 1918, Canada was asked if she could provide an infantry battalion, as troops with experience of a vigorous climate were required. This implied, as opposed to the first request for a Canadian quota to the 'Elope' party, that the men must be fit for general service; and since that would reduce Canadian ability to reinforce the western theatre, the invitation was declined.[37]

On the 30th, the War Office further requested eighteen Canadian officers and seventy N.C.O.s for a special mobile force being formed in the Murman area from Allied contingents and local levies. Infantry, machine gun, and artillery personnel were required to act first as instructors, and later for regimental or administrative duties in the units raised. A total of ninety-two officers and N.C.O.s—all volunteers—commanded by Lieut.-Colonel J. E. Leckie, sailed from Leith, Scotland, for Murmansk on 17th September. John Edward Leckie, a cheerful, energetic man in his middle forties, was a graduate of the Royal Military College and an experienced soldier. He had served in the South African War where he had won the D.S.O. On the Western Front, he had commanded a battalion and, for a period, a brigade, being awarded the C.M.G. in 1917.[38]

Nor was this the last request for Canadian troops to serve in northern Russia. The United States failed to include artillery in its Archangel contingent. On 3rd August Canada was asked to provide two batteries. The 16th Brigade, C.F.A., consisting of the 67th and 68th Batteries, was formed from the Canadian Reserve Artillery and left Dundee for Archangel on 20th September with a strength of eighteen officers and 469 other ranks; almost all had been on the Western Front and all elected to serve in Russia. Throughout the voyage the commander, Lieut.-Colonel C. H. L. Sharman, shared a table with Brigadier-General W. E. Ironside, the British officer who was soon to succeed General Poole. Charles Henry Ludovic Sharman was younger than Leckie. He was a fairly thickset man of middle height some forty years old; but his fresh, fair complexion and sandy moustache made him appear younger than he was until you knew him; then his manner and quick, sardonic wit showed him to be a man of experience well versed in exercising command. Commissioned in 1906, he was a major at the outbreak of war and had successfully filled various staff and regimental appointments in England and in France.[39]

Allied forces, at Murmansk and Archangel alike, were very mixed. Contingents were drawn from Britain, the United States, Italy, France, and Canada. These were joined by anti-Bolshevik Russians in both areas; and in the Murman area Finns and Karelians worked with the Allies, together with Serbians who had fought their way north from Odessa. An estimate of contributions compiled in December 1918 gave the following distribution:

	Murmansk	Archangel
British and Canadian	6,832	6,293
American	—	5,302
French	731	1,686
Italian	1,251	—
Serbian	1,220	—
Russian and other locally raised troops	4,441	2,715
	14,475	15,996[40]

Locally recruited Russian forces fluctuated considerably through recruitment and defection, but total Allied forces in the Murman and Archangel areas at no time exceeded 45,000 men.

The total Canadian contribution to North Russia, including both artillery and instructional personnel, was forty-one officers and 554 other ranks. Operations in the two areas were carried out independently of each other and each must be described separately.

THE MURMAN OPERATIONS

In the Murman Peninsula, as we have seen, the immediate task of the 'Syren' force was to prevent the occupation of Murmansk and Petchenga by German troops or by Finns co-operating with them. A further task was to pin down the German army in Finland as long as possible to prevent it from reinforcing the Western Front. Local forces would have to be raised if anything was to be accomplished, and it was therefore part of the duty of the commander at Murmansk to organize and train such troops to supplement the expeditionary force.

A factor which would undoubtedly affect the tasks of the force was the attitude of the Soviet Government. A small squadron of the Royal Navy had been based at Murmansk in 1917 to protect ships carrying supplies for Russia from submarines, and part of it remained there during the winter of 1917-18. In the early part of March 1918, when negotiations with the Germans at Brest-Litovsk seemed in a state of deadlock, the panic-stricken Bolshevik leaders ordered the local Soviet at Murmansk to co-operate with the British in defending the port from German 'robbers'. As a result of this the Murmansk authorities requested the help of the British naval commander, Rear-Admiral Thomas Kemp, and placed three Russian destroyers at his disposal. The Admiralty reinforced Kemp's squadron,[41] and in addition the first landings of marines at Murmansk were made at the invitation of the Soviets. The Bolsheviks, apprehensive of German intentions even after the Treaty of Brest-Litovsk had been signed and still smarting from its terms, had no wish to see Germans and anti-Bolshevik Finns in possession of Murmansk, and had raised no objections to the further Allied landings finally accomplished in May. Major-General F. C. Poole, who was Commander-in-Chief of all Allied troops in Northern Russia until the middle of October,* had arrived at Murmansk in May. During that month Bolshevik pessimism with regard to Germany was removed with the inauguration of official German–Soviet relations and the realization that Germany did not intend to crush Bolshevism by force provided Allied intervention was not encouraged.[42] By the end of May the Soviet Government had, in fact, received a German ultimatum requiring the immediate departure of Allied forces from Murmansk, and the opinion prevailed in Soviet circles that continued toleration of Allied intervention would result in a German march on Petrograd and Moscow.[43] Poole advised Maynard on 8th June that he had been informed by members of the Murmansk Soviet that Lenin had instructed them by telegram to warn the Allies to quit Murmansk; Allied occupation, said Lenin, was in contravention of the Treaty of Brest-Litovsk. A little later Trotsky (then Soviet Minister for War) had wired ordering the Council to eject the Allies by force. Despite this, Poole had received no official intimation of the severing of diplomatic relations between the Soviet Government and the Allies; officially there was no state of war between them. There was, however, evidence of increasing Soviet hostility and 'if', said Maynard, 'in addition to Germans and Finns, we were to be called upon to deal with the armed forces of Bolshevik Russia, we were likely to find our hands more than sufficiently occupied'.[44]

Allied troops, approaching the North Russian coastline, could hardly fail to be depressed. There were no buildings, no trees, and even in summer sea and land merged into a blur of featureless grey. Closer inspection merely confirmed the first impression—a grim, forbidding uninhabited land without trace of field or pasture. 'At length', reported a man who served there, 'the ship found a crevice,

* Independent commands were then set up, under Maynard at Murmansk, and under Ironside at Archangel.

crawled into it, and some thirty miles up a fjord, there was the port
—no recognisable town, no buildings of the slightest distinction. . . .[45]

Murmansk—a collection of drab, log-built huts plagued in summer
by heat, smells, and mosquitoes—lay on the eastern shore of the Kola
Inlet, thirty miles from the Arctic Ocean. Before the war it did not
exist. Kola, a fishing village at the head of the Kola Inlet, some six
miles distant, was the only inhabited centre in that area. The new
port came into being to handle war stores loaned to Russia by the
Allies, and rail communications with Petrograd had been established during the early war years.* The railway ran south from
Murmansk for 150 miles to Kandalaksha at the southern shore of the
Kola Peninsula on the White Sea, thence a similar distance, still
southerly, through the district of Karelia to Kem, an ancient town
on the western shore of the White Sea. From Kem it continued,
southward, through Soroki—Segeja—Maselskaya to Medvyeja Gora
at the northernmost tip of Lake Onega. The railway then followed
the western shore of the lake as far as Petrozadavodsk, where it continued to Petrograd across the neck of land between Lake Onega and
Lake Ladoga.[47]

The Finnish border ran from north to south roughly parallel with
the railway; at Kandalaksha it was fifty miles distant, and at Kem,
140. Finland had no port on the Arctic Ocean; the Finnish border
encountered the Norwegian some fifty miles before reaching the sea.
The prospect of seizing either Petchenga or Murmansk was, therefore, alluring to the Finns. Norway had a common frontier with
Russia at a point twenty miles north-west of Petchenga, which in
turn was about seventy-five miles north-west of Murmansk. The
country itself, 'devoid of soil in which even the homely radish could
flourish', was bleak in the extreme—'nothing but tundra and the
eternal forests of pine and fir'.[48]

Maynard found, in his opening conversations with Poole, that the
present distribution of Allied troops (excluding the force which he
himself had brought) was as follows:

Murmansk: 150 Royal Marines.
              400 Serbians (nearly all sick).
              150 Russians and Poles (just enlisted).

* By prisoners under Canadian engineers loaned to Russia for the purpose.[46]

Kandalaksha : French Artillery Group (ill-equipped and many
sick).
Serbian battalion (many unfit).*
Finn Legion† (of little use at present).

Kem :   250 Royal Marines.
250 of the Serbian battalion.

Petchenga :   150 landing party from H.M.S. *Cochrane*.[51]

The British commander had, after deducting the sick and totally
untrained, approximately 2,500 all ranks—including the 'Syren'
force—with which to oppose 100,000 German and White Finnish
troops. Nor was this all, for there was 'a prospect amounting almost
to a certainty, that . . . two Russian Red Guard divisions . .
would be added very shortly to the list of my opponents', and in
addition, there were certain to be strong pro-Bolshevik elements in
the town and along the railway—to say nothing of the 500 armed
and truculent sailors of the Russian warships in harbour.[52]

It seemed to Maynard that his task might with justice be regarded
as 'somewhat in the nature of a gamble', but the odds were not so
overwhelmingly against him as a mere comparison of numbers
seemed to indicate. From Kem no road suitable for military traffic
ran northwards; the only serviceable roads from the Finnish frontier
debouched on the railway at Kandalaksha and Kem. During the
summer months the swampy tundra would preclude the movement
of any but small bodies of troops, and thus an enemy advance in
strength from the south or south-west must be confined 'either to the
railway or to one or more of the several water-routes leading by lake
and river to the Kola Inlet'. These rivers, running through wild and
inhospitable country, were tortuous and rapid. Special boats would
be required to negotiate them, very probably a difficulty which could
not be surmounted; Maynard assumed, with reasonable confidence,
that any strong advance must come by the railway. Hence he concluded that to hold Murmansk he must hold the railway as far south
as possible. He accepted this violation of a principle of war—splitting

---

* This battalion had fought its way north through Russia from Odessa.[49]

† 'At Kandalaksha were collected 500 scurvy-stricken Red Finns, who had
been driven out of their country by the Whites. Their tendencies were probably
Bolshevik; but they would certainly be ready to oppose the White Finns, and
perhaps the Germans.'[50]

his force—for he realized that his best chance of frustrating a massed attack by Germans and Finns lay in fighting a series of 'delaying actions, under conditions favourable to ourselves'. These conditions would be supplied by the nature of the country and the railway itself.[53]

'The railway crossed innumerable streams and rivers, spanned by bridges up to nearly 200 yards in length—and all were built of wood. A few bundles of straw and dry branches, a liberal supply of paraffin, and a box of matches would suffice for the destruction of any one of them. And their reconstruction, even if unhampered by us, would entail in many cases weeks and perhaps months of labour. For the majority of the rivers were swift-flowing and deep, and many were spanned by no other bridge from source to mouth.'[54]

Maynard decided that Poole's selection of both Kandalaksha and Kem as the two main defensive centres on the railway had been sound. Both were possible concentration areas for hostile forces and use as such must be prevented. Furthermore, these towns were accessible from the White Sea, and thus their garrisons need not have to depend entirely on railway communications; for the Allies enjoyed command of the sea. 'With these posts held, and strengthened, as I hoped they would be shortly by the arrival of Allied contingents, we should have a reasonable chance of preventing Murmansk falling into German hands, so long as summer conditions prevailed.' But the Soviet attitude could upset these calculations. A Bolshevik force at Kem would be 'bad enough'; if at Kandalaksha, it would be 'doubly serious'; and if at Murmansk itself, the Allied position would be hopeless.[55]

Petchenga was considered by the Force Commander to be of secondary importance; access to it on the land side would be extremely difficult. In any case, Maynard did not have sufficient troops to reinforce it at present, and thus he decided that its garrison would only be strengthened at urgent call.

Having arrived at a plan, Maynard left Murmansk on 27th June to inspect the railway and its garrisons as far south as Kem. He took with him a Russian-speaking intelligence officer, two other staff officers and, as escort, a platoon of British infantry. The journey was important in that it forced Lenin to show his hand. Fifty miles north of Kandalaksha, Russian railway officials unsuccessfully attempted to delay the British train. At Kandalaksha itself the reason became clear. A trainload of Bolshevik troops, with engine attached and steam up, was about to leave for the north. Though outnumbered eight to one, the British commander bluffed his Bolshevik counterpart into inaction until Serbian reinforcements arrived from the local garrison who took over the train. Maynard gathered from his altercation with the Bolshevik commander that other Red Guards were following up this leading detachment. He therefore left the Bolshevik train under guard of the Serbs, increased his escort by fifty men from the Kandalaksha garrison, and continued on to Kem, which he found thronged with Red Guards from two recently arrived trains. At Kem the Allies had 500 men, a naval 12-pounder gun, and an improvised armoured train; to these were added the escort from Maynard's train, now numbering 100. There was therefore no doubt about the power of the Allies to detain the Red troops who complied with orders to detrain. Maynard ordered the officer commanding at Kem not to allow any Bolshevik troops to proceed towards Murmansk. He then returned to Murmansk via Kandalaksha where he learned that the Red Guards encountered were but the advanced guard of a large Bolshevik force whose purpose was to attack the Allies and drive them from Murmansk. On receipt of this information, Maynard ordered the Bolshevik troops at both Kandalaksha and Kem to be disarmed.[56] He took further action: first, he reinforced the Kem garrison by two British infantry platoons and a machine-gun section; second, Red Guard detachments at various localities between Murmansk and Kem—ostensibly to safeguard the railway—were also disarmed; finally, Maynard ordered a search for weapons at Kem, Kandalaksha and intermediate villages. Including the arms taken from Red Guards, some 10,000 rifles, sixty machine guns, and large quantities of ammunition were confiscated. The only threat Maynard now had to counter at Murmansk was German.[57]

The outcome of Maynard's actions was threefold. The Bolsheviks ceased to move north—instead, their leading contingents withdrew to Soroki, burning bridges as they went. Despite no official break in Allied–Soviet relations 'there was rupture, open and unmistakable'. And lastly, the Murmansk Soviet decided to sever relations with Moscow and support the Allied cause.[58]

Maynard returned to Murmansk from his first journey down the line on 3rd July. The next day, after discussions with Poole and the Murmansk Soviet (whereby he gained a free hand to take any

military measures possible to combat a Bolshevik–German–White
Finn combination), he started out again to make a more detailed inspection; this time with no escort—'convincing proof' he wryly observed, 'of our military poverty'.[59] At Kem, Maynard held a recruiting drive which was not immediately successful. There he learned
that Bolshevik troops at Soroki had commenced a series of outrages
against all suspected of Allied leanings. A British light cruiser,
H.M.S. *Attentive*, with a detachment of the Finn Legion, had been
sent from Kandalaksha. Maynard left Kem for Soroki. Several
smaller bridges had been sufficiently repaired to permit the passage
of a light locomotive and coach, but a few miles from Soroki an
eighty-foot bridge had been completely destroyed. Here, the British
commander abandoned the train, crossed the river by small boat, and
resumed his journey on a derelict railway trolley, by means of which
on 8th July he made 'an unheralded and somewhat inglorious entry'
into the outskirts of Soroki. The appearance of the British warship,
he found, had been enough for the Bolsheviks—the majority had retreated south. British sailors and the Finns combed out the few that
remained. Maynard decided to garrison Soroki, using for this the
long-suffering Serbian battalion, to be followed by the armoured
train from Kem as soon as the railway had been repaired. His decision was based on the necessity of securing recruits for Russian
units—it was only by rendering life secure in the large towns and
making Allied influence felt that he could hope to do this. On the
14th Maynard arrived back in Murmansk.[60]

So far, von der Goltz had made no move. Raiding parties from
Finland—who had reached the railway in June—had been withdrawn. This inactivity, in all likelihood, could be attributed to ex-
aggeration in the reports of enemy agents.

> 'In the early autumn for example, though my whole force had not
> then reached a total of 6,000, papers were found on a German
> agent instructing him to ascertain the number of divisions on the
> Murmansk side, together with the names of their respective com-
> manders.'[61]

Whatever the reason, it was highly satisfactory to Maynard, who was
thus afforded a breathing-space in which to raise and train local units
and to expand those already raised. Of the former, the Karelian*

---

* Karelia is the name given to the tract of country lying roughly between the
railway and Finland, from Kandalaksha on the north to Lake Onega on the

Regiment was organized towards the end of July; the latter units consisted of the Slavo-British Legion (made up of local Russians, enrolled by General Poole) and the Finn Legion.

'My chief concern for the moment was to enlist and give rudimentary training to sufficient numbers to ensure the establishment of an effective outpost system pushed out towards the frontier of Finland. This was accomplished within a surprisingly short period, the Finn Legion at Kandalaksha and the Karelian Regiment at Kem soon reaching a strength enabling them to watch all likely lines of advance and later on, to take a chief part in repelling attacks by considerable bodies of White Finns under German leadership.'[63]

General Maynard now visited Petchenga, travelling by sea.[64] He found it to be a tiny village consisting of huts and a substantially built monastery at the extreme head of the harbour. It was, in fact, a subsidiary monastery built to stage pilgrims landing by sea before they went farther inland to a larger monastery five or six miles away. There was a church with an onion-shaped dome, a detached belfry and a few large weatherproof timber resthouses, the whole place being surrounded by rocky hills thinly covered with birch scrub.[65] Its defences were entrusted to H.M.S. *Cochrane*—in harbour—and a landing party from the vessel in the monastery buildings, which had been held successfully against a recent raid by White Finns.

Petchenga has been improved since 1918. Finland received it from the Soviets under the Dorpat Treaty of 1920 (ratified in January 1921), named it Petsamo, and developed a nickel mine in the neighbourhood. Harbour installations were built as well as an Arctic highway connecting the new port with railhead at Rovaniemi, 200 miles to the south. During the Second World War, the Germans occupied Petsamo and from it inflicted considerable damage on Allied convoys bringing aid to Russia.[66] But at the time of Maynard's visit, no roads led to the village, communications being mere tracks, the best of which ran to the Norwegian frontier. The nearest railway centre in Finland was 200 miles away, there were no shipping facili-

---

south. Though coming originally from the interior of Russia, its people had developed a most independent spirit, regarding themselves almost as a nation apart. The Karelian Regiment was open for enlistment to Karelians only, and its strength eventually rose to over 4000.[62]

ties whatever, and Maynard concluded that Petchenga was in little danger.

> 'To capture Petchenga . . . would demand the equipment and despatch of an organized force, with guns, engineering material, and an immense quantity of supplies, since none . . . could be obtained on the spot. What this would have entailed, with the nearest railhead 250 miles away, and no roads available for other than the lightest of wheel transport, was fairly easy to calculate; and one hour's examination of the locality convinced me that von der Goltz would not waste men and material in a real effort to establish himself at Petchenga. Had the place held out any attractions as a submarine base, I might have been left in some doubt. But . . . it was inconceivable that such a base could have been established . . . without years of toil and concentrated labour, which must include the construction of 250 miles of railway. . .
> To me it seemed certain that if Germany were really bent on acquiring a North Russian base, she should and would concentrate against Murmansk. With Murmansk in her possession, Petchenga, if she desired it, was hers for the asking.'[67]

Maynard decided that the existing naval garrison, reinforced perhaps by a small party from Murmansk and backed by *Cochrane's* guns, would be sufficient to deal with any attack likely to be made.

On 30th July, with a landing force of about 1500 (including the Poles from Murmansk, 100 marines and a portion of the machine-gun company 'borrowed' from Maynard) General Poole sailed for Archangel which he succeeded in taking. Maynard was left in command at Murmansk.

Towards the close of July, work began on two major projects—a defence scheme for Murmansk, and on preparing accommodation.[68] The latter was needed for reinforcements requested by Maynard, as well as by the ever-increasing numbers enlisting in local units. The demand for buildings, furthermore, would be increased by changed dispositions at the onset of winter; for, from November on, the whole country would be passable for enemy troops, and no longer could reliance be placed on the railway as the main line of advance. Any future alteration of dispositions again meant building. Local workers, under the supervision of British sappers, took these tasks in hand. The defence scheme, to counter a break-through of German forces to the northern seaboard—a major Bolshevik attack was discounted—provided defences barring likely lines of advance in summer or winter. Vantage points were selected sufficiently far forward to prevent the enemy from bringing effective fire to bear on the port. On these, and the provision of mobile reserves, the scheme depended. In addition, the plan included a rallying point for all troops should the Allies be forced to evacuate Murmansk. For this Maynard selected Alexandrovsk, at the mouth of the Kola Inlet. From it, the Allied commander would be well placed to prevent the use of Murmansk as a submarine base; the telegraph cable from Scotland came ashore there, and thus communication with England and Archangel could be maintained; further, the little port possessed anchorage facilities, and some buildings for accommodation and storage. Supplies, stores, and ammunition for 2000 men for a month were collected and housed. By early October the whole defensive system, though not yet completed, had progressed sufficiently to be utilized in an emergency.

During the second week in August reports reached Murmansk of large enemy concentrations along the Finnish frontier with, it appeared, Kandalaksha and Kem as the immediate objectives. Though no Allied reinforcements had as yet arrived, Maynard determined to take the offensive. He based his decision on two factors : first, local recruiting had been brisk—the Finn Legion now numbered 800, and the Karelian Regiment stood at 1200—and secondly, von der Goltz's apparent misapprehension of Allied strength must be fostered. An active policy was imperative. The German commander must have actual evidence that the Allies were 'ready and willing to try conclusions with his army'.[69]

'. . . [The local troops were] totally ignorant of modern warfare, and their ideas of discipline were more than vague. But they could use their rifles in a fairly workmanlike way; were ready to obey orders according to their lights; and were accustomed to travel with a minimum of food and impedimenta. Moreover, as they were fed, clothed, and housed on a scale contrasting vividly with the want and privation of many months past, they were fully content with their lot. Added to this, the Finns were thirsting for a chance of paying off old scores on the Whites, who had driven them with such ruthless ferocity from their homes; while the Karelians, staunchest of patriots, would be fighting to rid their country of an invader.'[70]

The embroilment with the Bolsheviks was disconcerting, for it increased Allied difficulties by compelling a portion of a meagre force to be employed otherwise than against the main enemy. There was however, one favourable element even in this—the Bolsheviks, unlikely to minimize the strength of a force which had compelled them to evacuate hurriedly the whole Murman area, would tend to mislead the German commander still further in over-estimating his opponent.

Operations, accordingly, were ordered as follows:

1. A mobile column, composed of Karelians and Finns (with such backing of Allied troops as could be spared) would operate towards the Finnish frontier from Kandalaksha and another from Kem.

2. One hundred and fifty British and Serbian troops would operate southwards against the Bolsheviks from Soroki.

3. The existing garrison at Petchenga would be stiffened by adding 200 Serbians (who had been convalescing at Murmansk, now fit).*[71]

It is now necessary to follow the fortunes of the operations listed and which all commenced during the third week in August. The reinforcing of Petchenga merely rid Maynard's mind, so far as possible, of anxiety regarding its safety while Allied troops were engaged elsewhere.

To deal first with Soroki, we find that the three weeks' dash south was ordered for three reasons: first, in the absence of both an efficient intelligence service and planes, it was to establish what Bolshevik forces had been concentrated between Soroki and Lake Onega; secondly, by so doing, it would further mislead the Germans, causing them to assume the Allies had a sufficiency of troops to warrant an attack on two fronts; thirdly, it was to deceive the enemy still more by allowing false orders—referring to large formations to be employed in an Allied offensive on all fronts, scrupulously compiled by Maynard himself—to fall into the hands of the Bolsheviks. These orders, when passed over to the Germans (on which the Allied commander had shrewdly counted), subsequently fulfilled their purpose. The risk in launching this tiny force far to the south against unknown odds proved to be justified. Bolsheviks, encountered twenty miles south of Soroki, were driven back ten miles on to their supports. The Allied column then attacked these main positions boldly;

* The remaining Serbians at Murmansk, too sick to hold out any hopeful prospect of early recovery, were evacuated to England.

(*photo: Radio Times Hulton Picture Library*)

3　Major-General Edmund Ironside

4
The Czechs move
East, 1918

Men of the Czech
Corps turn over
their arms at
Penza

A Czech armoured
train showing
method of
camouflage with
boughs

after suffering heavy casualties the Bolsheviks withdrew, leaving behind quantities of stores and ammunition. They were pursued for twenty miles and finally reached the shelter of Povyenets, a small port on the northern shore of Lake Onega, 130 miles south of Soroki. The Bolshevik force was estimated at an infantry battalion, with 200 cavalry but no artillery. Thus, the sally had achieved its purpose; further, it seemed unlikely that the Bolsheviks in that area, after the rough handling they had received, would make any aggressive effort for some time to come.

Meanwhile the columns from Kandalaksha and Kem had advanced towards the Finnish frontier. From the very start, both experienced difficulties with the supply system; such tracks as existed were even worse than reported, rendering wheeled transport valueless; pack animals were unavailable. The only solution was to follow the waterways where possible, but shortage of boats and swift currents precluded efficient use; stores over much of the way had to be manhandled by civilian carriers or the troops themselves. Even at first, when numbers were small and bases within a score of miles, it was difficult enough; before the close of operations, local enthusiasm had swelled the strength of the columns—Kandalaksha to more than a thousand, and Kem to double that figure—adding to the difficulties. 'That these were overcome, and an unbroken series of victories gained, speaks volumes for the grit and determination of Finns and Karelians alike, and for the fine fighting qualities of the handful of British officers and N.C.O.s who led them.'[72]

The Kandalaksha column, consisting of Finns and led by a Canadian (Major R. B. Burton*) encountered White Finns during the second day of its move direct towards the frontier. The column made steady headway during weeks of desultory fighting in a waste of forest, lake and bog. The Finn Legion everywhere mastered their White compatriots, who, after many reverses, finally withdrew behind their frontier. Burton then turned south-west towards the Karelian column from Kem to clear the intervening country of enemy troops. On 3rd October he fought a decisive action on the western shore of Lake Pyavozero against the last formed body of the enemy in northern Karelia, routed them, and drove them back across the border.

---

* One of five officers contributed by Canada to the 'Elope' party, destined for Archangel. In view of his employment with the Finn Legion he was left at Murmansk.

C

The Kem column under Lieut.-Colonel Woods* (a British officer), advanced along the northern bank of the Kem River. It was opposed by White Finn Guards, but steadily pushed them back in minor engagements to their advanced base at Ukhtinskaya. There, on 11th September, a battle ensued. For some time the issue remained in doubt, until the Karelians contrived a turning movement across country deemed to be impassable. This decided the issue; the enemy, completely routed, abandoned the base and ammunition, rifles, trench mortars, and machine guns. The column then concentrated on clearing central Karelia of the enemy, effected early in October following a second batttle fought on 21st September at Voknavalot-skaya, 130 miles west of Kem, close to the frontier; there the enemy lost between 200 and 300 in killed alone, machine guns, trench mortars, 600 rifles, ammunition, thirty boats, and several hundred pairs of skis.[73]

The columns inflicted losses on the enemy estimated at 2,000. German officers and N.C.O.s found amongst the dead, but no German troops, led Maynard to conclude that von der Goltz, like himself, had refrained from throwing in his own regulars; he had used, instead, local troops under German leadership. It was likely that his Finn auxiliaries had been pushed forward to obtain, if possible, a foothold on the railway. Had they met with success, the chances were that they would have been followed up by German troops, and a determined effort made to drive the Allies from the Murman area.

The results of the Karelian offensives were out of all proportion to the size of the forces used; most important was the effect on Allied morale of an unbroken series of victories. The White Finns, on the other hand, having been 'badly mauled' and driven back for weeks, would hardly be in a condition to assume the offensive. Secondly, local forces had been more than doubled; some 3,000 were now fit to give a good account of themselves. Thirdly, vital ground had been gained—organized opposition to a German advance could now be established from thirty to 100 miles from the railway. Moreover, this country would not be familiar to German troops; transport arrangements for them would need elaborate preparations; and the ground lent itself to the guerrilla type of warfare favoured by Maynard's

---

* Woods, a patriotic Irishman, organized and commanded the Karelian Regiment. His wild but stout-hearted soldiers wore shamrocks, cut from 'Shamrock' plug tobacco tins, as cap and collar badges. As might be expected, these troops became known as 'Royal Irish Karelians'.

levies. For the present, the safety of Murmansk was assured.[74]

Offensive operations in Karelia, as we have seen, lasted from the third week in August until early in October. At the end of August, Maynard gave thought to the winter. The outcome in Karelia had not then become clear. With the enemy so much stronger in numbers, victory hardly seemed likely; the best that could be hoped for was to impose delay on the enemy, and it seemed almost certain that the two columns must be driven back eventually. This would of course give the enemy a hold on the railway, preventing both the supply and the extrication by rail of Allied garrisons at Kem and Soroki; and if late enough in the season (the end of September brought hard frost and snow), no reinforcements or supplies could be brought through the frozen White Sea. Prudence dictated the immediate retirement of both columns to Kandalaksha, as well as the garrisons at Soroki and Kem, whilst there was still time thus making Kandalaksha (the main gateway to Murmansk) extremely secure. Militarily, in face of heavy odds, the security of Murmansk demanded this course of action before the threat to the railway became a fact and the White Sea closed to shipping. Maynard, however, decided otherwise.

Strategically unsound as the retention of the southern posts might be, other considerations indicated that they should be held. First, the loss of a vast recruiting ground would destroy Allied hopes of reconstituting an appreciable Russian front against the Germans; even the Karelian troops might defect when faced with transfer north. Secondly, for the inhabitants of Kem, Soroki, and other smaller towns it would be utter calamity—the Bolsheviks would handle them savagely. Finally, all officials co-operating with the Allies at Murmansk and down the line would be against evacuation. There could be no compromise between two such alternatives; and events justified the bolder.

Contemplation at this time of winter conditions and the unrestricted movement they would bring led the Allied commander to another decision—to construct and man the defensive line at Murmansk. Troops available fell short of the 'absolute minimum' of 3000 for this even counting the Italian Expeditionary Force of 1200, due to arrive shortly. Only one solution presented itself, the complete evacuation of Petchenga and the utilization of its garrison (now 500, made up of Serbs, British sappers, and the landing party from *Cochrane*) at Murmansk. The War Office, influenced by the Admiralty, objected to this and promised reinforcements. Accordingly Maynard asked for one infantry brigade, three batteries of field artillery, two machine-gun companies, and one trench mortar battery. His estimate was accepted without demur; but due to shipping difficulties the first contingent (including the Canadian contribution) did not reach Murmansk until 26th September, and the last (the brigade head-quarters and two infantry battalions) arrived a fortnight after the armistice, which had, of course, removed all danger of a German attack. The Italians arrived on 3rd September but succumbed to the climate almost immediately. The net increase in strength during that month did not permit Maynard to man the Murmansk defences fully; a Finnish attack on 28th September against the Petchenga outposts on the Norwegian frontier caused him to reinforce that garrison with half the 11th Royal Sussex and one machine-gun company (almost all his first British reinforcements), and a fortnight later he added for patrol work sixty French skiers. Thereafter Petchenga ceased to cause anxiety, even after *Cochrane* was withdrawn at the end of October to prevent her from being frozen in.[75]

The Petchenga garrison remained there throughout the winter, warmly clad but on short rations at first since it was not known to what extent supplies could be renewed. Trawlers managed to get through, however (sometimes with the help of an ice-breaker) so that the ration was increased. Huts, whose double walls were insulated with moss or sawdust, were warm, and there was plenty of wood for fuel. To the east of Petchenga a crag jutted out from a hill, and on this marines had established an observation post. This two-man hut, commanding a wide view along the fjord as far as the coastal range bordering the Barents Sea and inland as far as the eye could reach, was enlarged by sappers who blasted a ledge to accommodate the bigger structure which camouflage rendered almost invisible from below. Here, perched on the lofty crag, an officer and nine men spent the winter in all kinds of weather with no deterioration in health or spirits. The weather was mostly of two kinds, clear and still with temperatures dropping to forty below, or the landscape would be blotted out by blizzards tearing at the snowclad hills. In December the nights were twenty-three hours long, but the superb display of the Northern Lights when it was calm and clear compensated to some extent for lack of sun. By May 1919 most of the garrison had been relieved and dispersed to various points along the Murman Railway.[76]

During the autumn of 1918 the situation at Murmansk came under the influence of events outside Russia. As October passed, it became evident that the German army in Finland was being reduced; this, indeed, had started in September. The great Allied offensive in France—completely unexpected by Maynard—compelled the German command to detach troops from the north to replace casualties on the Western Front. By the middle of October von der Goltz's army was 'so denuded as to preclude all thoughts of aggressive action on his part'; the armistice in November saw the successful completion of the initial Allied tasks.

It is now desirable to sum up Allied achievements at Murmansk to November 1918; subsequent embroilment with Soviet Russia will be dealt with separately. Most important, the Germans had been prevented from using either Murmansk or Petchenga as a submarine base. Without a footing on the North Russian seaboard, Germany could not intensify submarine operations in the North Atlantic. The Murmansk force was equally successful in its second task. After the Russian collapse in 1917, fifty-four German infantry divisions were transported from East to West during the nine months from September 1917 to the end of May 1918. 'The stream ceased abruptly with the first landing of the Allies at Murmansk'—no movement during June, July, and August. Over this period Maynard's small force, by means of bold operations and deceptive measures, tied down the German army in Finland, stopping the probable transfer of some 40,000* reinforcements, at a time when the war's final issue was still in doubt. German troops were withdrawn from Finland in September and October, after attempts to seize the North Russian ports had finally been abandoned; but by then it was too late for them to influence the final struggle in France and Belgium. The strategic policy of Allied intervention at Murmansk received ample vindication in the success of a mere handful of troops, who had 'done more to

---

* Though these figures have been taken from Maynard's account and checked against other reputable British sources, General von der Goltz disputes them. In a letter to Captain John Hundevad (editor of the Canadian *Legionary*) dated August 10, 1936, he contends that his Baltic Division in Finland originally numbered 12,000 men. Of these, 3,000 were ordered away in May 1918. He agrees, after the Allied landings at Murmansk, that there were no more transfers until September and that the Germans had organized and trained a new Finnish army. Even if von der Goltz's figures are accepted, a very small Allied force had still been successful in tying down a much stronger German force.

assist in the overthrow of Germany than could have been accomplished by many times their number employed in any other theatre of the war'.[77]

WITH IRONSIDE AT ARCHANGEL

Meanwhile, at Archangel, events had developed on different lines; there, the enemy was always the Bolsheviks.

The voyage from Murmansk had not passed without incident. Of the three naval vessels preceding the small convoy (the British light cruiser *Attentive*, seaplane carrier *Nairana* and the French cruiser *Amiral Aube*) the French ship went aground in fog on 30th-31st July, the first night out of Murmansk. Her guns and landing force of 200 French troops and 100 Royal Marines were thus lost to the expedition —a serious blow when it was not known what degree of opposition would be encountered.[78]

At this time of the year southerly winds blow the ice up north so that, apart from a few floes, the passage was clear. Daylight found the two British vessels anchored to the north-west of Modyuski Island, which, fortified with two batteries of four 6-inch guns and one of four 4-inch, guarded the seaward approaches to Archangel. Against these *Attentive* could bring to bear only two 6-inch and three 4-inch guns on a broadside; nevertheless, she sailed close in and called for the surrender of the forts. This the Red commandant at first agreed to do; he then changed his mind on receiving instructions from Archangel to resist to the utmost. *Attentive*, therefore, stood out to sea and opened fire with the almost impossible task of knocking out the well-protected guns or mountings while she herself remained conspicuous and wholly vulnerable. A Bolshevik shell struck the foremost funnel of the ship, putting two boilers out of action, but by now well-directed naval fire began to succeed beyond expectations. Under its cover seaplanes from *Nairana* swooped low to bomb the batteries, infantry and sailors landed, and by nightfall all was over. The way to Archangel now lay open.[79]

Anti-Bolsheviks in Archangel itself, heartened by the news of the approaching expedition and the fall of Modyuski, overthrew the Bolshevik administration on 2nd August so that when the Allied troopships steamed into the port that evening, the quays and river bank were crowded with welcoming townsfolk; tug-sirens, the whistles of other craft, and cheers greeted the arriving troops as liberators. The old Russian tricolour flags flew over the large but shabby town dominated by the cupola and four spires of the cathedral shining in the setting sun.[80]

The seat of the provisional Northern Government was immediately established at Archangel under a socialist, President Nicholas V. Chaikovsky, described by Ironside as 'a placid old gentleman of over seventy years of age, very tall and thin, but surprisingly active in body . . . completely and utterly unmilitary'; he did not seem to realize the Bolsheviks could not be defeated except by force. 'He was living quietly in the past.'[81] Chaikovsky himself was displaced by a conservative military *coup d'état* in September, but he was brought back as President with Colonel B. A. Douroff as Governor. Douroff did not last long. He was a man of about forty-five—short, with an untidy beard—who had never been entrusted with a command of any sort in the old army. His total efforts at recruiting had been to raise one company which, when ordered to parade for Ironside's inspection on 29th October, refused to turn out. Douroff, completely mortified, resigned and was sent on a mission to Paris by Chaikovsky. General Marushevsky, a tiny man about five feet tall who had commanded the Russian troops in France, succeeded Douroff on 17th November, and he too soon had troubles with a locally raised unit of Russian troops. A month after his appointment the new commander ordered the 1st Archangel Company to parade; it refused to leave barracks and was persuaded to do so only after other Russian troops had opened mortar fire. The ringleaders were found guilty of mutiny and sentenced to death, commuted by Ironside to terms of imprisonment. In January 1919 Chaikovsky left for Paris to join the White Russian Council there, and was succeeded by P. J. Zoubov. About the same time General Eugene K. Miller, a White Russian of Baltic origin, succeeded Marushevsky as Governor-General with the additional function of Commander-in-Chief. The provisional Government co-operated fully with the Allies throughout the intervention period.[82]

Canada's contingent for Archangel entrained in London on 19th September. The scene on that late summer day has been vividly described :

'The crowd on the platform at King's Cross was a riot of colour. . . . The troops of nearly every Allied nation, from bearded Russians in baggy uniforms with large gold epaulettes to French colonial infantry in *bleu d'horizon*, mingled with groups of khaki-clad British soldiers and individual officers and N.C.O.s from countries as far apart as Serbia and Japan.

'At one end of the platform, a part of this international throng, were the officers and men of the 16th Brigade, Canadian Field Artillery. Though newly organized, they looked smart and fit, for all were veterans of the Western Front. All, too, were volunteers.

'As they waited for the order to entrain the Canadians saw a familiar figure approaching them. Moving relentlessly through the press of soldiers was a very large British officer, whose general's forage cap did not entirely conceal the red hair, hearty complexion and strong features which the troops instantly identified as belonging to an old friend. This was Brigadier-General Edmund Ironside, fresh from commanding a brigade in France, whose early association as a staff officer with the 4th Canadian Division was well remembered. He was a gunner himself, and they gave him a cheer as he approached. He shook hands with several old friends in the ranks, and it made the Canadians feel a little less strange to learn that he was to accompany them on their bizarre adventure.'[83]

Sailing next day from Dundee, the Canadian field brigade reached Archangel on 1st October and disembarked two days later : Ironside arrived in the same convoy, and thus had a fortnight with General Poole before taking over command from him as Major-General. Ironside found that the Bolsheviks, after their expulsion from Archangel, had been closely pursued by Allied troops 'to make elbow-room for the enlistement of as many Russians as possible during the winter'. In the face of stiffening Bolshevik resistance, Poole's force was now consolidating its defences in case the Bolsheviks should turn to the attack. Five columns had been pushed forward. Of the two main columns, one had reached a point 100 miles down the Volodga Railway, which ran due south from Archangel. The second was upstream of the confluence of the Dvina and Vaga rivers, south-east of Archangel, with forces on both these waterways, those along the Vaga being closer to the railway. This column—about 240 miles from Archangel—was the most advanced, owing to the aid given by the Royal Navy. Brig.-General R. G. Finlayson, a British officer, commanded both columns—British, French, American and Russian troops—despite the wide distance between the river and the railway which, in the event of advance, would widen farther. Two smaller columns protected the flanks of the railway column, at the Yemtsa river to the east and on the Onega river (on the White Sea) to the west. The fifth column, a minor one, was at Pinega, on the river of that name, a hundred miles east of Archangel.[84]

Allied forces landed at Archangel were pitifully small. The War Office's appreciation of what troops should be sent to North Russia compiled in June 1918 called for a brigade of infantry with two or three batteries of artillery, a due proportion of engineers and technical troops, together with two or three flights of seaplanes to hold Murmansk and Petchenga; and, for the defence of Archangel, *at least*, an equivalent force. 'For any operations such as an advance to Vologda,' the appreciation went on, 'a force of at least one or two divisions would be necessary,'[85] but the detachment of such a force from the Western Front had, of course, been found impossible.

In August, General Poole had no more than two battalions of fighting troops—the French 21st Colonial Battalion, and a battalion of Royal Scots made up of category C3 men who were unfit for active service in France and whose use in Russia, therefore, was limited. These were by no means enough for the effective defence of Archangel, by War Office reckoning, yet with them Poole had nevertheless boldly followed up the retreating Bolsheviks in an attempt to gain as much territory as possible before winter set in. A deep advance would not only gain recruiting ground; it would also facilitate junction with a hoped-for advance from Siberia and it was in this direction along the Dvina that the British battalion made most progress.

During the first week in September an American force made up of three battalions of the 339th Infantry Regiment and three companies of engineers, numbering in all some five thousand men, reached Archangel under the contingent commander, Colonel George E. Stewart, enabling Poole to reinforce the Dvina column and the minor Yemtsa River column, as well as that formed by the French battalion operating along the Vologda Railway. The Americans, who had been sent to Archangel from England instead of going to France, were Middle Western draftees recruited at Fort Custer, Michigan, in 1918 and as such were completely devoid of battle experience. But at least they were able-bodied, and not battle-weary as almost all the British and French troops were after four years of war.[86]

Proceeding south along the Vologda railway in boxcars, the men of the American 3rd Battalion reached the town of Obozerskaya, eighty miles from Archangel, on the morning of 7th September. This

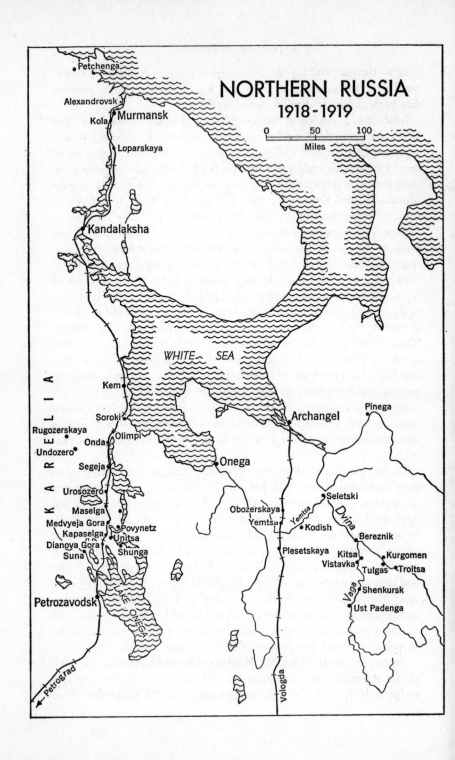

NORTHERN RUSSIA
1918-1919

0   50   100
Miles

Petchenga

Alexandrovsk

Kola   Murmansk

Loparskaya

Kandalaksha

WHITE   SEA

Kem

K A R E L I A

Soroki

Rugozerskaya

Onda   Olimpi

Undozero

Segeja

Urosozero

Maselga

Medvyeja Gora

Kapaselga

Dianova Gora   Unitsa

Suna   Shunga

Povynetz

Petrozavodsk

LAKE ONEGA

Archangel   Pinega

Onega

Seletski

Obozerskaya   Yemtsa

Yemtsa   Yemtsa   Kodish

Dvina

Bereznik

Plesetskaya   Kitsa   Kurgomen

Vistavka   Tulgas   Troitsa

Vaga   Shenkursk

Ust Padenga

Vologda

← Petrograd

town had been captured by the French the previous day. The main Bolshevik supply base on the railway front was at Plesetskaya, some fifty miles south, and this was set as the first objective.[87] A British armoured train on the front, however, was matched by one brought up by the Bolsheviks, who also had planes for reconnaissance and bombing. An attempt to reach Plesetskaya at the end of September failed.

Meanwhile the 1st Battalion of the 339th Infantry reinforced the British on the Dvina river on 17th September. The Americans caught up with the Scots in the vicinity of Chamova, a village thirty miles south of Bereznik and about 150 miles from Archangel along the river.[88] The Dvina was navigable by barges as far as Kotlas, situated 400 miles south-east of Archangel. A branch of the Trans-Siberian Railway, 200 miles long, connected Kotlas with Viatka on the main Trans-Siberian line. General Poole's plan of advancing as far as possible along the Dvina before winter would therefore greatly facilitate a link-up with the friendly forces expected to move westwards from Siberia by way of the Trans-Siberian Railway.

The Dvina Column pushed on upriver along the bank of the mile-wide stream through low, marshy country and mud. The next village, Seltso, was occupied on 20th September after a short bombardment by a few White Russian field guns in support of the Allied infantry. They then paused to permit a British gunboat and supplies to be brought up, and meanwhile two American platoons, which had been left at Bereznik while the remainder of the battalion went on to Seltso, were ordered up the Vaga. The river Vaga, a narrow and swift stream, flows into the Dvina at Bereznik; Poole rightly appreciated that he must hold the approaches which this river would afford against Bolshevik troops moving to cut off his Dvina force now at Seltso. With the few troops at his disposal he had been unable to attempt to do so before the American troops had arrived. A small American column, therefore, was directed on the Vaga town of Shenkursk, after Archangel the second largest place in the area, and therefore an objective important for reasons of prestige as well as strategy. The column, of less than two hundred men, left Bereznik by riverboat on 16th September and on the following day took the town without a shot being fired. The Bolshevik garrison fled in panic at the first news of the column's approach.[89]

Shenkursk, a popular summer resort, was built largely of brick. It had a monastery, fine churches, schools and an army barracks. Its population included the cultured owners of summer homes who had moved into permanent occupancy to ride out the Bolshevik storm. Here the Americans, quartered briefly in comfortable barracks, enjoyed the social life which the town provided. When winter came, this included skating on the Vaga, skiing, afternoon teas, dancing, and the company of lovely young *barishnas*. Pony sleighs, bearing bearded men and fur-clad women, cantered briskly through the hard white streets towards brightly lit engagements behind steamy panes of glass. Like Brussels before Waterloo, there was the sound of revelry by night and, as in the Belgian capital, it was short-lived. While it lasted, however, the gaiety of Shenkursk afforded a tantalizing glimpse of what life must have been like in the old Imperial days.[90]

Reinforced with British and Russian troops, the column pushed on after garrisoning Shenkursk, and at the end of September had consolidated in the face of stiffening Red resistance at Rovdino, a village thirty miles south of Shenkursk and about 240 miles from Archangel. By this time the Dvina column had got forward to Tulgas some fifty miles south-east of Bereznik, and thus not much farther than the Scots had managed alone, and it was here that the Canadian 67th Battery joined the force. Bereznik continued to be the supply base for both the river columns.

Before the arrival of Canadian gunners, the main river column had been dependent on the Navy for its artillery apart from a few Russian guns; for long-range fire it continued to be until the arrival of 60-pounder guns in 1919. The river was too shallow for large ships, and at first the enemy had better vessels than the extempore gunboats contrived by the British from local river steamers; his guns considerably outranged our own. A monitor mounting a 7.5-inch gun was brought up from Archangel after it had been lightened to negotiate sandbanks and bars, and this 'veritable dreadnought' proved a match for the Red flotilla. Thanks to this vessel the column had been able to achieve its long advance, but even then progress had been slow. The withdrawing Bolshevik flotilla left mines behind which had to be cleared; troops were forced to halt to avoid outstripping their artillery and water transport. Again, if the troops floundering waist-deep through marshes or plunging through forest in the sub-tropical summer heat were held up, the Navy, thus deprived of flank support, would not dash on up-river into ambushes of concealed batteries and machine-gun fire.

Another disadvantage became clear with the onset of winter, and this was a factor of decisive importance to the campaign. The Allies suffered from being dependent on more northerly water communications than the enemy, and these froze over sooner, preventing the Navy from supporting the ground troops at the end of 1918 and in the spring of 1919 for a short period when enemy ships were free to move. Ironside, unlike Poole who had failed to do so, saw the need for 60-pounders with the ground forces to give support when naval vessels had to withdraw if they were not to be frozen in, but these did not arrive from England until 1919. Our ships, in order to reach Archangel, had to be clear of the river by 7th October, whereas the Bolsheviks did not retire until three weeks later and those three-week periods in the autumn and the coming spring were very critical.[91]

The front was not continuous; in fact, the front of the Vologda railway column amounted to little more than a thousand yards. The troops occupied block-houses protected by wire. Administrative arrangements were complicated in that all supplies, except for the railway column, must be brought up by water and then be transferred to carts. Snow would necessitate the use of sleighs to reach the advanced positions. Russian ponies and sleighs had not as yet been organized, a point of immediate concern to Ironside. Meanwhile it was necessary to ship as much of the winter supplies as possible before ice sealed the rivers. Communications between the isolated columns in a vast forest—a swamp in early and late summer, with deep snow in winter—were extremely difficult. The only troops trained in skiing or snowshoeing were the Canadians, and these were not as yet brought forward.

Before assuming command, Ironside learned from the Dvina and Railway columns that the local population was apathetic, showing no desire to fight the Bolsheviks. On his return to Archangel, he discussed with General Poole the subject of raising Russian forces, and inspected two local units—the Slavo-British Allied Legion numbering 500 men, all volunteers, and the Polish Legion. The former 'did not lend themselves to being formed into a fighting unit'; but the latter, 300 strong, 'would very soon be ready to take their place in the line'. The reports of Allied liaison officers, unanimous in saying that little was being done by the Provisional Government to raise local forces, appeared to be correct. Ironside resolved to approach the government on the subject as a matter of supreme importance.[92]

Despite advances made, the overall situation was not reassuring.

A great area was held by very few troops. An Arctic winter approached, its effect on men and weapons unpredicted. One thing was certain—ice would shut off Archangel from Europe all winter, so the force must subsist on what it had. The tenuous columns, thrust forward as they were and vulnerable to Bolshevik infiltration, caused most concern. Positions would have to be wired in all round and made into fortified areas, which could hold out until relieved.

Ironside's immediate decisions were these: in view of transport difficulties in the winter, the two main columns must be placed under separate commands. Finlayson was to command on the Dvina, the more important column, and another commander for the railway column would have to be found.* It was urgent that the two Canadian batteries should strengthen the Dvina forces. The War Office should send out 60-pounder guns on the next ship. Finally more troops must be raised locally. In an effort to recruit more Russians, Ironside visited the gaols of Archangel during October and began to expand into a battalion a company of the Slavo-British Allied Legion under Captain Dyer, one of the Canadian instructors. This unit was later known as 'the Dyer battalion' in honour of its founder, subsequently killed in action on the Dvina front.

The 16th Brigade C.F.A. was temporarily split, three officers and twenty-six men joining the Vologda railway column to man an armoured train under command of a British naval officer until January 1919. The train formed part of the Vologda railway column and was composed, in order, of a flat car with sandbag machine-gun emplacements, a coal car mounting an 18-pounder and machine guns, the locomotive, a second coal car with two naval pieces and machine guns mounted, and cars for accommodation. During October the railway column achieved a slight advance, and the position reached was maintained while the Canadians were on this front. In January the gunners rejoined the 68th Battery which, with the exception of the Seletski detachment, was now at Shenkursk on the Vaga.[93]

The 68th Battery was not complete, having left the guns of one section at Dundee. A party under Major W. C. Hyde, the battery commander, was detached to Seletski in support of American infantry of the minor column operating on the Yemtsa river between

---

* Ironside offered the command to Colonel Stewart, commanding the American contingent, who refused it; Colonel Lucas, an officer of the French contingent, was then appointed.

the river Dvina and the railway. There it saw constant action, although there were no major operations before the end of the year. It was not until December 1918 that this party rejoined the brigade, leaving one section in action until April 1919 when the brigade was complete again. Meanwhile the balance of the brigade, consisting of the 67th Battery and what was left of the 68th Battery, proceeded by barge to the junction of the Dvina and Vaga rivers. Columns were fighting about forty and seventy miles respectively up each of these rivers. The 67th Battery was assigned to the Dvina river, and the truncated 68th to Shenkursk, the most southerly defended town on the Vaga. Lieut.-Colonel Sharman was appointed Commander Royal Artillery to the Dvina Force comprising both river-columns.[94]

On October 14, 1918, the 67th Battery (Major F. F. Arnoldi) was deployed with one section on the left bank of the Dvina in the village of Tulgas, and one opposite on the right bank at Kurgomen at a time when ice in the north had forced the Royal Navy to withdraw. 'We found we had facing us some twenty-two armed water craft, including several gunboats armed with 6″ and 4·1″ naval guns . . . three batteries of field guns and as far as we could find out, approximately 3500 troops facing our force of one six gun 18 pounder battery . . . one naval 5·1 gun mounted on an old iron barge, . . . and a grand total of between 900 and 1,000 all ranks.'[95]

Worse than this disparity in numbers was the fact that the Canadians were hopelessly outranged. The naval gun barge kept the enemy at a respectful range until 20th October, when it was sunk by the Bolshevik flotilla. The Bolsheviks then brought craft forward within easy range for their guns, yet well out of range of the Canadian 18-pounders, and 'cheerfully shelled us over open sights'. Even the field guns which the enemy brought into action outdistanced Canadian guns; 'his field guns ranged up to 9,000 yards, while our old type buffer 18 pounder . . . was not graduated above 6,600 . . .'. Ice appeared on the river in this area on 24th October, the Red naval craft were withdrawn, affording some respite until 10th November, when mild weather permitted gunboats to reappear as a prelude to the Bolshevik attack on Tulgas the next day.[96]

November 11th—Armistice Day—was a day memorable in the annals of the Canadian artillery. The village of Tulgas, where a garrison consisting of 300 American infantrymen, a company of the 2/10th Royal Scots, and fifty-seven Canadian gunners in the village itself were barricaded in blockhouses and peasant huts, had been surrounded the previous night. A Bolshevik force 600 strong had infiltrated through pine forest and thick underbush, effectively cutting the Allied line of communications with Bereznik, fifty miles to the north. The main Bolshevik force had established itself south of the village, while to the east Soviet gunboats, unchallenged by any Allied craft, covered any possible escape route across the Dvina with 4-inch and 6-inch guns.

At daybreak a heavy enemy bombardment on the Tulgas defences opened from the gunboats, followed at eight o'clock by a frontal Bolshevik infantry attack from the south. The two right section Canadian guns, already laid in that direction, were immediately engaged in support of the Allied infantry. A short time afterwards, while still heavily engaged in front, the defenders were astounded to hear Soviet volleys and machine gun fire in *rear*, and it was in this area that the two Canadian guns had been emplaced, virtually unguarded save by the men of the artillery section themselves and by an American Lewis-gun squad. It seemed that nothing could prevent their capture. The Bolshevik surprise attack, however, was discovered by the twenty drivers of the section when only 200 yards distant. Armed with rifles the drivers rushed out, temporarily checking the Bolshevik advance, then fell back to the gun pits, fighting all the way. Their action gave warning to the gun crews, firing to the front, so that one gun was run out of its pit and reversed, opening up on the enemy with a quick-bursting shrapnel charge fired into the mass of charging Bolsheviks at point-blank range. The slaughter was indescribable and the survivors wavered. Herded on by their officers, however, they charged again to meet a second withering blast which stopped them. Due to an unfortunate rise in the ground in front of the gun the Bolsheviks were still able to crawl forward in dead ground to within 100 yards of the pits, where they formed a circle and opened up with machine guns and rifles, while gunboats kept up a continual bombardment from the river in an attempt to silence the stubborn pieces. Covering fire for the Canadian gun crews was provided by the American machine gun squad and by other artillerymen not needed on the guns, all firing hotly as fast as they could reload. A platoon of Royal Scots, detached from the main defences to support the Canadians, suffered heavy casualties on their way to the position, but those who arrived held the enemy at bay until late afternoon when dusk permitted the second gun to be reversed—impossible before because of sniping. With nightfall the enemy withdrew into the woods on both fronts—the southern assault had been easily contained—leaving sixty dead and wounded, including one battalion commander, in Canadian hands. Two Canadians—a corporal and a driver—and ten Scots were killed. Colonel Sharman, who was visiting the 67th Battery at the time, was able to congratulate the Section on the spot. Of the Canadian action he said later : 'General Ironside told me . . . that the exploit of the 67th Battery at Tulgas on November 11th, when the drivers saved the guns . . . is one which has only occurred twice before in the history of British Artillery, once in the South African War and once in 1811.' One Military Cross, three Distinguished Conduct Medals, and three Military Medals were awarded.[97]

The Allied position at Tulgas, though temporarily stabilized, remained critical for three more days. Americans, British and Canadians, clad in ankle length duck ulsters lined with fur, eyed their abnormally long rifles with permanently-fixed bayonets* speculatively; ammunition would not last for ever, leaving them only the bayonet as a last resort. The Reds had cut the telegraph line from Tulgas to Archangel, so there could be little hope of reinforcements.

But the Reds had counted greatly on the surprise blow from the rear. After this had failed, they had no stomach to face the Canadian guns again and contented themselves on the 12th with attacks against the more easily defended south coupled with a methodical pounding of the defences by long range artillery. Every attack was held, but the ceaseless bombardment—it is estimated that 1,500 heavy shells fell on Tulgas that day—was taking its toll. The defenders were almost collapsing from sheer exhaustion. Night brought some relief, but even then sporadic shellbursts punctuated the hours of darkness. The 13th brought much of the same—repeated attacks and a deluge of shells—so that when night came it was clear to all that time lay on the enemy side. Under these circumstances an Anglo-American conference arrived at a desperate plan for the 14th which called for a counter-attack against the vastly superior enemy. This would be mounted against the enemy flank. Before dawn, in bitterly cold weather, American infantry moving through the forest fringe posi-

* These rifles, manufactured in the United States for the Imperial Russian Army, bore Russian markings. They were issued to American, British and Canadian troops for North Russia on the assumption that large stocks of ammunition would become available at Archangel—not, unfortunately, realized.[98]

tioned themselves correctly without discovery, and moved in against the Bolshevik positions. An observation post barred the way, but its occupants, completely surprised, were quickly overcome. An ammunition dump at the post was deliberately fired, and the Americans now advanced boldly creating as much noise as possible to give the impression of a much stronger attack than it actually was. To this the blazing dump contributed—ammunition exploded in all directions adding an inferno of noise which burst on the startled enemy like a thunderclap. Convinced that reinforcements had arrived, the Bolsheviks broke and ran, leaving the Americans in possession of the southern approaches.[99]

At least a respite had been gained. Nature now conspired to convert what might have been but a temporary withdrawal into a full retreat. A sudden drop in temperature which had begun in the night continued throughout the day, glazing the mile-wide river with ice. Red gunboats, deprived of their prey, reluctantly turned and nosed their way south, to where the ice would be thinner, upstream to Kotlas. Without artillery, the Bolsheviks abandoned their attempts on Tulgas and for the next few days attempted to pull back the force which had infiltrated to the north of the village. Some of these soldiers, lost in the trackless bush, perished from exhaustion while others blundered into villages miles behind the Allies' lines, half dead from cold and hunger. These reported that Trotsky himself had directed the attack, swearing to drive the foreign invaders 'beneath the ice of the White Sea', and with his predilection for sudden descents on the various fronts, this is not unlikely. If so, he must have steamed away on his gunboat a very disappointed man. The Reds lost more than 300 men against the Allies' twenty-eight killed and seventy wounded.[100]

The General Armistice of November 11, 1918, brought no relief to the troops in North Russia. It found the Allies settling in for the winter, using defensive wire around gun positions and defended localities as a precaution against further infiltration, still fighting an enemy against whom no declaration of war had ever been made. Allied operations, however unwittingly, had now become a phase of the Russian Civil War.

CHAPTER III

THE SPREAD OF CIVIL WAR

Throughout the summer of 1918 fighting against the Bolsheviks took place in other regions of Russia. The Volunteer Army embarked on a second Kuban campaign which eventually freed from Bolshevik control the area north of the Caucasus mountains between the Black and Caspian seas. A body of Czechs, operating eastwards from the Volga, succeeded in taking over the Trans-Siberian Railway and by this action liberated an area in European Russia stretching from the Volga to the Urals, and the whole of Siberia from the Urals to the Pacific. These actions—especially that of the Czechs—influenced future Allied intervention and will therefore be described.

THE VOLUNTEER ARMY'S SUCCESS

In April 1918, following failure at Ekaterinodar, the Volunteer Army remained undisturbed on the frontier between the Don and Kuban territories. News of the clearing of the Bolsheviks from the Don by Cossack and German forces reached Denikin at the end of April. On 16th May Krasnov succeeded Kaledin as Ataman of the Don Cossacks, and following his election, sought the co-operation of the Volunteer Army in a projected drive against Tsaritsin on the Volga. Alexeiev, the White leader in the South, favoured this course, but was opposed by Denikin, his field commander, who advocated a return to the Kuban territory. It is worthwhile to review the arguments of the two generals at that time.

Alexeiev, sound in strategy, saw the Volga as the vital theatre of the war. There, as we shall see, a corps of Czechs was embroiled with the Bolsheviks and had set in train operations which eventually led to a Czech takeover of the Trans-Siberian Railway from the Volga to the sea. On the Volga, Alexeiev foresaw, the Bolsheviks would concentrate all their efforts in defeating the Czechs to prevent the formation of an Eastern Front. Thus the centre of events decisive for the fate of Russia was there, and the Volunteer Army, he concluded, 'must not be late in leaving the Kuban and appearing at the principal theatre of the war'.[1] At this distance, armed with hindsight, one can safely conclude that an early link-up between the Czechs and the White Russian forces fighting with them, and the Volunteer Army and the Don Cossacks from the South, would have been too much for Trotsky's hastily improvised formations which then ineffectually barred the route from the Volga to the Russian capital.

Denikin, however, had strong reasons for a second Kuban campaign, and in the end his view prevailed. First of all, he wanted a territorial base on which he could feel independent of Krasnov. The new Ataman made no secret that he was co-operating with the Germans in the Don territories in return for munitions, whereas the Volunteer Army consisted in very great part of members who had joined it in disgust when the Bolsheviks had taken Russia out of the war. These men—and Denikin sympathized with them—persisted in loyalty to the Allies and antagonism to Germany; co-operation with Krasnov, therefore, might well alienate a large part of the Volunteer Army. Further, another part of that army consisted of Kuban Cossacks and any attempt to abandon the liberation of their territory in favour of an advance to the Volga would antagonize these troops also and make probable an occupation of the Kuban by the Germans. Thus, Denikin reasoned, to cancel the Kuban offensive in favour of a desperate throw on the Volga might well mean the break-up of the Volunteer Army; a more piecemeal attack, taking the Kuban first, would in the end achieve the same results, and with more safety.[2]

The Kuban region lay between the Sea of Azov, the Black Sea, and the Caucasus. In 1918 nearly 3,000,000 Kuban Cossacks lived in the area—about forty per cent of the total population of Cossacks, Tartars, and Ukrainians. Into this territory the Volunteer Army, numbering about 9,000 with twenty-one guns and only limited ammunition, went forward on 22nd June to begin its second Kuban campaign. Against them were Red troops estimated at more than 80,000 with an abundance of artillery and shells. But, since Kornilov's first drive into the Kuban, familiarity with Bolsheviks and their methods had aroused hostility—even amongst the townspeople who had previously supported them—so that Denikin's ranks swelled as he marched southwards.[3]

Aiming first at Bolshevik communications, Denikin gained speedy success, first on 25th June at Torgovaya where he broke the enemy communications between Tsaritsin and Ekaterinodar forcing the

Soviet North Caucasian Government to depend on its own resources. Three weeks later, he defeated the Reds at the railway junction of Tikhoretzkaya, where the main Moscow–Caucasus line intersects that from Tsaritsin to Novorossisk, thus gaining freedom to develop further operations in any of three direction.[4]

Denikin next struck at Ekaterinodar, the Kuban capital, and this fell on 16th August after a three-day battle. The occasion was marked by a victory parade which Alexeiev reviewed, by banquets and speeches, public prayers and thanksgiving services. But all this could not hide a rift which opened between the Kuban Cossacks and the leaders of the Volunteer Army.

The Volunteers had one goal in mind—the restoration of Russia 'great, united, undivided'; their struggle lay with Bolshevism in the whole of Russia, not only in the Kuban territory; but they could not win without the support of the Cossacks. The latter were primarily interested in freeing the Kuban from the Soviets, and saw as their object a federation of liberated autonomous provinces embracing the Terek, the Kuban, the Don, and certain sections of the Caucasus. This achieved, they wanted peace, little realizing that the Kuban (which had no natural frontier to divide it from the rest of Russia) would hardly have been permitted by the Soviets to exist as an independent state. Both the Volunteer Army and the Kuban Cossacks were dependent on the other, for the Cossacks could not preserve any independent way of life without the military support of the army. But neither side seemed to realize this interdependence; resentment against interference by the leaders of the Volunteer Army in the internal sovereignty of the Kuban Territory, culminating in the use of military force by Denikin against the Kuban Rada in November 1919, weakened the strength of the common cause against the Reds.[5]

Kuban territory, however, had been by no means wholly freed from the Bolsheviks, although the Kuban capital had been captured. Disputes between the government and the Volunteers were not as yet sufficiently serious to affect this purpose, undoubtedly in the interest of both. Denikin's advance continued during August with Cossack support.

On 26th August the Whites gained an outlet to the sea with the capture of Novorossisk. At this port, two months earlier, the Soviets had deliberately scuttled half the former Russian Black Sea Fleet to prevent the ships from being handed over to the Germans in conformity with the terms of Brest-Litovsk. Other vessels, in defiance of

Bolshevik orders, sailed to Sevastopol for surrender to the Germans; these later passed into the possession of the Whites, and with the final collapse of White forces, of the French. Now, with the capture of Ekaterinodar and Novorossisk, the West Kuban was under White control, and Denikin's little force had grown to some 40,000 as a result of mobilizations carried out in the occupied territory. The entire North Caucasian Red Army was estimated at 150,000 men.[6]

Despite this disparity in numbers Denikin decided to strike for the natural boundaries of the North Caucasus—the Caucasus Mountains in the south and the Caspian Sea in the east. The Red Army blocked the way at Armavir, but this town fell to the Whites without difficulty. Then, on 21st September, Denikin met his first reverse. The Taman Army (a force of about 30,000 forming part of the Red forces in the area) which had been raised on the Taman peninsula to fight insurgent Cossacks, moved southward along the Black Sea coast, struck overland south of the Kuban river, and wrested Armavir from the Whites after hard street-fighting. Red Army leaders now felt strong enough to embark on an offensive, but differences of opinion developed between the Commander-in-Chief, Sorokin, and the commander of the Taman Army. The former proposed the recapture of Tikhoretzskaya to restore rail communications with Tsaritsin, aiming first easterly at Stavropol. The Taman leader agreed with the objective, but proposed to march there directly along the main Caucasus–Moscow railroad line. Sorokin's plan carried, but the commander of the Taman Army continued to protest, and was shot for his stand. Stavropol, attacked by the combined Red forces, fell on 30th October, but its loss was more than counterbalanced by a political crisis which had broken out at Pyatigorsk, the temporary Soviet capital in the area. There Sorokin, on 21st October, fearing a plot by the authorities to depose him, struck at the Government first, seized the President and other prominent members, and had them shot. Other members of the Government, who escaped arrest and execution, succeeded in rallying the army against Sorokin—the Taman portion was already alienated by his execution of its leader—and the Commander-in-Chief was himself shot in Stavropol, where he had gone to use his own influence with the army.[7]

Sorokin's mutiny, though of brief duration, had serious influence on Red fortunes. Without leadership or organized direction, the force at Stavropol waited for instructions and supplies, and made no effort to advance. White forces cut the line between Stavropol and

Pyatigorsk (the source of orders and supplies) and surrounded Stavropol, which, after a three-week battle, capitulated on 20th November. This battle was decisive for the North Caucasian campaign. Though half the Taman Army—the only Red force which could match the Whites in fighting quality—struggled through the enveloping cordon, its physical and moral condition was badly shattered; the other half had been destroyed.[8]

During October 1918 the Whites, apart from the temporary military set-back at Stavropol, had suffered a disastrous blow. Alexeiev had been invited to Siberia where, it was confidently expected, he would take supreme command of all counter-revolutionary forces, planning and co-ordinating operations of the Whites in every theatre, not only the south. He became ill before he could leave, and died on 8th October. No White supreme commander ever functioned as such —after November the Siberian leader Kolchak filled the position in name only—and this was a lacuna which spelled final defeat for their cause. A strategist of the calibre of Alexeiev, in a central controlling position, would hardly have permitted the isolated thrusts by various White armies into the heart of Russia which occurred later, and which, though temporarily successful, were mere pinpricks against Red forces operating on internal lines of communication. On Alexeiev's death Denikin assumed the complete leadership in the south, taking charge of financial and political affairs in addition to commanding the army in the field.

Another figure appeared within the Volunteer Army at this time— Baron Peter Wrangel, who had lived in the Crimea during the German occupation. This man, a born cavalry leader, well over six feet tall, had formerly commanded the Czarevitch's own regiment of Ussurian Cossacks which had distinguished itself in Galicia. He offered his services to Denikin and was given command of a division with the rank of Lieutenant-General.[9]

Following the capture of Stavropol, the Whites occupied much the more favourable position. Behind them lay the fertile Kuban Valley, whereas the desert stretching from Astrakhan to the Caspian lay behind the Reds. The Red command in Astrakhan lay far from the theatre of operations and had received an unrealistic order in December for an offensive designed to achieve the port of Petrovsk on the one side and to wrest from the Whites the Tsaritsin–Tikhoretskaya–Novorossisk railway on the other, both objectives to serve as bases for further advances north and south-east. Before an advance could be made, Wrangel hurled his cavalry against the remnants of the Taman Army on the right of the Eleventh Red Army, which formed the main body of the enemy. The Taman force broke, and by 27th December it was no longer worth reckoning. The Eleventh Army, however, launched its offensive as ordered, and succeeded in reaching Batalpashinsk. Low morale and short supplies—the latter came from Astrakhan and were intercepted by the Whites—precluded further success, and a sweeping counter-offensive by Wrangel broke through the Bolshevik line and swept it back. Pursuit disorganized the Reds still further, and by 24th January the Eleventh Army had ceased to exist. By February no further opposition to Denikin was possible—50,000 prisoners, 150 guns, 350 machine guns, and considerable stores had fallen into his hands. Red troops who escaped death or capture straggled through the Caucasian passes into Georgia or entered the desert in an effort to reach Astrakhan. Bitter weather, typhus, and lack of food and water completed the Bolshevik defeat, strewing rocky defiles and the desert wastes with Soviet dead.[10]

Through superior leadership, organization, and skill, combined with high morale, victory had gone to the numerically weaker force. Red forces in the south of Russia had collapsed. The Volunteers and the Kuban Cossacks had been united as a White Russian army under single command. Had the same applied to the Volunteer, Kuban, Don and Siberian Armies, the Whites would have had no trouble with Trotsky's newly created forces which, though growing rapidly, were as yet largely disorganized with a string of defeats behind them.

Now the Armistice on the Western Front gave rise to hopes of Allied assistance, and it seemed to the southern Whites that the tide of fortune had turned in their favour. The hardworking General Denikin, still in his mid-forties, had at his back a region to which peace had been restored—an untroubled rear protected by the massive range of the Caucasus mountains. He could now strike northwards at the heart of the Soviet stronghold in pursuit of his sole purpose—the creation of a Russia free from Bolshevism, a Russia strong and undivided.

THE CZECH CORPS

In the heart of Russia events were taking place which eventually brought Allied intervention to Siberia, the theatre most strongly recommended by General Knox. Those events came about through the efforts of Czech troops, stranded in Russia by the Bolshevik defection from the war, to join the Allies on the Western Front. The nucleus of the Czech Corps was already in Russia at the outbreak of hostilities in 1914. At that time some thousand Austrian subjects, resident in Russia, openly declared their disapproval of the policy of Vienna, renounced allegiance to Austria, and offered to join the Russian Army. The bureaucratic Russian government at first frowned on this demonstration of independence; Russia, like Austria-Hungary, was a multiracial empire and feared that its own minorities might emulate the Austrian Czechs. Declared Russian war aims, however, included the right of small oppressed Slav nations to decide their destiny. A denial of the Czechs would violate this policy; thus the Czech volunteers were grudgingly accepted. In August 1914, at Kiev, they formed a unit known as the Hussite Sharpshooters Brotherhood, and in October appeared at the front in the Third Army sector as the 1st Czecho-Slovak Battalion.[11]

The Russian Third Army commander, Duntriv, was wise enough to welcome them; he foresaw, moreover, that use could be made of the Czechs out of all proportion to their strength, and he broke the unit up into small detachments which were parcelled out to all divisions of the Third Army as front-line scouts. Their instructions were explicit. Thousands of their countrymen were serving as unwilling conscripts in the Austrian armies, needing little persuasion to bring them over to the Russian side; this the scouts did. On March 21, 1915, near Skorov, nine Czech scouts entered the Austrian trenches and brought back practically the whole 28th Regiment of Infantry— some sixty officers, 2000 men—and thirty-two machine guns. In May, when a party of scouts led a Russian battalion into the Austrian rear, 7000 men came over. Such wholesale desertions of Czecho-Slovak soldiers aroused bitter hatred in Austria and led to reprisals against the civil population of Bohemia and Moravia.[12]

But the new 'recruits' were not allowed to join the Russian army and strike a blow at their late masters. Instead they were diverted to munition factories and to farms; some, indeed, found their way into prison-camps along with German and Hungarian captives. The most which was done was to allow the Hussite Sharpshooters to make up their losses from the pool of military prisoners. At the beginning of 1916, however, the atmosphere changed. A second battalion was permitted; by May, the 1st Czecho-Slovak Brigade was formed; then, with the revolution in March of the following year, all obstacles towards the forming of larger Czech forces were at once swept away. Prison gates were flung open. Czechs from all parts of the vast Russian territories streamed into Kiev to form a force numbering 40,000 men, which then awaited the guidance of the Czech apostle of freedom—Jan Masaryk.[13]

Professor Masaryk was the guiding spirit and inspiration of the Czechs as Mazzini had been for the Italians. During the first three years of the war he had lived in London, a refugee from Austrian suppression. This man, born in 1850, apprenticed to a blacksmith in his youth, had struggled for education and risen above his humble origins. After graduation from the universities of Vienna and Leipzig, he was offered a chair at the University of Prague in 1882. In 1907 he was elected to the parliament of the Dual Monarchy, where he loudly protested against the annexation of Bosnia and Hertzogovina in 1908. His whole life was devoted to the freedom of the Czechs. For this he was arrested in Vienna at the outbreak of the war. He subsequently escaped to Switzerland, and thence to London when he 'kept alive the conception not only of Bohemian nationality but of a considerable Czecho-Slovak state'.[14] To the Czech troops in Russia, separated from homeland and families, surrounded by alien peoples in a world of confusion and passion, he was the 'little father'. They sang his praises round their campfires, decorating huts and box-cars with his picture, and through him preserved their faith in ultimate freedom.[15]

After the revolution Masaryk went to Russia; there he consolidated the Czech units into what was virtually a corps, placed them under the red and white flag of Bohemia, and in Paris procured for them the status of an Allied army.[16] Thus the real Czecho-Slovak Army was formed, and it was not long before it proved itself. In Brussilov's June offensive the Czechs, at least, could be counted on; they captured some 4000 Austrian prisoners before the Russian armies melted away around them, and drew from Brussilov a glowing tribute : 'The Czechoslovaks, perfidiously abandoned at Tarnapol by our infantry, fought in such a way that the world ought to fall on its knees before them.'[17]

The disorderly retreat of Russian forces at this time, when men literally threw away their arms and scrambled back from the front to rape and plunder, was profitable for the Czechs; they were able to seize discarded machine guns, rifles, and ammunition and to build up a surplus for distribution to their volunteers still arriving at Kiev.[18]

When the Treaty of Brest-Litovsk ended Russian resistance to Germany, the Czecho-Slovaks demanded to be transported to the Western Front where they were badly needed by the Allies. In face of the German wall of steel stretching from the Baltic to the Black Sea, the only safe route was by way of the Trans-Siberian Railway to Vladivostok, across the Pacific, and thence through the Panama Canal to the battlefields of France. An understanding was reached with the French Government whereby the Czechs were to be brigaded with the French armies, and France was to become responsible for shipping and equipment. The Bolsheviks—no less anxious to see them go—promised Masaryk a free exit for the Czechs, which promise was later embodied in a formal agreement between the Allies and the Soviet Government in Russia on 26th March. Masaryk, after accomplishing his task, left for Japan to arrange for ships; from there he sailed for Canada en route to Europe, arriving at Vancouver on April 29th, 1918.[19]

German reaction to these arrangements was instant disapproval. Ludendorff, in a bitter passage, said :

'In Russia events had developed along lines of their own, illustrative of the lying propensities of the Soviet Government. With the consent of this Government the Entente had formed Czecho-Slovak units out of Austro-Hungarian prisoners. These were intended to be used against us, and were therefore to be conveyed to France by the Siberian railway. All this was sanctioned by a Government with whom we were at peace, and we actually took it lying down!'[20]

True, no formal declaration of war against the Soviets resulted, but the German army now advancing into the Ukraine had orders to smash the Czechs before they could withdraw from their positions around Kiev. The Czechs now numbered 50,000 men, and these, side by side with the more steadfast of the Red Guards, were able to give a good account of themselves by carrying out delaying skirmishes. At Bachmach, where the Germans succeeded in blocking the railway ahead of them, they fought their way through in a hotly contested action, extricating all their trains to Kursk. There they reorganized.[21]

Soviet–Czech relations, despite an auspicious beginning, became strained soon after the Czechs had arrived in Russia from the Ukraine. The German Ambassador in Moscow, Count Mirbach, began to exert pressure on the Bolsheviks as a result of which the Czechs were partially disarmed. They were permitted only a specified number of weapons for defence against counter-revolutionary attacks. Other arms, not without misgivings, were turned over in an act of good faith—their journey through Siberia had been guaranteed by the Bolsheviks and it was agreed that a Bolshevik representative should accompany each train to facilitate their journey. But the trains, ordered to move by stages in an attempt to destroy the cohesion of the corps, travelled at a snail's pace. There were eighty trains, separated at distances of about fifty miles, and some took two months to cover what should normally have taken two days. An atmosphere of suspicion and hostility developed, intensified by Soviet efforts to persuade the Czechs to join the Red Guard and thus break up the corps; indeed, some 300 did so.[22]

The Czech Corps, at the beginning of May, was already strung out over thousands of miles of Trans-Siberian railroad. Then, on 2nd May, the Supreme Allied War Council approved a French suggestion that all Czech forces west of Omsk should be sent to France by way of Archangel, and to this Trotsky agreed. Paradoxically, the agreement between the Allies and the Soviet authorities played a part in increasing the estrangement between the Czechs and the Bolsheviks, for, due to defective communications, it appeared to the Czechs that the initiative had come—not from the Allies—but from the Soviets. Early distrust now hardened into a firm conviction that the Bolsheviks intended to divide them further; that this was a first step towards total disarmament and later internment. Cecek, Gaida, and Syrovy, young men holding only the rank of lieutenant or captain yet leaders of the Czechs (officers of high rank had been Russian), advocated making their way through to the Far East, by force if necessary.[23]

At Cheliabinsk, on 16th May, a minor incident provoked hostilities which were soon to free vast areas of Russian territory from Bolshevik control. A Hungarian prisoner-of-war, returning by train towards Europe, threw a piece of iron at a Czech soldier on the station platform at Cheliabinsk, severely injuring him. The men of the 6th Czech Regiment dragged the Hungarian out of the train and killed him. The local Soviet summoned Czech witnesses, then arrested them. Following this, a deputation from the Czechs marched into town to demand their release; the head of the deputation was also arrested. The Czechs then raided the Soviet building, released their comrades by force, occupied the station, and disarmed the Red Guards. Menaced on every side, the Czechs convened a military council to discuss the situation. Delegates were summoned from every unit which could be reached but this took time.[24]

Trotsky, informed of these events, sent a telegram calling upon the Czechs to give up their remaining arms, which was rejected. Then, on 21st May, he instructed the local Soviet to request the Czechs to create trade-union organizations and to enter the Red Army. This also was rejected.[25] Two days later, Trotsky called for the detention, disarming, and dissolution of all Czech units, followed on 25th May by a still sharper order : 'We demand . . . that they should be disarmed. Those of them who do not do so voluntarily will be shot on the spot . . . reliable forces are to be sent in the rear of the Czech troop trains, and these are commanded to suppress the insurgents.'[26]

The Czech military congress, in truth a council-of-war, had, on 24th May, reached a momentous and heroic decision—they would fight their way from the heart of Russia to the Pacific, practically with their bare hands. An executive committee to supervise the move to Vladivostok was formed, with Captain Gaida, a man still in his twenties commanding the 7th Regiment, at its head.[27]

Several towns claim to have seen the first fighting in the ensuing struggle. The Czechs themselves, when interviewed at Vladivostok later, said it began at Penza, the last place of importance in European Russia before the Volga river. Five trains were collected there on 26th May when delegates returned from Cheliabinsk. The decision to continue the journey was announced; arms, which had been stacked in readiness to hand over to the Red Guards, were redistributed. An attack on the town was decided on, but this was delayed to await the arrival of the main body of the 4th Regiment whose commander (Lieutenant Cecek, the hero of Bachmach) was already at Penza with advanced elements of the regiment. On the night of the 27th-28th three enemy trains arrived; the following day yet another train brought armoured cars and machine guns, which were in position when the Czechs attacked before dawn on the 29th. After a day's stubborn fighting, the town fell, yielding more artillery, machine guns, rifles and ammunition than could be dragged away.[28]

Paradoxically, the very dispersion of the Czechs now became a source of strength. Prisoners in the interior of Russia had joined them at several locations, swelling their numbers to some 60,000 men. After Cheliabinsk and Penza town after town came into their hands with amazing rapidity : Novo-Nikolaevsk, in Central Siberia; Syzran and Tomsk at the end of May; on 7th June Omsk, the largest town in Western Siberia; and Samara, the central point of the Middle Volga, a day later. Thus, at the end of the first week in June the Czechs and other anti-Bolshevik forces controlled about 1000 miles of vital communications in European Russia from Penza (some 400 miles from Moscow) to the Urals, and in Asia a similar distance from Cheliabinsk eastwards as far as Krasnoyarsk.[29]

These swift victories were due to many causes. The Soviets, without trained and reliable troops, were almost completely unprepared. The Czech attacks took place practically simultaneously at widely separated points to which the Bolsheviks, dependent on the railway, were in many cases unable to rush reinforcements. The desperation of their case made the Czechs daring, and their early successes were largely due to prompt action and surprise. Additionally, they were disciplined, and their supply service efficiently organized. The capture of a Bolshevik train containing gold gave them purchasing power. The attitude of the local people was also important. Towns contained secret organizations which in any case were preparing an uprising and the appearance of the Czechs made their task easy. Even workers showed indifference, if not hostility, towards the Soviets.[30]

The news of these victories astonished the Allied leaders. When their full implications were realized, a reappraisal of the Russian situation became imperative. Intervention was in the air—was not this then, the right moment when so much of Russia was daily passing into Allied control? As Churchill said, 'An immense area . . . several hundreds of miles broad and 3000 miles long, including the backbone connections from the Volga river almost to Lake Baikal, was in the effectual possession of these strangers thus foully attacked when seeking to leave the country in virtue of signed agreements.'[31] At the end of June, Allied orders reached the Czechs. No longer were they destined for France; instead, they were to remain where they were, gathering around them all the Russian elements who wished to see order restored. The Trans-Siberian Railway was to be completely occupied.[32]

The immediate task of the Czechs was now to consolidate the

scattered elements of their corps and secure full control of the Trans-Siberian Railway. Their units in European Russia linked up with those east of the Urals at Cheliabinsk on July 6, 1918. A force whose first members had reached Vladivostok in April seized the port on 29th June and struck out west into Manchuria to meet Gaida's units pushing east.[33]

The last great barrier lay in the Lake Baikal region, east of Irkutsk. The Red Guards could have asked no greater assistance from nature than this long inland sea with its mountainous and rocky shores. The town of Baikal was situated on the western shore fifty miles from Kultuk, at the southern tip of the lake, and between these towns the railway skirted the shore, running for the most part on a ledge on the precipitous mountain-side above the water; there were thirty-nine tunnels. Gaida took Baikal station without difficulty and chased the Bolsheviks through the tunnels towards Kultuk. Only the last tunnel had been blown; in fact a Soviet train carrying explosives to blow the others had been destroyed by Czech storm troops. This last tunnel, however, thoroughly wrecked, completely blocked the Czech advance. Beyond it the Bolsheviks rallied, augmenting their forces with reinforcements from East Bakalia and other provinces.[34]

The Czechs were now in an impossible position. To go back was unthinkable. To go on meant clearing the tunnel and the excavation of loose rock would take a month; unless this was done their trains could not continue. Every ferry and boat was in the hands of the Bolsheviks, and these, with guns mounted, virtually prevented movement along the exposed ledge between Baikal and Kultuk. Meanwhile the enemy forces continued to grow. Work commenced on the tunnel, and after three weeks labour in July it was cleared sufficiently to permit the passage of hand-carts. Gaida, however, realized that even with the rubble completely removed, the Bolsheviks ahead were in overwhelming force. In these circumstances he decided on a bold, even desperate, plan.[35] Part of his force, under cover of darkness, was to infiltrate by mountain trails to a deep valley through which the railway passed; his main force would retreat, giving every evidence of a disorderly retirement, to lure the enemy into this valley to the south of the tunnel; both forces would then attack from front and rear; and finally, a special detachment was to destroy the track behind the Soviet trains thus preserving them for use on the onward journey.[36]

The plan was put into effect on the night of 3rd-4th August. Dawn found 1300 men in position to ambush the enemy if they advanced. Enemy scouts reported the main Czech forces in retreat and throughout the day Red troops began to move—cavalry scouts, an armoured train, again a cavalry detachment, a thousand infantry, then artillery, followed by two more armoured trains, two hospital trains, two supply trains, and nine empty troop trains. Not until after sunset did the enemy troops reach the prearranged point, and then the trap was sprung. It was a black night with pouring rain, and the sudden explosions and sounds of firing to the rear were too much for their shaky discipline. A frontal assault did nothing to allay their fears. Completely surprised, the Reds panicked. The execution continued throughout the night, but with daybreak the enemy forces rallied and tried to break the Czech cordon. Fighting was bitter on the 6th, and it was not before evening that Bolshevik resistance finally crumbled. All the trains were captured, and after the track had been repaired the Czechs continued eastwards; they joined the Vladivostok force towards the end of August. The last Soviet towns in Eastern Siberia fell to the Czechs and the Red forces either dispersed or broke up into partisan bands. Railway communications had again been established along the whole Trans-Siberian route,[37] and with that 'the whole of Russia from the Volga river to the Pacific Ocean, a region almost as large as the continent of Africa, had passed as if by magic into the control of the Allies'.[38]

But in Siberia, as in other liberated regions, experience soon showed that it was easier to overthrow the Soviets than to replace them with a government having popular support. Following the Czech successes, two main governments emerged—the West Siberian Commissariat at Omsk, and the Government of the Committee of Members of the Constituent Assembly in Samara. The former, proclaimed on 1st June, was largely Socialist Revolutionary in character and aimed at the re-establishment of democratic government, restoration of normal goods exchange, a sufficiency of food, and an early resumption of the work of the All-Russian Constituent Assembly. Siberia was to be autonomous with its own flag of white and green, symbolic of the snows and forests of the country. But the Commissariat did not last long. It had tolerated the Soviets (not as agencies of government but as working-class organizations) and had gone slowly about the denationalization of factories and the abolishment of land committees. On 30th June a new and more conservative government which annulled all Soviet decrees took over. Through-

(*photo: Imperial War Museum*)

ace Parade, Vladivostok, November 15, 1918. Canadian soldiers march past

nadian troops at Vladivostok from a painting 'Canadians outside the Depot, Siberia'
Louis Keene

(*photo: National Gallery of Canada, Ottawa, Canadian War Memorials Collection*)

6
Bolshevik prisoners clea[r]ing snow from the stree[t] of Archangel, April 191[9]

Transports carrying the North Russian Relief Force to Archangel, making their way through a sea of ice, May 1919

General Lord Rawlins[on] and General Ironside o[n] the Quay at Archange[l] 1919

Unloading Allied stores at Murmansk, June 1919

(*photos: Imperial War Museum*)

out July and August the new Siberian Government, with a conserva-
tism that would ultimately deepen into reaction, began to swing
more and more away from Bolshevism and even from moderate
socialism.[39]

The occupation of the town of Samara by the Czechs on 8th June
saw a more radical type of government dominated by Socialist Revolutionaries who had been members of the Constituent Assembly.
This Assembly soon controlled a large area in the middle Volga. The
new government, like the West Siberian Commissariat, strove for a
re-established Constituent Assembly, but in contrast it quickly dissolved the existing Soviets and put down Bolshevik opposition with
pitiless severity. Against weak opposition it was militarily successful
and extended its territory. Contact was established with the Ural
Cossacks who had been waging guerrilla warfare against the Reds
for several months. Ufa was taken on July 4th, and Simbirsk, Lenin's
birthplace, fell a fortnight later.

At Ekaterinburg (threatened in July and captured by the Czechs
later) the former Czar Nicholas II and his entire family were exterminated on the night of 16th-17th July at the decision of the Ural
Territorial Soviet. The massacre was carried out with revolvers in
the basement of the Ipatiev House and the bodies were then conveyed
to an abandoned mine some thirteen miles distant, where they were
destroyed as completely as possible by fire. From there, the remains
are said to have been transported to a swamp. No trace of them was
ever found by persons who investigated the killings. The thorough-
ness of the slaughter almost certainly precludes the possibility that
one of the Czar's daughters (Anastasia) escaped, as some have supposed.[40]

To the south Volsk was captured and then, on 6th August, the
occupation of Kazan—500 miles from Moscow—came as a serious
shock to the Bolsheviks, for with the town, the troops of the Constituent Assembly captured the gold reserve of the former Imperial
Government which had been transferred from Petrograd for safety.
This gold later passed to Admiral Kolchak, the White leader in
Siberia, who used it to buy supplies and munitions abroad.[41]

Despite extension of territory and military success, however, the
outlook for the Samara Government was far from hopeful. Popular
enthusiasm, the expected flow of recruits necessary for a victorious
march on Moscow, and a triumphant re-opening of the Constituent
Assembly were all lacking. Army officers and the middle classes, de-

D

sirous of pre-Revolutionary conditions, considered the new government too radical. Though the Socialist Revolutionaries constituted a peasant party, peasants were too ignorant to lend it support; primitive instincts prompted them to pay no taxes and to give no soldiers to any government, Red, White, or of any other hue. Then there was another unfavourable factor. Samara was an obscure provincial town without large reserves of arms and munitions. Nor did the Samara government co-operate with that at Omsk against the common enemy—instead, antagonism existed which led to transportation difficulties between them and a customs war along the indefinitely defined frontier. Yet a third regional anti-Bolshevik government emerged at Ekaterinburg, the capital of the Urals. This Ural government leaned to the right and gravitated towards Omsk, not Samara, in its political allegiance.[42]

The Czechs viewed these rival authorities with scepticism; to them it seemed that political and military unity was essential if anything was to be gained. Largely at Czech instigation, a state conference opened on 8th September at Ufa, a small town in European Russia between Omsk and Samara, which was attended by representatives of the Omsk and Samara governments, as well as by those from other regional authorities—all summoned to create a new and all-embracing government.[43]

The conference started badly. A hopeless divergence of viewpoint between right and left-wing elements arose. The struggle against Bolshevism had brought no unity to its opponents. On 10th September the Red Army, revitalized by Trotsky who had arrived at the Volga front in August, seized Kazan from the White and Czecho-Slovak forces—hailed by Trotsky as the turning-point—and went on to take Simbirsk two days later. Samara itself (though it did not fall until 8th October) was clearly threatened and indeed the capture of Kazan was a prelude to the clearing of anti-Soviet forces from the whole of the Volga region. This was the first victorious campaign of the new Red Army. Its immediate effect on the Ufa Conference was to weaken the position of the left wing of the Assembly, represented by the Samara Socialist Revolutionaries, so that they were forced to accept a government, a Directory of five persons, of whom only two were Socialist Revolutionaries. The Directory regarded itself as the successor of the fallen Provisional Government and, as such, an all-Russian authority. It had no administrative apparatus, no financial backing, and could only be described as a shadow government. At

Omsk it lived under constant threat of dissolution by *coup d'état* on the part of militarist reactionaries.[44]

The *coup* soon came. On 18th November the Directory was overthrown by Cossacks; Admiral Kolchak, War Minister in the late cabinet, became dictator with the title of Supreme Ruler and commander-in-chief of all the land and naval forces in Russia. The establishment of Kolchak's dictatorship marked the end of the democratic phase of counter-revolution in Russia. It was plain that in the ruthless conditions of a class civil war, Russia was far from ready for democratic methods of government. From now on the main burden of the struggle against Bolshevism fell on conservative nationalist dictators such as Kolchak and Denikin. The government under Kolchak at Omsk was eventually to be recognized as the all-Russian National Government by the other outstanding White leaders—General Denikin in South Russia, General Miller at Archangel, and by the North-western Government associated with General Yudenitch.

The rise of Kolchak had an unfortunate effect on the attitude of the Czechs who were democratically disposed and who favoured the Socialist Revolutionaries rather than the conservative military 'reactionaries'. They had, moreover, displayed an almost proprietary interest in the Directory, so largely their own creation. From the time of its overthrow and replacement by Kolchak, the Czechs relapsed into sullen inaction—with the exception of some of their leaders, including Gaida, who joined Kolchak in the hope of making a career in the Russian service—and soon withdrew altogether from the front. From that time their employment was merely passive, consisting of guarding part of the Trans-Siberian Railway.[45]

The Czechs had done much. They had freed two-thirds of Russia from Bolshevik control. They had made possible the establishment of anti-Bolshevik governments. Their action was decisive on Allied intervention from the East. And lastly, they had faced the Bolshevik leaders with a grim alternative : either they must create at once a disciplined army, or they must accept defeat and bloody retaliation from the classes they had persecuted so mercilessly.

TROTSKY BUILDS THE RED ARMY

During the summer of 1918 the very existence of the Soviet régime was precarious. Czech victories, German occupation, the success of the Volunteer Army, and Allied intervention had restricted the

Soviet Republic to an area roughly equal to that of the old Muscovite principality of the fifteenth century. To guard even this territory, no trained army existed; and maladministration and lack of food appalled even those who had favoured the Bolsheviks. Factories were idle, towns empty as workers streamed into the country to hunt for food. Lenin, ever a realist, recognized the period as 'the highest point of this critical situation', and in the light of the apathy or paralysis that prevailed it is incredible that his régime survived.[46]

In the few provinces that remained to the Soviets conditions gradually declined to famine level and on 11th June it was decided that 'Committees of the Poor' would be set up all over the country. These committees were established for two purposes: to distribute grain, other agricultural products, and agricultural machinery, and to assist in taking surplus grain away from the richer peasants. They were, in fact, little better than foraging parties whose services were paid for with a proportion of the foodstuffs seized. Armed force would be used if necessary. Abuses crept in. In some cases committees attracted criminals who used their arbitrary powers to rob and commit acts of violence; in others, these new powers were misused to pay off old scores. There was bitter resentment. The Commissariat for Internal Affairs recorded twenty-six peasant uprisings in July, forty-seven in August, and thirty-five in September, where 'people were cut to pieces, beaten to death, burned alive in these unknown battles over the country's last crusts of bread'.[47]

The political situation, too, was tense. The Bolsheviks declared martial law in Moscow on 29th May. Anti-Bolsheviks seized the town of Tambov on 17th June, only to lose it again two days later, when fifty of the insurgents were executed. Disaffection developed in Petrograd, where the Obukhov Factory (the Russian Krupps) was ordered closed, and where the torpedo-boat squadron of the Baltic Fleet had to be disarmed. Strikes occurred in Tula and Sormovo (near Nizhni Novgorod) and at Lublino, a suburb of Moscow, and the Bolsheviks were forced to declare a state of emergency on the Nikolai Railway which connected Moscow with Petrograd.

The 6th July witnessed another serious outbreak against the Bolsheviks—or Communists*—this time on the upper Volga. White

---

* The official name of the Bolshevik Party was changed to Communist Party in 1918. Both have been used interchangeably throughout this book. Similarly, though 'Allies' did not in strict parlance include the United States, it has not been felt necessary to make distinction.

officers seized the artillery base of Yaroslavl from Red soldiers of indifferent quality. Stubborn fighting set in which lasted for thirteen days; though the Red forces were numerically superior to the few hundred ex-officers and their hastily recruited men, they had no capable leaders. The uprising failed to command general support. Workers, however much they hated the Bolshevik régime and the hunger it had brought, could not bring themselves to fight at the side of old officers. Other classes rallied to the side of the insurgents, offering themselves as volunteers. Under bombardment by artillery and planes, the Whites eventually collapsed, and 350 participants in the uprising were put to death.[48]

On August 30th the head of the Petrograd Cheka (Secret Police), Uritsky, was assassinated on the way to his office. That same evening, Lenin narrowly missed a similar fate. He had been addressing a factory meeting of workers, and as he walked towards his car two women stopped him to complain of the action of food search-detachments. As he began to explain, three shots sounded and Lenin fell, wounded in the chest and left shoulder. The woman who had fired was caught by the Cheka and shot next morning. She proved to be a Dora Kaplan, a sympathizer with the Constituent Assembly.[49]

These two acts plunged Soviet Russia into terrorism exceeding that of the French Revolution and scarcely matched in human history for barbarity. It was done deliberately to safeguard the rear for the Bolsheviks and, with famine, it served its purpose. Two cogent weapons—terror to break the spirit and famine to induce indifference to anything but food—enabled the Soviets to remain in power.

This was vital policy for the Bolsheviks, but much more was required. Hemmed in by enemies, they recognized the need for an armed force that could defend the country. A revival of the old army was impossible for it had virtually demobilized itself; the Red Guard had been sufficient to back the revolution, but now could do little more than put down unrest at home. A new Red Army to be raised on a voluntary basis—the main appeal of the Bolsheviks was that they were bringing peace, and any compulsory mobilization so early in the revolution must have failed—was decreed as early as January 28, 1918, but the attempt was not successful. By April the Soviets had recruited a mere 100,000 into an army whose fighting quality and discipline were extremely poor. War Commissar Trotsky began to build from this a Red Army on which the Soviet régime could depend, and he had firm ideas. The main objectives were the substitution of conscription for voluntary service; the creation of a central military authority; the destruction of partisan spirit—so common in the Red Guards—and imbuing instead the traditions of a regular force; the enlistment of old officers for intelligent direction; and finally, the restoration of discipline. Even under normal conditions this would have been a tremendous task; in accomplishing it when he did, Leon Trotsky deserves to be rated the outstanding leader of the civil war—despite what later detractors, after his fall from power, have said—and the decisive factor in eventually bringing the whole of Russia under the Hammer and Sickle.[50]

Step by step, Trotsky went methodically forward. A Supreme War Council was created in Petrograd on March 1, 1918. Decrees of 8th and 20th April set up war commissariats, responsible for the general military training of the population, all over Russia; on the 22nd, part-time compulsory military training for workers and peasants was ordered and the practice of electing officers abolished. The bourgeoisie, who could not be trusted with arms, were mobilized on 10th July for labour in the rear. As yet there was no conscription, but the closing of factories and the shortage of bread led thousands of disillusioned workers to enlist in the new Red Army where, at least, they would not go hungry. Czech successes, however, convinced Trotsky that it was a race against time and his programme must be stepped up. He decided to break with the volunteer system. The mood of the country would not yet permit overall conscription, but in Moscow and Petrograd, where the Bolsheviks were strongest, a partial mobilization was forced through. Later, with authority firmly established through terror, national conscription was decreed. From 331,000 on 1st August, the Red Army increased to 550,000 in September and to 800,000 by the end of the year. Indeed, a year later, Trotsky had 3,000,000, and even then growth continued until, during 1920, the army amounted to 5,500,000 men.[51]

The provision of officers was of special concern to Trotsky, for these must be both professionally competent and politically reliable. He strongly advocated the employment of old officers and met with considerable opposition; it was argued that these officers were hostile to the Soviet régime and would betray it at the first opportunity—besides, they would occupy positions which would block loyal soldiers from promotion. In the absence of sufficient Bolsheviks with professional military experience, especially in the artillery and technical branches, Trotsky enrolled 50,000 veteran officers between June 1918 and August 1920. He guarded against defection by merciless punishments, not only of the officer, but also of his family, and by appointing to units political commissars who simultaneously kept an eye on the loyalty of officers and carried on propaganda and education among the recruits. The ex-Imperial officers were, as Trotsky said, flanked both left and right by two armed commissars. Through the use of commissars a political organization developed throughout the army, sufficiently strong to keep the Party supreme and the army loyal.[52]

With the increase in size of the Red Army, the organization became more complex. On 2nd September the Revolutionary Military Council of the Republic, headed by Trotsky, was established to direct the operations and administration of the armed forces. Secondly, an Extraordinary Commission for Supply was created on 10th November to control the output of munitions, and—purely theoretical—to place orders for munitions abroad. Finally, with a view to coordinating the work of the Revolutionary Military Council and other agencies of government, a Council of Workers' and Peasants' Defence was set up on 30th November under the presidency of Lenin, with five other members including Trotsky and Stalin.[53]

Supply problems were always serious. Industrial production had greatly declined. Soviet territory, through the Brest-Litovsk treaty, was cut off from important sources of minerals and raw materials, and rail transportation was hopelessly disorganized. Though the Bolsheviks had inherited considerable stocks of war material these would not last for ever. By the summer of 1919 there was an acute shortage of bullets and only victories over the Whites, who were supplied from abroad, enabled stocks to be replenished. Nor could supplies be obtained from other countries. Soviet Russia was formally blockaded by the Allies from the time of active intervention in the summer of 1918 until November 1920. The Bolsheviks could carry on no international trade of any importance throughout the civil war. The effects of the blockade, the collapse of production and the breakdown of the transportation system at home, all rendered the supply of the Red Army extremely precarious, but what was produced went largely to the Red Army. Soldiers were allotted the highest rate of rations and, unlike civilians, generally received the prescribed scale.

The first real test of the new Red Army lay in stemming the advance of the Czechs and the anti-Bolshevik forces of the Samara Government in late August and September 1918. Trotsky had done his spade-work, but now was the crucial point—could the new troops defend themselves and the revolution? Behind the Czechs lay an unbroken series of victories climaxed by the seizure of Kazan on 6th August. This corps, in fact, represented the most formidable military force in the whole of Russia at the time by virtue of its discipline and fighting spirit. Red troops, hopelessly demoralized, had streamed back from Kazan to Sviazhsk and taken position there. The destruction of the Red Army at Sviazhsk would leave no organized force to check the further advance of the Czechs on Nizhni Novgorod and on Moscow—only 500 miles away. Trotsky, aware of the decisiveness of the impending battle, left Moscow on 7th August for Sviazhsk, the first of thirty-six long journeys which he made in a special train to the widely separated fronts of the civil war—a symbol both of his lashing energy and of his individual contribution to Red Army victories. An observer who was with him at the time (and who subsequently opposed him) recorded the impact of the War Commissar on the despondent Reds: 'The general condition of the Sviazhsk group of troops at the beginning of August could be briefly described as lack of confidence in their own strength, absence of initiative, passivity in all work and absence of discipline from top to bottom. The arrival of Trotsky brought a decisive change into the state of affairs. In the train of Trotsky arrived at the backwoods station [of] Sviazhsk firm will to victory, initiative, and decisive exertion in all sides of army work.'[54]

The appalling conditions at the Red front are hardly surprising. Czech and White morale, stimulated by victory, could not fail to be high. That of their opponents had declined accordingly. The Red Army, hastily improvised and bedevilled by supply problems, was a rabble. The masses of troops—peasants and workers quickly flung together—needed more inspiration than the handful of Communists thrusting them into action could supply. A new spirit and desire to win somehow had to be breathed into the amorphous body to give it life. This was recognized by Trotsky:

'Every detachment led its own life. The one common desire was for retreat. . . . The earth itself was seized by panic. Fresh Red detachments, which arrived in good sentiment, were immediately caught up by the mood of retreat. . . . Everything was breaking in pieces; there was no longer any firm point. The situation seemed hopeless.'[55]

He did not shrink from firm measures; each commissar in a regiment which fled—and the commander—would be shot. A raiding party of Whites put to flight a regiment recruited from Petrograd workers. The Red unit then seized a ship to escape up the Volga. Trotsky ordered the ship surrounded by vessels of the Volga flotilla, dragged the deserters ashore, and brought the commander, the regimental commissar, and every tenth soldier before a firing-squad. Through such ruthless methods, combined with promises and hasty reorganization, he transformed a panic-stricken mob into a fighting force which became the nucleus of the Fifth Army, probably the best of sixteen Red Armies raised during the Civil War.[56]

On the night of 28th August, Kappel, the leader of the White forces on the Volga, attempted to destroy the enemy at Sviazhsk by infiltration from the rear. Such tactics, carried out with daring by Kappel, had previously been successful—as at Simbirsk in July. On this occasion however, the Red troops (outnumbering the Whites by two to one)* held firm; Kappel withdrew, and the Bolsheviks moved on Kazan. Skirmishing ensued, protracted until 10th September, when a combined assault by the Red land force and the Volga river flotilla overcame the defences and Kazan fell.[57] Simbirsk followed on the 12th, and on 3rd October the Reds marched into Syzran. Five days later they captured Samara.

It was during this period that the Czechs were attempting, at Ufa, to forge from various regional governments a single anti-Bolshevik government. Such a government, the Czechs realized, was absolutely necessary if a united stand was to be made against the advancing Reds.

The revitalized Red forces, though small, had been too much for the White troops and the government at Samara, which moved to Ufa, then to Omsk, until Kolchak's *coup* in November swept it away. The Whites, now as demoralized as the Reds had been before Trotsky's arrival, gave ground east of the Volga, losing Izhevsk, Ufa, and Sterlitamak before the end of the year.

The Red advance was important. Materially it gave the Bolsheviks rich agricultural provinces which could relieve to some extent the food shortages in the rest of Soviet Russia; an outlet to the east had

* The forces involved were small—about 2000 Whites against 4000 Reds.

been gained with the reopening of the Volga which could be used to transport grain and stocks of oil from Astrakhan. These operations, small though they were, marked the first victorious campaign of the new Red Army[58] and this was of great significance for the survival of Bolshevik Russia.

CHAPTER IV

INTERVENTION IN SIBERIA—
TO THE ARMISTICE

GENERAL DESCRIPTION OF SIBERIA

The vast expanse of Siberia, stretching from the Urals to the Pacific, had but a sparse Russian population amounting to not more than 9,500,000 in 1917.[1] Yet the country was fast developing, and was not unlike Canada at that time. The climate is harsh, with long cold winters, but contrary to popular misconceptions, Siberia is by no means barren. The frozen tundra of the north gives way to a forest region, and south of that lies a continuation of the black-earthlands of the Ukraine; the land is rich in minerals. An important geographical feature is Lake Baikal which, extending 430 miles north-east to south-west, is the largest freshwater body in Asia. This lake, surrounded by mountains, cuts directly across the southern agricultural belt, imposing a difficult natural obstacle to lateral communications.

Russia had furthered her influence in Siberia through the Cossacks who were given freedom to form and administer military settlements. Behind them came the Russian state organization which built forts or fortified towns on the sites of nearly all the present Siberian cities. As the Cossacks moved farther east a protective screen was thus established, which permitted settlements to grow under two distinct elements of the population. The first, which refused to accept church reforms made in the seventeenth century, went willingly to seek a region where they could worship in the old way. The second was made up of political exiles and convicts whose fates were mixed. Some were forced to develop the country by working in labour groups on public works or in the mines; others could select their own places of residence on condition that they would not leave the province for various periods of time and of these many enjoyed the freer life and remained to swell the growing ranks of pioneers when their terms were over.[2]

The slow process of colonization was speeded up when, by the

Treaty of Peking in 1860, Russia compelled China to cede the whole area from the Ussuri river to the Pacific. Two years before, in the same way, Russia had already acquired the left bank of the Amur river. Now, in the southernmost part of the region, the Russians built the fortress town of Vladivostok and, with this place established as a seaport, brought in colonists by sea from Odessa to settle the coastal region as well as the Amur and Ussuri areas farther west. Cossacks moved in to protect the new areas; their strength increased by extending Cossack rights to willing settlers, by moving thousands of Ukrainian peasants to join them, and by enrolling reliable Buryats and other Asiatic tribesmen. Thus, towards the end of the century, the Siberian Cossacks had split into three main groups, the Trans-Baikal Cossacks in the area east of Lake Baikal, the Amur Cossacks, and the Ussuri Cossacks. For the most part, the new settlements flourished. Peasants owned their own land and were free in a very real sense. They could increase their capital by their own exertions, and by doing so they developed an independent spirit in sharp contrast to that prevailing in the rest of Russia.[3]

Just as railways in Canada opened up the west, so the Trans-Siberian really opened up Siberia for development. This railway, having a total length of 5542 miles, ran from Moscow to Vladivostok, the through service being inaugurated in 1903. East of Lake Baikal, in order to avoid following the great curve of the Amur river, Russia obtained a concession from China to construct the line from Chita straight across a part of Mongolia and northern Manchuria to re-enter Russian territory not far from Vladivostok. This branch became known as the Chinese Eastern Railway and was controlled by the Russian Government.[4] The short cut through Manchuria looked far less dependable after Japan emerged victorious from the Russo-Japanese war in 1905, and an alternative route to Vladivostok was started in 1908. This route, the Amur Railway, opened in 1914.[5]

The Trans-Siberian, even before the through road was fully open, could be used partially to populate Siberia. Three million Russian peasants were moved east of the Urals by the government between 1896 and 1909. The population of western Siberia almost doubled between 1897 and 1911[6] and in 1912 alone the Board of Emigration settled 400,000 persons on lands in Siberia.[7] Unlike the agricultural classes, skilled workers brought to the mining centres and cities included amongst their numbers members of the Social Democratic Party, both Bolsheviks and Mensheviks, and these provided a nucleus for revolutionary activity. This was strongest in Krasnoyarsk, on the Yenisey river, and in the Suchan coal mines north of Vladivostok.[8] But in 1918 the number of Bolsheviks in Siberia was extremely small, and this must be remembered when liberation by the Czechs and subsequent intervention by the Allies are considered. In 1922, after emerging victorious in the civil war, Communists constituted only one half of 1 per cent of the population of western Siberia. East of Lake Baikal the figure was about 8000 party members according to official statistics, or a mere 0·13 per cent of the population at that time. Four years before the number was undoubtedly smaller.[9]

ARGUMENTS FOR INTERVENTION

Operations in Siberia were discussed by the Allies soon after the Bolsheviks seized power in November 1917. It was already plain that Russia could no longer be counted upon to hold significant German forces on the Eastern Front. British troops at Hong Kong were alerted for movement to Vladivostok, but no movement was ordered at that time. In December 1917, after the Russo-German truce, the Allied military representatives at Versailles held out no hope of aiding resistance to the Germans in South Russia without intimate communication with that area, and this could best be provided through Vladivostok and the Trans-Siberian Railway. A month later the British Foreign Office urged upon the American Government the view that only by means of the Siberian railway could effective help be given to the anti-German factions in Russia, suggesting that Japan could furnish most of the help required. Not only were Japanese troops available and near at hand, but the strength of a pro-German party in Japan made it desirable to bring Japan into direct conflict with Germany, thus forestalling any possible German-Japanese rapprochement. In February the War Office followed up with a submission to the French calling for a resolute Japanese intervention in Siberia which would support anti-German Russian forces, save Roumania, and put a stop to German troop-movements from East to West.[10] But, through American reluctance to countenance intervention, the question came up time after time throughout the first half of 1918 without decision.

Every military argument seemed to point to intervention in Siberia. A War Office appreciation made in June 1918 summed up the British view, which, as no early end to the war could then be foreseen, was based on the continuation of campaigns throughout 1919 and 1920. Intervention, it was stated, would have little effect on the campaign of 1918. The Central Powers had at that time fifty-eight divisions in Russia deployed along a line Tiflis–Kertch–Rostoff–Kursk–Smolensk–Pskoff, a thousand miles west of the Urals. Even if intervention was sanctioned at once, it must be some weeks before an expedition could land at Vladivostok, and however quickly troops could move forward, they could scarcely hope to reach the Urals (3500 miles distant) before the cold weather set in. Consequently such an advance, from the purely military point of view, need not cause the Germans the slightest anxiety that year, and they could 'continue their agreeable task of absorbing the richest resources of the Ukraine, the Donetz coalmines, the Baku and Grosni oilfields, and the Caucasus manganese deposits'. It was on the 1919 campaign that intervention would have far-reaching, and perhaps decisive, effect.[11]

In June 1918 the Germans on the Western Front had an estimated superiority of between thirty-five and forty divisions. And a year later, though America by then hoped to have a further thirty-five trained divisions, they would still have a slight superiority and could continue to fight in 1919 with considerable chance of success *if they were not obliged to withdraw troops to meet a threat from the East.* Therefore, while the intervention of the Allies could have little effect on the present military situation, it should be undertaken at once in view of the ultimate issues of the war. Unless an adequate force could be reconstituted in Russia sufficiently powerful to menace the German hold on Russian resources, forcing Germany to withdraw troops from the Western Front to oppose this threat, the military superiority of the Central Powers in Europe would continue. Not only would the Allies have little chance of securing a victory in 1919, but for the early part of that year they would still be in danger of defeat.[12]

This, then, was the main argument for intervention. But there was another, equally important. Would the objectives for which the Allies were fighting be secured, even if Germany should be heavily defeated in the West, if an Eastern Front was not reconstituted? The German armies might be driven out of France and Belgium, but it was difficult to see how such terms could be imposed on the Central Powers as to force them to give up the prey they had secured in the East. Nothing but adequate armed force in the eastern theatre could compel the Germans to disgorge the wheat and coal, the oil and minerals, of the Ukraine and Caucasus. Such force must in the first instance be provided by the Allies, but an essential object would have to be the reconstitution of Russia as a military power so that, *when the Allied armies were withdrawn, Russia herself would be able to defend her liberty, honour, and national existence from German spoliation.*[13]

This spoliation would not only be of material resources but also of manpower for industrial purposes and to swell the ranks of their armies. Such a double increment of strength would increase the recuperative power of Germany enormously, and it was feared that she would be able completely to outstrip the rest of Europe in the reconstruction of economic and military resources so that at no distant date Germany would once again be in a position to threaten the peace of the rest of the world (as indeed, even without Russian resources, Hitler did twenty years later).[14]

The British did not suggest a weakening of the forces in the West to provide an intervention force in Russia. The bulk of the troops in Siberia must be furnished by Japan, with small detachments of American and British troops to mark the international character of the undertaking, and to reassure the Russians of the disinterestedness of Allied motives. Operations undertaken by the Japanese (based on Vladivostok) along the Trans-Siberian Railway would be strategically sound because they would bring to bear great military forces which could not be employed on the Western Front and which would otherwise be lying idle. The aim of Japanese forces should be to reach the Volga and deploy a striking force on the line Vologda–Samara with detachments at Archangel and Astrakhan. There they would control the Volga waterway and the cotton railway from Tashkend. As a first step to deployment on this line an advance along the Trans-Siberian Railway from Vladivostok to the Urals would be necessary, establishing a compact force of one or two divisions at Cheliabinsk and Ekaterinburg with light troops pushed west of the Urals to Perm and Ufa. Siberia would thus be occupied. Siberian wheat and Ural minerals would be secured against German acquisition; the repatriation of German and Austrian prisoners who would otherwise be used as reinforcements on the Western Front would be rendered difficult; *and it would have the most far-reaching political results which would in all probability extend westwards.*[15]

Behind the Allied front, Russians would rally to any movement for the restoration of order and sane government. Russian forces would be large and constantly increasing. These forces, when organized, could be used to carry out the next 'bound' from Cheliabinsk to the Vologda–Samara line. An Allied advance through Siberia would almost certainly be followed by the development of partisan warfare in European Russia. A Russian revival would be brought about by intervention which would rally to the standard of freedom and good government those sections of the Russian population which had those ideals at heart.[16]

The British envisaged the need for a Japanese force of eight and a half divisions—six and a half would suffice to guard the railway from Vladivostok to Cheliabinsk leaving two to establish the necessary forward line. It was estimated that fifty railway trains would be required to transport a single Japanese division; and one train per two divisions would serve for maintenance. The capacity of the Trans-Siberian, though impaired, was considered to be at least equal to the task.[17]

The Supreme War Council at Versailles, meeting in July, fully endorsed the British view. By then the astounding feats of the Czech Corps had become known. Their control of the railway 'proves that the bulk of the Siberian population are no longer sympathetic to the Bolsheviks'; Siberians must be well disposed to the Allied cause. It removed any apprehension that Allied intervention would be opposed—as might have been the case had intervention forces been composed almost entirely of Japanese—and rendered penetration to the Urals particularly easy. The Czechs, it had been reported by the Czech National Council to the Allied consuls at Vladivostok, were in danger of being cut off by German and Austrian prisoners of war at Irkutsk, and an appeal for immediate military assistance had been made which could not be ignored. 'Intervention in Siberia, therefore, is an urgent necessity, both to save the Czecho-Slovaks and to take advantage of an opportunity of gaining control of Siberia for the Allies which may never return.'[18]

The major reasons given for intervention echoed the British appreciation, stating that the primary object of Allied action was to co-operate with the Russian nation in recreating the Eastern Front as a first step towards freeing Russia and preventing the domination and exploitation of that country by Germany. Failure to intervene immediately would be 'disastrous to the Allied cause'; it would destroy all hope of the resuscitation of Russia as an ally; it would mean the permanent impairment of the blockade of the Central Powers; and finally it would bring 'the indefinite prolongation of the War, and the surrender of any real prospect of victory for the Allies in 1919'.[19]

In considering the composition of an Allied intervention force, the Council found it imperative that the force should be *'adequate in number,** military in character and Allied in composition'*, and that, above all things, 'it should operate immediately'. Owing to geographical and shipping conditions, Japan should furnish the bulk of the force, but, in order to maintain its Allied character, 'it must include both American and other Allied units'. The force should be 'under a single command appointed by the Power that provides the largest number of troops'—that is, Japan. The Japanese had already been sounded out, and had agreed to go into Siberia provided they were assured of 'the approval and active support of the United States Government'. They had not committed themselves to go beyond Irkutsk but the Council had no grounds for thinking this represented the limits of their effort. Furthermore, they had accepted the two conditions which the War Council considered it important to impose —disinterestedness in Russian internal politics, and guarantees to evacuate Russian territory after the war. Only the consent and co-operation of the United States was now required to set the policy of intervention in motion.[20]

'Therefore', the report concluded, 'in view of:

'(i) The unanimous opinion of General Foch and the Allied military advisers of the Supreme War Council that immediate despatch of an adequate Allied force to Siberia is essential for the victory of the Allied armies:

'(ii) The facts that no adequate expedition can be sent without Japanese co-operation and that Japan will not undertake effective action without the encouragement and support of the United States Government, and

'(iii) The shortness of the time available before the winter for initiating action in Siberia, and the rapid German penetration into Russia,

'the Supreme War Council appeals to President Wilson to approve the policy here recommended, and thus enable it to be carried into effect before it is too late.'[21]

* Italics supplied.

In the face of this appeal Wilson finally sanctioned, with modifications, a form of intervention. But before we examine the vague and misleading document issued by the State Department in Washington which initiated action, we must turn to considerations other than military. Many a good military plan has foundered in the stormy seas of politics and public opinion; so it was to be in Siberia.

AMERICAN POLICY IN THE FAR EAST

The American policy in eastern Asia had been that of a balance of power, which resolves itself basically into the relationship of three nations—Russia, Japan, and China. China, as a power, had until recently been unable to match her neighbours in strength, and it was there that rivalry between Russia and Japan was focused. The United States, anxious to prevent unification of the Far East under one power which would threaten her trade and the security of her Pacific coast, traditionally supported the independence of China.[22]

The American annexation of the Hawaiian and Philippine islands in 1898 drew no Japanese protest, for at that time Japan earnestly desired American friendship and support for action in Korea following the Sino-Japanese War of 1895. The United States, alarmed that Russia's force appeared overwhelming in northern China, favoured Japan; and in the Russo-Japanese War of 1904-05 (fought mainly for control of Korea and China) the United States, though officially neutral, was in reality a spiritual ally of Japan through the actions of President Theodore Roosevelt. Japan defeated Russia, thus preventing the emergence of a great Far Eastern empire controlled from St Petersburg; and as part of the spoils Japan received the southern half of Sakhalin Island.[23]

During this period the aggressive policy and actions of Russia in China also resulted in the signing of the Anglo-Japanese Alliance in 1902[24] which, twice renewed, was to assume some importance when operations in Siberia were contemplated by the Allies in 1918.

For the next few years (1906-14), Russia and Japan seemed to balance each other, and no real threat was apparent to the United States. But Russia's defeat had released Japan's aggressive impulses; the Roosevelt administration, having supported Japan against Russia, reluctantly permitted Japan to consolidate its position on the Asiatic mainland in return for guarantees of America's Pacific possessions. The United States was powerless to prevent the closing of the 'Open

Door' in Korea and the expansion of Japan into Manchuria which, for practical purposes, was lost to China and divided between Russia and Japan. (A way was sought by diplomatic means, without success, to prevent the expansion of either Russia or Japan at the expense of China.) The attitude of the United States towards China was benevolent rather than beneficent during this period.[25]

On August 23, 1914, Japan declared war on Germany. A month later, Chinese President Yüan Shih-k'ai remarked to the American minister, 'Japan is going to take advantage of this war to get control of China'.[26] A disorganized China did not see fit to enter the war on the side of the Allies—she was as suspicious of Russia as of any other power—and while she hesitated, Japan seized the German port of Tsingtao. On January 18, 1915, Japan served on China 'Twenty-one Demands' (which secured Japanese control of large parts of the Chinese economy and defence) following this up with troop movements on the Manchurian–Mongolian border which would enable her to move in any direction without regard to the wishes of China. Washington viewed these developments with alarm; nevertheless, on 13th March, Secretary of State Bryan, when referring to Japanese 'demands' relative to Shantung, South Manchuria, and East Mongolia, conceded that 'the United States frankly recognizes that territorial contiguity creates special relations between Japan and these districts'. And in August 1917, following China's declaration of war on the Central Powers, Japan sent Viscount Ishii to the United States with the object of negotiating a new understanding with that country which was accomplished by an exchange of notes between Secretary of State Lansing and Ishii on 2nd November. The understanding incorporated Bryan's concession of two years earlier by stating 'that Japan has special interests in China, particularly in the part to which her possessions are contiguous', but both countries declared opposition 'to the acquisition by any Government of any special rights or privileges that would affect the territorial integrity of China or that would deny to the . . . citizens of any country the full enjoyment of equal opportunity in the commerce and industry of China'.[27]

This convention marked the limit of American concessions to Tokyo;[28] in fact it provided an indication that the United States from now on intended to block the aggressive policies of Japan.[29]

Throughout the war years Japan's power had grown while that of Russia was on the wane. In 1914 the German possessions in China had fallen to Japan. The German archipelagos in the Pacific had followed, and then in 1915 the 'Twenty-one Demands' had given Japan a predominant influence over China. The entry of the United States into the war, and her preoccupation with the Western Front, left Japan practically unchecked in the Far East. Yet it was quite clear that in view of treaty arrangements between the powers at war with Germany, Japan could hardly move against the Russian zone of Manchuria or the Chinese Eastern Railway as a means of extending her influence in the Far East. Then came the Russian revolutions of March and November 1917 which removed the influence of the only other great power in the adjoining lands and seemed to offer Japan an opportunity to control the Russian Far East as well as northern China.[30]

After the March revolution, Japan watched and waited, making no decisive move. Then, following the November revolution, local soviets began to seize power in the cities of the Far East; a Japanese warship appeared at Vladivostok on 30th December.[31] Throughout the spring of 1918 Britain, France, and Japan continued diplomatic preparations for intervention, and simultaneously exerted pressure on the American Government. On 4th April two Japanese were killed in Vladivostok. Next day a few Japanese marines were put ashore to protect their nationals, and Britain took similar action.[32] The next step by Japan occurred in May, when military and naval agreements (May 16 and 19) were signed with China, to be followed by a further military agreement in September. By their terms, Chinese forces were put under Japanese command for joint action in Siberia; the Chinese Eastern Railway would be used for the transportation of troops.[33] Only after it had become clear to President Wilson that with or without the co-operation of the United States intervention was practically certain, did he consent to carefully limited participation by the United States, the main purpose of which was to act as a check upon Japan, to counteract Japanese moves, and to thwart Japanese attempts to impose themselves upon the country.[34]

Thus the political background to an intervention which would contain as its main contingents troops from America and Japan militated against any united policy or action; it served to render absolutely useless the broad purposes which Britain and France had in mind when intervention was so strongly advocated. But there was worse to come. The issue was confounded still further by the American attitude towards Russia.

AMERICA, RUSSIA, JAPAN—AND AMERICAN–JAPANESE INTERVENTION

It may be doubted if Wilson really understood the nature of Bolshevism. He had enthusiastically acclaimed the March revolution which had been the culminating factor in his determination to enter the war—though diplomatic relations with Germany had been severed on February 3, 1917, there had been no anticipated declaration of war; Russian developments provided Wilson with a real ideological basis for this. A hated autocracy had been eliminated from the Allied ranks, a new revolutionary democracy added. Significantly, the United States was the first nation to recognize the new Provisional Government of Russia (22nd March) and on 22nd April, in his speech to Congress concerning the declaration and prosecution of the war, Wilson turned to Russia. Now all the Allies were fighting for freedom, he said, and 'Here is a fit partner for a League of Honor'.[35]

In March 1918, shortly after the signing of the Treaty of Brest-Litovsk, the Americans still regarded Russia as an ally despite all evidence to the contrary, and despite the fact they themselves had not recognized the Soviets as a government, even *de facto*, nor accepted any of their acts. The American attitude was made plain by the State Department to the Japanese—'we should continue to treat the Russians as in all respects our friends and allies against the common enemy'.[36] Two months earlier, in a speech to Congress which contained the first statement of 'The Fourteen Points', President Wilson had even lauded Bolshevik insistence on open meetings at Brest-Litovsk which were intended to stir up workers' revolutions throughout the world as being 'in the true spirit of modern democracy'.[37] Again, in May, Wilson said, 'I intend to stand by Russia as well as France. The helpless and the friendless are the very ones that need friends and succor'.[38]

That Wilson's attitude at this time struck an unreal note, though an idealistic one, is hardly surprising. Recent events in Russia had been almost completely misinterpreted in the United States. Two conflicting points of view, both in American public opinion and in the reports from Americans in Russia, were reflected in Washington.

The first condemned the Bolsheviks—considerable credence was given to the view that the Soviets were German agents—and this group included most of the State Department representatives. As early as December 10, 1917, Secretary Lansing advised Wilson that he had studied the Russian situation and had drawn these conclusions:

'That the Bolsheviki are determined to prevent Russia from taking further part in the war.

'That the longer they continue in power the more will authority in Russia be disorganized and the more will the armies disintegrate, and the harder will it become to restore order and military efficiency.

'That the elimination of Russia as a fighting force will prolong the war for two or three years, with a corresponding demand upon this country for men and money.

'That with the Bolsheviks' domination broken the Russian armies might be reorganized and become an important factor in the war by next spring or summer.

'That the hope of a stable Russian Government is for the present in a military dictatorship backed by loyal disciplined troops.'[39]

It will be noted that these views were largely shared by the British and the French. It was a mistake, however, on the part of some of the leading members of this group to brand Lenin 'a German agent'. If an opponent is to be beaten, the first prerequisite is to understand his game. The danger of Lenin lay in the fact that he was the convinced and absolutely dedicated fanatic of a false idea, sincere enough to hold the masses firm in the belief that all the blood and tears would one day cease with the 'Millennium'. The only way to disarm him was to expose him for what he was, not to attack him for being a hired instrument of the Central Powers, which, though he took money from them, he obviously was not. Yet the American Committee on Public Information published a collection of documents, 'The German–Bolshevik Conspiracy', which endeavoured to show that 'the present Bolshevik Government is not a Russian Government at all, but a German Government, acting solely in the interests of Germany and betraying the Russian people, as it betrays Russia's natural Allies, for the benefit of the Imperial Government alone'. They show no such thing—rather the incompetence of those to whom the job was entrusted. As an example, one facsimile included by way of corroboration purports to be a document put out by the 'General Staff' of the German High Sea Fleet. Now the German navy had no 'General Staff', and in eighteen lines of the document are two mistakes in grammar, seven in spelling and seven in phrasing. This, in itself, throws grave doubts on the authenticity of the whole collection, of which even anti-Bolshevik Russians said : 'They produce an uneasy impression of forgery'.[40]

The second group, composed largely of radicals, intellectuals, and idealists, accepted Bolshevik statements at their face value and vehemently condemned all interference with the Soviet régime. Colonel Raymond Robins, the American Red Cross representative in Moscow (with whom the Soviet leaders dealt in the absence of the American Ambassador from Moscow) who was generally regarded by the Bolsheviks as the leader of the pro-Soviet party, shared the opinions of this group.

On February 15, 1918, Robins reported : 'Great values for Allied cause in resulting situation depend on continuance of Bolshevik authority as long as possible. No other party will refrain from ac-cepting German peace or so deeply stir internal forces opposed to German government.'[41] He advocated (as also did Bruce Lockhart, a British agent in Russia) recognition and support of the Soviet government as the most effective means of restoring it to a position of such authority that it could once more take the field against Ger-many. But the State Department did not agree. In the first place, the Bolsheviks were, in fact, a minority party in Russia; recognition of them would alienate the vast majority who opposed them. Secondly, there was little confidence in the durability of the Soviet régime. Third, and most important, German and Austrian intervention was already in progress and this made Robins's proposal seem totally valueless.[42]

Robins also advocated economic assistance to the Bolsheviks, and on May 14, 1918, Lenin invited the United States to take over as much of the Russian foreign market as she desired.[43] Robins recom-mended that the offer should be accepted, as in his opinion economic co-operation would open the way for a friendly intervention after which the Eastern Front could be effectively rebuilt.[44] But to the United States Government, not unaware of such Bolshevik measures as the destruction of public order, the confiscation of personal goods and property, and the abolition of money, it seemed that the invita-tion should be declined. And perhaps wisely. The offer in all proba-bility was a realistic device by Lenin to stave off American interven-tion and to embroil that country with Japan and the other Allies who would have looked jealously at the sole execution by America of such an all-inclusive plan. Later, in 1920, when Japan alone remained in

Siberia, the Soviet Government granted large concessions to Americans with the dual object of using American capital as a means of achieving recognition, and of promoting American–Japanese rivalry until the area should once again come under Soviet domination. In the end, all American firms lost their investments. When Lenin had effected a final settlement with Japan in 1925, the Communists took over the properties of the International Harvester Company with a loss to the firm of 31,000,000 dollars, while Singer Sewing Machine lost 84,000,000. Other firms, including Parke, Davis and Company, Victor Talking Machine, Westinghouse Electric, and New York Air Brake, all lost substantial sums.[45]

Meanwhile, Robins and the American Red Cross in Petrograd and Moscow continued to hand out milk and medical supplies with the full approval of Lenin. As a practical expression of Wilson's principles, this was laudable. 'At the same time', comments a student of this period, 'it was evident that such philanthropic work was not solving any of the major problems.'[46]

Under prevailing conditions, the real choice open to the United States lay in either accepting the Bolsheviks as representing the people and including Russia among the Allies (or for that matter as supporters of the Central Powers) or in disregarding that government and trying to set up a friendly government in its place. But beset by widely differing reports, Wilson became more and more uncertain as to the right course to follow. He was firmly resolved not to interfere in the internal affairs of Russia. It seemed to him that in a short time the leaders of the various factions would unite to form a national government which would renew the war. How this could be done in view of the Bolshevik terror, their hold of the major towns and communications, and the universal disorganization, is not clear. In a letter to Colonel House on July 8, 1918, Wilson gives some indication of his preoccupation with the problem. 'I have been sweating blood', he wrote, 'over the question what is right and feasible to do in Russia. It goes to pieces like quicksilver under my touch.'[47] But a few days later (17th July) he evolved what he thought was the correct formula, and embodied it in an *Aide Mémoire*, a document which was presented to General Graves before he left to command the American contingent in Siberia, and which was made public to the Allied governments on 3rd August.* Detailed analysis of the

* In view of its importance, the full text of this document is given as Appendix I (p. 145).

Aide Mémoire will not be attempted, but consideration of even parts of it will show at once that it was so vague and unreliable that as a practical guide to a commanding officer the document was singularly worthless.

In the first place, nowhere are the Bolsheviks and the Soviet régime mentioned. There are many references to 'Russia', the 'Russian people' and to 'Russian forces' but there is nothing specific as to what is meant by these terms. The Bolsheviks, neither criticized nor denounced by the document, might even contend that as Russians they qualified for aid just as much as their opponents. Yet the State Department, as Secretary Lansing repeatedly declared, refused to recognize the Soviets as a Russian government even *de facto*; the document did not say so, and thus Graves was left with the task of not recognizing and not fighting forces with which he must inevitably clash. That there would be clashes must have been quite obvious—for though the document specifically denies that the American contingent was to be used for military intervention, there could be no doubt that the Soviets would regard the landings of American troops as intervention and would oppose them. Let Graves assume that by 'Russians', groups other than the Bolshevik were meant, then which of these? Was he to read into the document support of the defunct Provisional Government? Or of the dispersed Constituent Assembly whose Ambassador still remained in Washington? What of the separatist 'governments' then in being which represented only parts of Russia? Was only some overall government to be supported? Wilson gave no guidance and the anti-Bolshevik Russians would inevitably read into the document their own desires. They fought bitterly even between themselves—each claiming to represent the people of Russia—so that each would expect American aid against the rival factions as well as against the Bolsheviks. And if that help was declined, they would turn against the Americans for deceiving them, and obviously all of them could not be satisfied. It seems that one body should have been picked out for support, the only alternative being to win universal ill will, but no clue was given Graves as to what that body should be.

Similarly, military instructions with regard to the Czechs were equally vague. Help to this corps had been seized upon by Wilson as the major admissible reason for military action in Russia. His plans 'for safeguarding the rear of the Czecho-Slovaks operating from Vladivostok . . . in co-operation with a small military force like its own from Japan' were quite unrealistic. The Czechs at this time were fighting their way forwards west of the Urals towards the Volga, but there was no mention of their offensive in the *Aide Mémoire*, nor any hint that they were so far distant from Vladivostok. Was Graves to move 3500 miles inland to protect their rear? Was he to protect some part of the railroad which formed their communications? Or was he to hold the base at Vladivostok? They should be helped to 'consolidate their forces'. This was interpreted at a later date as 'consolidate their forces at Vladivostok', but events at the time the document was written all point to another interpretation—to consolidate their forces on the Volga front.

In summary, the *Aide Mémoire* at best can be described only as a vague guide, open to different interpretations by different persons. The President alone could say what the phrases really meant, and during the intervention period, when widely differing interpretations were placed on them by the State Department on the one hand and by the Army on the other, no clarification was ever made. This remarkable document has been described as follows:

'It breathes President Wilson's well-known spirit of disinterestedness and idealism. It is in every sense of the word for the most part a sermon embodying the President's views on the duty of one nation to another in the time of misfortune and of chaos. It deserves an honored place in the development of international obligations but it is singularly unclear in its practical application of these principles. As a guide to the activities of diplomats or troop commanders moving either to Siberia or North Russia, it is throughly unreliable and it places upon the diplomats and commanding officers the task of deciding exactly what action they should take in any conceivable situation.'[48]

A singularly unrealistic touch was added by Wilson's proposal to send representatives of the Y.M.C.A., who, in Churchill's words, would 'offer moral guidance to the Russian people'.[49]

The final part of the document which states that it was not contemplated by the United States that intervention should involve 'interference of any kind with the political sovereignty of Russia, any intervention in her internal affairs, or any impairment of her territorial integrity . . .', and the call for like assurances on the part 'of the governments uniting in action', needs no interpretation. It was pointed at Japan.

The Japanese were, in fact, in a difficult position in view of their designs upon Russia's Far East. Nevertheless, they had the satisfaction on 3rd August of being *invited* by the American government to 'send a small contingent of 7000 men to assist the Czecho-Slovak troops in Siberia'—the initiative actually came from the United States—and were told that they would 'have the high command'.[50] It has been stated that Japan agreed to the American suggestion to restrict her troops to 7000, but this is erroneous. Ishii, the Japanese Ambassador in Washington, informed the Acting Secretary of State that:

'. . . his Government for political reasons could not bind itself to limit the force to 7000 as it would be said by the people of Japan, and particularly the opposition, that the limitation was being imposed because of lack of confidence in Japan and its motives. . . .'[51]

That the Americans understood that Japan would exceed this total is clear; for on Japan wishing to include in her declaration regarding sending troops to Siberia a statement that she enjoyed a 'special position', the Americans considered such a statement unnecessary 'in view of the fact that they [the Japanese] would have supreme command and larger number of troops than all the other powers put together . . .'[52]

The Japanese declaration dated August 3, 1918, said in part:
'The Government of the United States, equally sensible of the gravity of the situation, recently approached the Japanese Government with proposals for the early dispatch of troops to relieve the pressure weighing upon the Czecho-Slovak forces. The Japanese Government, being anxious to fall in with the desire of the American Government, have decided to proceed at once to make disposition of suitable forces for the proposed mission, and a certain number of these troops will be sent forthwith to Vladivostok.

'In adopting this course, the Japanese Government remain constant in their desire to promote relations of enduring friendship, and they reaffirm their avowed policy of respecting the territorial integrity of Russia, and of abstaining from all interference in her internal politics. They further declare that upon the realization of the objects above indicated [relief of the Czecho-Slovaks] they will immediately withdraw all Japanese troops from Russian territory, and will leave wholly unimpaired the sovereignty of Russia in all its phases, whether political or military.'[53]

In view of subsequent Japanese action in Siberia, the sincerity of this document may be doubted.

Meanwhile Masaryk, in the name of the Czecho-Slovak National Council, had already instructed the Czech forces to remain in Siberia. 'The Bolsheviks', he said, 'keep their power only through the weakness and incompetency of their opponents.' He admitted that the Czecho-Slovak troops could be used 'with advantage' in Russia. 'Our men know Russia and Russians : but it would be a distinct loss to use our forces for a more police than military duty, more so, that they would not like it themselves. That of course depends on the further development of the Russian situation and then on the plans of the Allies in Russia. Meanwhile, the army will stay in Russia and co-operate with the Allies.' Realistically, he saw the purpose of military intervention as being aimed at the Bolsheviks, and was disturbed at the inconsistencies in the American attitude. 'I abstain from criticizing the action in Siberia,' Masaryk went on. 'I am not informed about the size of the military help and I do not know what political and administrative plans the Allies are pursuing. Judging from the reports I receive, and from the news I read in the papers, I am obliged to say that it seems to me that the Allies must send a considerably greater force, and that their policy towards the various Russian parties and governments (a rather dreary symptom of the Russian disorganization and lack of political maturity) should be clearer and more energetic. A precise political (and administrative) plan is also necessary for the success of the military operations.'[54]

Thus, the Americans and Japanese were avowedly proceeding to Siberia to safeguard the Czechs. The Czechs, who were advancing westwards in an offensive, were to remain in Russia to co-operate with the Allies. Yet no overall plan stating clearly how the various forces would work together or specifying what their objective or tasks would be, was ever formulated. It is hardly surprising that the expedition was conspicuously unsuccessful; it had been formed in a way that doomed it to failure even at the outset.

The British and French, however, welcomed the American move. The French, already committed to Czecho-Slovak and Polish independence, and desperately anxious to have an eastern front reconstituted, saw the declaration as a preliminary step towards all these objectives. The British, who had seen Wilson move from neutrality in the war to active participation, who had seen his attitude towards

Siberian intervention change from hostility to participation, had little doubt that events in Russia would, willy-nilly, force America to play an active part. But neither country could know at this stage that their expectations would founder on the personality of the American commander, General Graves.

THE AMERICAN COMMANDER

Major-General William S. Graves, appointed to his present rank as recently as July 18, 1918, was commanding the 8th Division in California when Wilson at last decided to send a force to Siberia. He had served in the Philippines, in the American West, and along the Mexican border. On 2nd August he was ordered to Kansas City, where, at the Baltimore Hotel, he was to ask for the Secretary of War. He arrived on the 4th, and found the Secretary (Newton D. Baker) at the station preparing to leave. During the course of a brief interview in a private room at the railway station, Baker informed him that he had been appointed to command the American contingent in Siberia and handed over a copy of the *Aide Mémoire*. This was the only briefing Graves ever got, though he did receive a warning from Washington later that the Japanese would oppose any move to bring the various Russian armies together since they wanted, for their own purposes, a collection of weak and separated forces. He had no access to State Department or War Department information and reports, and was told nothing other than was contained in Wilson's document and the later communication from Washington. But he had no questions. He read the *Aide Mémoire*, and knowing nothing of Siberian conditions—the document did not enlighten him as to what these were—he found everything perfectly clear. 'This', said Baker, 'contains the policy of the United States in Russia which you are to follow. Watch your step; you will be walking on eggs loaded with dynamite. God bless you and good-bye!'⁵⁵

On September 2, 1918, when he arrived in Siberia, Graves inevitably found conditions different from what he had expected. But in a confused situation he soon displayed the qualities for which, no doubt, he had been selected—qualities which were at once both limitations and virtues. These were a rigid obedience to orders, and a readiness to act only on that part of the order which was clear. Where an interpretation of the order on his own initiative was called for, he did nothing. According to the *Aide Mémoire*, he was not to interfere in Russian affairs; his task was to extend aid to the 'Russian people' acceptable to them for their own defence. To Graves, that meant that he was to do nothing until an accepted Russian government had come into being and asked for help—he was not to assist any faction to become an all-Russian government. As for the Bolsheviks, he did not, as the State Department did, adopt an openly anti-Bolshevik position; they were Russians, and formed part of the Russian people. Finally, he was to guard the rear of the westward moving Czecho-Slovaks, a task impossible without moving forward and becoming embroiled in the fighting. He contented himself, therefore, with guarding part of the Trans-Siberian Railroad and military stores at Vladivostok. Having adopted this policy, he maintained it throughout, no matter how the situation changed and fluctuated. He said himself : 'I have often thought it was unfortunate that I did not know more of the conditions in Siberia than I did when I was pitchforked into the mêlée at Vladivostok. At other times I have thought that ignorance was not only bliss in such a situation, but was advisable.'[56]

The British and French, faced with this intractability, soon left Graves out of the reckoning; it was always found impossible to carry the Americans along on any course of positive operational action in Siberia. These nations may, in fact, have regretted that the Americans had participated at all—without a contingent from the United States they would in all probability have scraped together larger bodies of troops than they actually did, and would have taken more positive military action themselves against the Bolsheviks.

INTERVENTION FINALLY BEGINS

British and French detachments were the first to arrive at Vladivostok. On 3rd August the British landed the 25th Battalion of the Middlesex Regiment from Hong Kong. France sent 500 men from Peking. Then, on the 8th, Japanese landings began on a large scale.[57] By the 27th, 18,000 Japanese troops had already disembarked at Vladivostok, while 6000 additional troops had been moved to the Manchurian frontier at Manchouli. At the beginning of November Japan had dispatched 72,400 men into Siberia and northern Manchuria, of whom 44,700 were combatants.[58] The Japanese commander, General Kikuzo Otani, assumed command of all the Allied forces on 18th August.

The 27th United States Infantry Regiment, with fifty-three officers and 1537 men under Colonel Henry D. Styer, arrived from the Philippines on 16th August. Then came the 31st Infantry Regiment while Graves, as we have seen, arrived from San Francisco on 2nd September. The American contingent finally contained 7500 men. A small body of Italians (2000) followed, and, in addition to them, 12,000 Poles, 4000 Serbs and a similar number of Roumanians were all dispatched to Siberia.[59]

CANADIAN PARTICIPATION

A week after the Americans had announced their decision to send troops to Siberia, the War Office sought the views of Sir Robert Borden, the Canadian Prime Minister, on the availability of Canadian troops for such an expedition. British resources, sadly depleted by the German offensive in the West, were overstretched. Overtures had been made before, and the British had been given to understand, unofficially, that two battalions of discharged soldiers could be raised in Canada; this would be quite in keeping with the present policy 'not to divert any appreciable body of troops from the Western front'.[60] Borden and the Minister of Militia (General Mewburn) were in London at the time of the request and were able to examine the British suggestion on the spot.

Borden studied the General Staff appreciation and that prepared by the Supreme War Council. The cogency of the arguments impressed him. Furthermore he saw future trade benefits for Canada across the Pacific if a friendly Russian government could be established; he was favourably disposed to the dispatch of a small force to Siberia. 'Intimate relations', he said, 'with that rapidly developing country will be a great advantage to Canada in the future. Other nations will make very vigorous and determined efforts to obtain a foothold and our interposition with a small military force would tend to bring Canada into favourable notice by the strongest elements in that great community.'[61]

Mewburn, who had returned to Canada, put in hand the organization of a brigade headquarters, two infantry battalions, a battery of field artillery, a machine-gun company, and certain other troops. The Middlesex battalion, already in Siberia, would join these troops, the combined force being known as the Canadian Siberian Expeditionary Force; it would represent the British Empire in the collection of Allied and Associated forces operating in Siberia and would come under Canadian command—thus marking the first occasion a Canadian had exercised overall command of an imperial venture.[62] It was not before 12th August, however, that the privy council authorized the dispatch of the troops; thus a month had intervened between the British request and the final Canadian approval of participation. Meanwhile the War Office had grown impatient. Militarily, swift action is often the essence of success, and a battalion in a few days is often worth a brigade in a month. Prompt action in this case awaited the political decision, but in the end delay made little difference. An attempt was made to expedite the matter through the Governor General, causing Borden, who had thus been circumvented, to cable angrily '. . . no reply shall be sent to the British Government's message except through me'.[63]

The approved contingent, 5000 strong, consisted of Headquarters Canadian Expeditionary Force (Siberia), H.Q. 16th Infantry Brigade, a base headquarters, and the following major units:

'B' Squadron, Royal North West Mounted Police (Cavalry),
85th Battery, Canadian Field Artillery,
16th Field Company, Canadian Engineers,
6th Signal Company,
259th Infantry Battalion,
260th Infantry Battalion,
20th Machine Gun Company,
No. 1 Company Divisional Train,
No. 16 Field Ambulance,
No. 11 Stationary Hospital,
No. 9 Ordnance Detachment.[64]

It was hoped that men would be raised by voluntary enlistment, but this was not found possible. Conscripts under the Military Service Act were taken and concentrated on the West Coast in readiness for Vladivostok, but it was not until 11th October that an advance party of 680 all ranks actually sailed from Vancouver under the force commander, Major-General J. H. Elmsley, an experienced officer who had commanded a brigade on the Western Front.[65] He had led the 8th Canadian Brigade during some of the sternest fighting of the war—at the Somme, Vimy Ridge, Hill 70 and Passchendaele.[66]

Canadian troops were to be under the control of the Allied Commander-in-Chief (General Otani) but Elmsley had the right to appeal to the War Office, with a copy to the Canadian Government,

7
Archangel 1919.
The barrel of a
badly-needed
60-pounder gun
in transit to the
front

One of the 60-
pounder guns that
held back the
Bolsheviks

The Archangel
Front, 1919.
Canadian field gun
in action

8
Canadian gunners,
Archangel Front,
during the winter of
1918–1919

(*photo: Canadian War Museum, Ottawa*)

A Canadian 18
pounder equip
for winter con
tions, Archang
1919

(*photo: Directorate of History, Canadian Forces Headquarters, Ottawa*)

Canadian gunners,
Archangel, June 1919

(*photo: Canadian War Museum, Ottawa*)

against any order which appeared to him to imperil the safety of his force. Further, no appeal could be decided against Elmsley without the approval of the Canadian Government. In addition, the Canadian commander was authorized to correspond directly with Canada without reference to the War Office or any outside body. The force, including the Middlesex, would be administered from Canada through Canadian service units in Siberia.[67]

The War Office gave as the objectives of the Allies in Siberia, first; to restore order and a stable government; second, to reconstitute an eastern front; third, and most immediate, to support the Czecho-Slovaks in their present positions. Elmsley would naturally be subject to the orders of Otani, but as regarded all local political (or military political) questions, he would be in close touch with (and guided by) General Alfred Knox, who had been selected, on account of his unrivalled knowledge of Russia, to be the British Military Representative at Allied Headquarters.[68]

The advance party arrived at Vladivostok on 26th October to find that the best accommodation had been taken over by the Japanese and Americans, making it necessary to find billets outside the town.[69] During November, however, the Russian military authorities made available barracks of brick construction at Gornostai and Second River, some twelve miles from the harbour. Both places required a considerable amount of work which the advance party put in hand at once so as to have it completed before the arrival of the main body in January 1919.[70] Office accommodation was obtained more readily; at the end of October, Force Headquarters and Base Headquarters opened in the Pushinskay Theatre, centrally situated in Vladivostok.[71]

ALLIED INTERVENTION FOUNDERS ON DIVERGENT NATIONAL POLICIES

Meanwhile the French Military Mission, which had moved up country to join the Czechs, prepared a report dated September 27, 1918, which considered the military factors involved in providing aid to the much-tried corps. Political considerations were purposely avoided 'lest they arrest us in the study of the purely military situation or falsify our judgment'.[72]

The Russian situation at the end of September was briefly this. Two Czech groups were operating, one on the Volga, and the

E

second in the northern Urals. In South Russia, White forces under Denikin had captured Ekaterinodar, but these troops were effectively separated from the Volga group of Czechs by a German division from the Ukraine which had been interposed at Novo Cherkassk; other White forces around Orenburg, with some Czech reinforcements, were seeking to prevent a Bolshevik breakthrough at Ufa. British troops had temporarily abandoned Baku on the Caspian. In the north, the Allies had seized Murmansk and Archangel and were now pressing south, while in eastern Siberia large Allied contingents had landed.[73]

The Volga group of Czechs, reinforced by Russian troops, was based on Samara. This force, by means of bridgeheads, held the west bank of the river and the town of Syzran at the centre of its front. Simbirsk, to the north, was partly in the hands of the Czechs and partly in the hands of the enemy. Kazan had been evacuated. From Simbirsk, north-east, the front followed the Volga and Kama river lines. To the south, the front was marked by the Volga as far as Khvalinsk, some 100 miles south-west of Samara, where the Bolsheviks had crossed the river. On this front, the Czechs were opposed by the 1st, 5th, and 4th Bolshevik 'armies'.[74]

A second Czech force, the North Ural group, based on Ekaterinburg, held about 500 miles of the Trans-Siberian Railway from Tioumen to Sarapul. The group was engaged in two operations, the first aimed at cutting the railway beyond Perm between Perm and Viatka, while the second moved on Perm itself. Some Russians, though poorly organized, worked with the Czechs, who faced the 2nd and 3rd Bolshevik 'armies'.[75]

In all, about 104,000 men opposed the Czechs and this number was being steadily augmented. Yet, despite being outnumbered and the length of the front, the Czechs were holding their own and even pushing the enemy back to Perm. Their success was due to two main factors : the existence of easily defensible river obstacles, and the superior organization and morale of their troops.[76]

This, the French contended, could not last. A month or two hence, rivers would no longer constitute an obstacle; even heavy artillery could cross the ice. Nor would the Czech successes be tolerated much longer by the Germans who had already occupied the Ukraine and pushed out towards the Caucasus. German military interest would prevent farther westward penetration towards the old Eastern Front, and there would be no question of the Czechs resisting even one German division of regular troops provided with artillery, just as the Bolsheviks would never be able to resist a regular division provided by the Allies. *Success would go to the side which could first furnish a fully equipped division on the North Ural Front.* If this should be German, the Czechs would be obliged to evacuate the Volga, for otherwise the Germans would be behind them; the reconstitution of Russian forces would be cut short. If Allied, the Red Army troops would literally vanish, and an advance along the northern branch of the Trans-Siberian Railway through Viatka to Vologda, linking up with the Allied force in North Russia, would be perfectly possible.[77]

On the assumption, therefore, that the presence of an Allied division at the front was essential to success, what of transport? The Trans-Siberian Railway would of course be used to bring up troops from East Siberia as had already been done to permit a Japanese division to move from Vladivostok to Baikal. But conditions on the railway were critical. The move of the Japanese division alone had necessitated fifty trains (2500 cars) which were still at the disposal of the Japanese. The Czechs were using others, leaving on the whole of the line between three and four thousand cars only. Nor could Czech rolling-stock be taken away until their front was sufficiently reinforced, for cars provided their only means of withdrawal in case of need. 'We must be at least at Perm, if not Viatka, before we can dream of liberating any part of this rolling stock.' The line permitted the use of only eight trains a day, thus it would take a week to put one Japanese division into motion, and it would be a month before the complete division could reach the Urals, even if no time was lost between the order and the execution. Should other divisions be sent, only one division a month could be counted upon.[78]

Despite these difficulties, the French report continued, Allied troops should be concentrated in the Urals as soon as possible. Concentration in Eastern Siberia, 'even if there are twenty divisions, would not advance us one iota', and would be a military error. Units should be transported west at once from the port of disembarkation, thus freeing rolling-stock for the transportation of others. The use of Allied troops to garrison towns along the Trans-Siberian Railway would be 'a simple waste of time', for garrisons at Chita, Irkutsk and so on would either retain their rolling-stock and immobilize it, or release their cars and be immobilized themselves. The immobilization of active troops, provided with artillery, 'constitutes the most deplorable use possible'; instead, new Russian formations should be used to keep order along the route.[79]

A firm base in the west could be found very easily. The Trans-Siberian was made up of a double line as far as Omsk; beyond Omsk the line branched into two single lines running north-west through Vologda and south-west through Samara. Intermediate towns on these lines were Ekaterinburg in the north and Cheliabinsk in the south, separated by some 150 miles of the Ural Mountains proper. The linking of Ekaterinburg and Cheliabinsk by a defence-line would thus form a triangle, Omsk–Ekaterinburg–Cheliabinsk, served by two railways; a line *de rocade* behind the Urals. This triangle, it seemed to the French, fulfilled the classical requirements of a good base, and a concentration should therefore be effected at Omsk, the capital of the richest province in Siberia, which had been garrisoned by 80,000 Russian troops and which possessed a sufficiency of barracks and administrative buildings. Furthermore, should the Czechs be obliged to withdraw from the Volga, they could re-establish themselves on the short Ekaterinburg–Cheliabinsk line and be reinforced from Omsk. What, then, would be risked by concentrating at Omsk at once, instead of waiting until obliged to do so in haste, beset by transportation difficulties and the fear of being too late?[80]

Every military argument favoured a forward concentration of the Allies. 'Clearing-up' in Eastern Siberia did not require 100,000 troops, whereas the Czechs on the Volga and in the Urals were wearing themselves out in an unequal struggle. Two divisions would be enough—one to defend the base, and the other to advance with the Czechs. It would not appear necessary to have to plead for an Allied force in the Urals.[81]

The British battalion moved forward to Omsk, in October, as did the French and Italian contingents, but what of the Americans and the Japanese? They remained west of Lake Baikal to wage the private battle for which they had come—the battle for Eastern Siberia.[82]

At first, the Japanese had been willing to move forward to support the Czechs.[83] As early as August 19, 1918, at an Allied Military Conference called by General Otani, the general situation was discussed. At that conference Otani stated that if the Czechs in Siberia were to be saved from defeat before the winter, 60,000 to 70,000 troops should be made available *immediately* for operations, and that if she were asked to do so, Japan was ready to send the troops required.

He requested the various military representatives to inform their governments of this and obtain their consent. 'What would be said of the Allies in future history', he concluded, 'if, owing to Allied failure to take the military measures necessary to relieve them, the Czechs were crushed?'[84]

No action to ascertain the attitude of his government was taken by the American representative at the time; instead, he awaited the arrival of General Graves, but it was already obvious what the American attitude would be. Five days earlier it was reported that the Americans had prevented the dispatch of Japanese reinforcements to Lake Baikal. In consequence, the Acting British Military

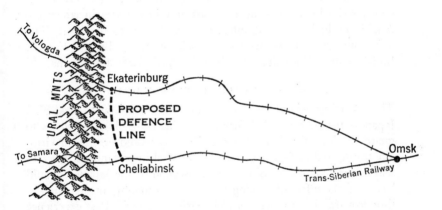

Representative reported, 'owing to American opposition, the Japanese 7th Division cannot be used for operations in Transbaikal, and no more Japanese troops can be sent for the same reason though the remainder of the 12th Division is mobilized. . . . There seems to be a fair prospect of proper military measures . . . being interfered with by political considerations.'[85]

On 8th September, General Graves was officially informed that the Japanese, British and French wished to move west to the Volga before winter set in; he was asked to ascertain the attitude of America. Eleven days later, Graves cabled Washington to convey a remarkable glimpse of the obvious: 'French and English are, undoubtedly, trying to get the Allied forces committed to some act which will result in the establishment of an Eastern Front.'[86]

The American commander received word from the War Department on 27th September that his force was not to proceed west of Lake Baikal, and that if the Czechs were to continue their westward move, American responsibility would consist only of guarding the railroad. On the same day Wilson declared that America could not participate in any military activities west of the Urals, and suggested that the Czechs should withdraw east of the mountains. That same month, when the Czech leader, Gaida, and his French advisers came to Vladivostok to plead for Allied help, Graves informed him explicitly that he could not count on America west of Baikal.[87] Japan would take no effective action at the front without the encouragement and support of the United States, and thereafter followed her own policies in the Russian Far East only in the area in which the Americans had expressed interest—from Baikal to the coast. The only contingents to go west of the lake were the British, French, Italian, Polish, Roumanian, Serbian; and, of course, the Czechs.

THE AMERICAN—JAPANESE DUEL

The reasoning behind the American decision is not far to seek. Had Japanese troops proceeded forward to the Urals, leaving others to guard the line, the Trans-Siberian Railway would have been virtually transferred to Japan; in view of the vital importance of this railway to the economy of Siberia, its possession by the Japanese would have had the effect of placing the Siberian economy in their hands, thus jeopardizing the territorial integrity of Russia. Past experience in China—where the Japanese had taken over the railways of Southern Manchuria—had already shown that 'ownership by a foreign government of a railway . . . in practice destroys equality of commercial and industrial rights',[88] and this was as true of the Trans-Siberian and Chinese Eastern Railways as of those in South Manchuria.

American business was active in Siberia; it was, in fact, an integral part of the economic development of the country. Steel manufacturers had sold cars, locomotives, and rails to the Russian railways; ships, bridges, and dry docks had come from American firms. The International Harvester Company in 1918 had its own plants and over two hundred branches throughout Siberia. Elsewhere in Russia, Westinghouse had a factory in Petrograd and made air brakes for railway cars. In July 1918, 60 per cent of all the cotton thread in Russia was still being turned out by the J. M. Coates Company of

America. This was a valuable market to preserve, and it could only be done by keeping the railway open and preventing it from falling into the hands of a nation which, the Americans feared, would force a monopoly by military methods.[89] It is perhaps not surprising that these aspects struck the Americans very forcibly when confronted by the Russian Revolution of March 1917.

In the summer of 1917, at the invitation of the Provisional Government, two railway commissions were sent to Russia by President Wilson. The first, under John F. Stevens, was known as the United States Railway Advisory Commission to Russia, and had the task of surveying all the Russian railways, making recommendations regarding improvements in management and technical changes, and finding out what was required in the way of supplies and equipment. The second, the Russian Railway Service Corps, consisted of about 300 technical experts who were to function in key positions in railway operation. The November Revolution prevented their assignment to duty until March 1918, when they began operations on the Chinese Eastern Railway. Both commissions were an American attempt to run the railways for the benefit of Russia and their presence was a strong factor in blocking Japanese efforts to assume control. As Stevens was to say later, on his return from Siberia, 'after matching wits for four long years—secretly of course—I prevented the Japanese from taking the Chinese Eastern Railway'.[90]

These commissions, and another which arrived at Vladivostok on June 3, 1917, under Elihu Root with the purpose of finding out what material support Russia needed to carry on the struggle against Germany, seemed to Japan to provide evidence of sinister intentions on the part of the Americans. Large quantities of construction materials and rolling-stock ordered from the United States raised the question of how the Russians would pay; Russia must grant, the Japanese thought, commercial interests in mines, railways, forests and other enterprises, in return. The commercial rivalry between Japan and America was often mentioned by members of the Soviet Government as the one thing which stood between them and the loss of Siberia. Lenin contended that the rivalry between the two nations rendered a struggle for supremacy absolutely inevitable. Japan would not stand idly by while American experts took up strategic locations along the railway.[91]

The Japanese–American duel for the railroad, as we shall see, continued throughout the period of intervention; the year 1919 was filled with incidents between the two countries which hindered efficient operations, prevented or slowed the forwarding of military supplies to the anti-Bolsheviks, and which, in the end, were a major factor in the return of the Soviets to Siberia.

Meanwhile, upon his arrival in Vladivostok with the *Aide Mémoire*, Graves made the opening move in his own personal battle against the Japanese. He was incensed to find that there had been an unfortunate misunderstanding of his instructions even before he came with them. Colonel Styer, on being informed by the Japanese that the American Government had placed the American contingent under General Otani, had committed his troops to an attack on Khabarovsk in co-operation with the Japanese. This, to Graves, was highly unusual and improper. In the end, however, as the operation was to be carried out mainly against Austro-Hungarian armed prisoners, he allowed it to proceed, and the 27th Infantry took part in the successful attack, going on to another on Blagoveshchensk which fell on 18th September. These were the only joint operations in which the Americans participated—all future requests from the Japanese were turned down flatly. Graves made it perfectly clear to Otani at their first meeting that, though he might be the senior officer, he was not Allied Commander-in-Chief so far as the Americans were concerned; his own instructions were that the American forces would remain an independent unit. It must be assumed that General Graves was never informed that the Japanese were to 'have the high command' as the State Department had explicitly stated; but he asked for no clarification; he never recognized an authority over his troops higher than his own.[92] The lessons of the Western Front, where the pressure of events had forced the appointment of Foch as Commander-in-Chief, had not been learned. Despite general agreement that Otani, commander of by far the largest contingent, should have the supreme command, Graves was able to circumvent the arrangement either through ignorance or design. This marked the first real rift, in a military sense, between the Americans and the Japanese. Thereafter, no common policy was ever achieved.

While operations against Khabarovsk and Blagoveschchensk were proceeding, a mixed Allied force, largely Japanese, had also proceeded to the Ussuri region (on 18th August) to relieve the Middlesex battalion—which had moved northwards to the 'Ussuri front' immediately on its arrival—and to clear the area of Bolsheviks; it was estimated that here 15,000 armed prisoners were co-operating actively with the Reds.[93] The force met with early reverses, and reinforcements from the recently landed Japanese 12th Division had to be sent. These, assisted by troops furnished by Kalmykov, Ataman of the Ussuri Cossacks, routed the enemy, halting Bolshevik uprisings in the Maritime and Amur Provinces of Eastern Siberia for several months.[94] With the Amur Railway under anti-Bolshevik control, the Japanese 14th Division occupied the Amur district with Kalmykov and his Cossacks operating out of Khabarovsk as a protégé of Japan.[95] The Soviet forces, as elsewhere in Siberia, disappeared into the forests and there formed partisan bands.

Czech successes in Trans-Baikal permitted the Japanese to enter that area without fighting, and there they linked up with another protégé—Semenov—who had entered from Manchuria. In the six weeks prior to October 25, 1918, American reports stated that 40,000 Japanese troops had moved through northern Manchuria, 20,000 of whom were preparing to winter at Chita. The remainder were scattered along the Chinese Eastern Railway, raising the Japanese flag over railway stations, evicting Russian employees, and in general taking the control of the railway out of Russian hands. Semenov also made his headquarters at Chita from where he could dominate both branches of the railway towards the coast, as well as the main Trans-Siberian line to Lake Baikal. He was thus in an admirable position to interrupt communications between Vladivostok and Omsk at any time.[96] The Japanese and their collaborators by this time were completely dominant in the area east of the lake. 'Along the railway they guarded every village, city, railway bridge, and almost all public buildings. Their gunboats were in every navigable stream and river, . . . by October, Japan had Siberia and Manchuria entirely under her power.'[97]

The Americans, after the joint action at Khabarovsk, had contented themselves with taking over guard duties along the railroad from Khabarovsk to Vladivostok with their main body at the port. They had other units along a branch line to the Suchan mines, and one at Harbin. They were to hold these positions throughout the winter.[98]

By the end of October it was already obvious that Japan, discouraged from sending troops to the Urals to aid the Czechs and suspicious of America's railway and economic commissions, was following a monopolistic policy of her own. Another factor determining the attitude of Japan had been the course which economic assistance, promised by Wilson in his *Aide Mémoire*, had taken. Although officially described as relief, the aid was in fact, a commercial venture. Licences were granted for private persons to conduct business in Russia. Japan opposed all the efforts of the United States at Siberian trade, and began to use her army as well as the forces of her protégés, Semenov and Kalmykov, to exclude American goods, and force those which she herself supplied into Siberia.[99]

Semenov and Kalmykov deserve some description. Grigori Mikhailovich Semenov was born in the Trans-Baikal in 1890, and was said to be half Buriat; at any rate he had Asiatic blood in his veins. He served in the Imperial Russian armies from 1908, and in 1917 was in the Trans-Baikal at the order of the Provisional Government to recruit Buriats to be used on the Eastern Front. Upon the fall of the Provisional Government, he moved into Manchuria with the detachment thus far recruited and it is probable that at this period he first made contact with the Japanese. In January 1918, he took the field against the Bolsheviks, moving back into the Trans-Baikal with about 600 men; though he met with little success he kept Soviet forces in this part of Siberia occupied until the middle of May, when, defeated, he withdrew once more into Manchuria. Not until the Czechoslovaks overcame the Soviets when they seized the railway, was he able to move again into the Trans-Baikal. At Chita and throughout the surrounding countryside he soon became notorious. For three and a half years he led an irregular army which, at its peak, mustered more than sixty thousand men, including Buriats, Yakuts, and Cossacks, officered very largely by reactionaries of the old Imperial school. For the support of these troops, besides being heavily subsidized by Japan, he robbed and pillaged, tortured and killed. There were three standard charges : being a Bolshevik; aiding the Bolsheviks; or hindering mobilization. Few communities remained immune from Semenov's grim riders. Sturdy Siberian peasants again and again rose against his oppression in defence of their lives and property and, in desperation, joined the Bolshevik partisans.[100]

Semenov, strategically situated at Chita, seized cars and locomotives for his own use, creating confusion in railway traffic; worse, he blocked the movement of arms and munitions consigned westwards to the front, retaining whatever he wanted for his own purposes.[101]

Another notorious participant in the civil war, again sponsored by Japan, was Ivan Pavlovich Kalmykov whom we last saw on the

Ussuri front at Khabarovsk. Little is known of his early career, save that he served with Semenov in a Cossack unit on the Caucasus front during the war. Nominally, Kalmykov was a subordinate of Semenov, but in fact played a lone hand, responsible only to the Japanese who armed and supported him. His career was comparable only to that of Semenov, though Graves said of him that he murdered with his own hands where Semenov ordered others to kill![102]

The Japanese seemed to have two main objectives in mind with regard to Russia, and in attempting to fulfil them, Semenov and Kalmykov had their parts. The first aim was to create disorder which would not only prevent the emergence of a strong Russian government, but would also render necessary the retention of Japanese troops in Siberia with the excuse of establishing order. Secondly, Japan hoped to create a buffer state based on the Buriats, a Mongol people who were living within the former Russian Empire in the western, southern, and eastern areas surrounding Lake Baikal. Adjoining this territory, to the south, were the Barga Mongols of northwest Manchuria and the Khalka Mongols of Outer Mongolia, with yet other Mongol peoples beyond. If all these Mongols could be assembled into a single political entity under Japan's protection, it would not only mean the addition of a vast territory, but would effectively deny to Russia access to the Pacific. The breakdown of Russian authority seemed to promise success to such a venture. Semenov, himself part Buriat, was selected to implement the Japanese plan, and a Pan-Mongol movement was assiduously fostered throughout the summer and fall of 1918. But, though conferences were held, the plan came to nothing early in 1919 through internal jealousies of the leading role to be played by the Buriats, and the inability of Semenov to obtain any tangible support for the proposed government.[103]

Another, and closely allied Japanese objective, was to increase trade with Asiatic Russia, largely at the expense of the Americans. Under the protection of her military forces, Japan sent thousands of businessmen and merchants into Siberia to impose a monopoly on the area. By working closely with the military, custom duties were evaded, consignments were forwarded as Red Cross supplies, and American goods were held up on the sidings while cars loaded with Japanese merchandise went forward. Japanese protégés such as Semenov and Kalmykov confiscated goods (but never from Japan) and the captured goods were sold only at prices suitable to the Japan-

ese in retail stores set up for the purpose. No longer was the railway
a through route permitting a free interchange of goods; it was now
broken into sectors, each 'used as a military weapon by some upstart
general or brigand'.[104] In 1919, these strong-arm methods had given
so great an advantage to Japan that her export trade to Siberia was
five times that of the United States, and her imports sixteen times as
large.[105]

This misuse of railway traffic brought chaos in its wake. Commerce dwindled, speculation ensued, and there was a rising cost of
living. Basic necessities became unobtainable. Food became scarce;
for although there were grain surpluses in western, central, and the
Amur regions of Siberia, a fish surplus at Vladivostok, and surpluses
of meat, eggs and dairy products between Irkutsk and Kurgan, the
breakdown in transportation meant that these items were unavailable outside their own districts. As Colonel Ward, commander of
the Middlesex battalion, passed through the Maritime Province on
his way to Omsk in October 1918, he saw hundreds of miles of un-
harvested grain left in the fields to rot.[106] Such conditions could
only provoke disorders, for as the rouble decreased in purchasing
power, peasants became increasingly reluctant to give up farm surpluses. Raids, carried out to enforce requisitions, led to peasant uprisings which destroyed faith in the government and benefited only
Bolsheviks. Railway workers struck for wage increases to combat the
high cost of living and further impeded railway traffic. This again
could be turned by the Bolsheviks to political account.[107]

The economic and political chaos which Japan wanted was soon
achieved. In the long run it worked against Japan for it made more
certain the ultimate success of the Bolsheviks in Siberia.[108]

POLITICAL DEVELOPMENTS IN SIBERIA

Meanwhile, what of political developments in Siberia? At first no
fewer than nineteen governments hoped to succeed the defeated
Bolsheviks as the recognized authority in Siberia. These included the
Amur Government of Blagoveshchensk, the Ural Government at
Ekaterinburg, and the Horvath Government at Harbin. But, as we
have seen, the contest eventually resolved itself into the struggle between the government established at Samara by the Committee of
Members of the Constituent Assembly and the one set up at Omsk by
the Siberian Provisional Government. One hundred and seventy rep-

resentatives from these and other governments gathered at Ufa on September 8, 1918, to create a new unified administration. At this time the anti-Bolshevik front on the Volga seemed in danger of collapsing under enemy pressure; the Czechs, who had received no help from the Allies and little from the Russians, were threatening to abandon it, and the military elements in the various governments pointed to disunity as the reason for lack of Russian fighting strength. The circumstances forced agreement. The outcome was a Directory of five persons—Arksentev, Astrov, General Boldyrev, Vologodsky, and Chaikovsky—who were charged with trusteeship of sovereign authority until a new all-Russian Constituent Assembly could be convened. An army was to be organized to carry on the war against the Central Powers and the Bolsheviks. Democratic institutions were to be set up in all areas liberated from the Bolsheviks—civil liberties, private enterprise, and the recognition of trade unions. On 9th October the Directory moved to Omsk, where on 3rd November it assumed responsibility for a theoretically united Siberia.[109]

One of the first acts of the Directory was to make overtures to General Alexeiev in the south to command the forces of the new government, but he died before he could reach Siberia. It is perhaps idle to speculate what would have been the ultimate outcome of the Civil War had he lived to accept the position; it is, however, certain that with a strategist of the rank of Alexeiev in the central control of operations, the power of the Whites would not have been dissipated in a series of unco-ordinated offensives on the Bolshevik stronghold of Muscovite Russia, as happened in 1919. In his absence, General Boldyrev, one of the Directory's five members, was appointed Commander-in-Chief of the new government's army. The portfolio of Minister of War was entrusted to Admiral Kolchak, who despatched General Ivanov-Rivov to represent him in the area east of Baikal, and to command all Russian troops in the Russian Far East. Ivanov-Rivov put the provinces of Amur, Primorskaya, Sakhalin, and Kamchatka under martial law; and he assumed almost dictatorial powers. Shortly afterwards, he himself came under the influence of Japan, and was of little further use to Kolchak.[110]

The Directory found itself split by rival factions which frustrated any positive action. On the one side, the Socialist-Revolutionaries, especially the more radical of these, found little satisfaction in the composition of the Directory, its policy, the membership of its Cabinet, or its location at Omsk; these men were undoubtedly 'hampering in council, feeble to help but powerful to embarrass'.[111] Ranged against them were the conservative elements, including the military, who believed the new government to be too revolutionary—run by the Socialist-Revolutionaries. In this group, the idea of placing absolute authority in the hands of one leader who would have the powers of a military dictator was rapidly gaining ground.

Certainly, the Directory made mistakes. On one subject there was agreement—that foreign help would be necessary to sustain the government, and that in a bid for this, as well as to hold back the Bolshevik forces, a strong Russian Army would be necessary. But no effort at a planned mobilization was made. Instead, the former practice of rushing men to the colours, before equipment was ready or training schools established, was continued. Officers, many of whom were unwilling to go to the front, donned uniforms with the hated epaulettes, and lounged at Omsk. Prisoners-of-war were improperly guarded and no proper measures were taken to safeguard the railroad, vital to the security of Omsk and the front. General Knox, the British Military Representative now at Omsk, was not happy with the situation. He suggested to Boldyrev the following measures: reduction of the 200,000 men who had already been mobilized by 40 to 50 per cent in order to render possible the equipment and training of the remainder; troops at the front to be equipped before those at the rear; calling-up all officers—those found unfit for service to be deprived of their uniforms; prisoners to be concentrated into camps and properly guarded; the disarming of the civil population along the railway; any disorders along the railway to be put down sternly; and finally, that wide powers should be given to Kolchak as Minister of War. Boldyrev replied, said Knox, 'as Kerensky did, that these things will be done in time'.[112]

It is perhaps significant to note that Denikin, the acknowledged leader of the White Russian military party, withheld recognition from the Directory, as did the Allied and Associated Powers.[113]

OMINOUS PORTENTS

As we approach the time of the general armistice—whose effect was deeply felt in Siberia—the events which had occurred in the Russian Far East since intervention forces had landed may be briefly summarized. Most important, there was no united policy between the various contingents which had, in fact, split into two groups: the

Americans and the Japanese on the one hand, who were battling each other for control of the railways and the economic resources of Siberia; and the other contingents, which had aid to the Czechs and the reconstitution of the Eastern Front as their aims (with the overthrow of the Bolsheviks implicit in this) on the other.

The Czech and White Russian forces still held the front, now running from north to south as follows: from Verkhoturie on the Tura river, to east of Perm, east of Sarapul, west of Bugurusla, west of Busuluk, west of Uralsk, and from thence along the Ural river to Gurisy on the Caspian Sea.[114] The offensive on Perm had been abandoned for the time being. In the absence of the expected Allied support, the Czech forces were becoming discouraged. On the home front the many governments of Siberia had achieved a union of dubious strength and seemed to be moving towards dictatorship. On the railways there was dual control by America and Japan, with Japan controlling more sections than the Americans. Japan interfered with operations, creating economic chaos from which only the Bolsheviks could profit. It should be added here that an American proposal that Stevens and the American railway commissions take over full operations—a proposal which Britain supported 'in the hope that this would obtain fuller military co-operation from them and ensure the despatch of material and equipment to the front'—had been turned down by Japan.[115]

General Knox, in remarkably clearsighted, frank, and prophetic notes which he compiled for General Elmsley in November, had this to say:

'The Allies have never agreed. American forces . . crowd the Barracks in the Far East.

'The Japanese have landed 70,000 but owing to lack of American pressure, they refuse to go beyond Irkutsk. In relation to the policy of Great Britain, France, and Italy, America may be said to be neutral, while Japan is actively hostile.

'The Japanese do all in their power to weaken Russia by subsidising every freebooter in the Far East and so enable them to defy the central government which the other Allies wish to strengthen. They irritate the local population beyond endurance and among the Allies they make nothing but enemies. Their opposition to the American railway scheme [that Stevens take over] has indefinitely postponed the provision of economic assistance and so immeasurably increased the difficulties of the much tried Russian Government; Russia and the Allied cause would benefit if every Japanese were withdrawn and . . . Americans only were left in garrison along the railway from Vladivostok to Baikal.

'Owing to the failure of the Americans to understand the situation and owing to the purely selfish policy of the Japanese, Allied assistance to the Russians and Czecho-Slovaks has so far been reduced to a few British sailors, one British garrison battalion, one French battalion, and a battery and a couple of Italian battalions. . . There are also Roumanian, Polish [and] Serb units in formation.

'Yet the present situation, though difficult, shows what magnificent results might have rewarded a sane and united policy. There can be no reasonable doubt that one Allied division or even a brigade, if pushed through to the Volga when the railway was opened in early September, would have reached Moscow before the winter, shattered Bolshevism and delivered the starving peasantry of northern Russia. . . .

'Where we modestly hoped for a Russian contingent of 50,000, the Russians have raised and maintained for several weeks an army of upwards of 300,000. . . . The British Government has promised equipment for 100,000 and this is now en route. Equipment for another 100,000 will probably be sent. . . . The one thing wanting is tangible Allied force at the front. . . . [The Czech Corps] is tired and wants to go home. Its principal complaint is the failure of the Allies to send help to the Urals. . . .

'The arrival of such a force would give new heart to the Russians and Czechs. The delay and hesitation in sending such a force is endangering the whole position. It has lost us the Volga Bridgeheads. The Russians now hold the enemy at the front, but more is required, for against a rabble like the Bolsheviks, to stand still is to confess weakness.

'If we keep our promises we have a reasonable hope of reconquering European Russia in the spring. . . . If we fail to rise to the occasion, what will be the result? Bolshevism will once more overrun Russia and all Siberia. All those who trusted us will be massacred.'[116]

APPENDIX I

AIDE MEMOIRE

The whole heart of the people of the United States is in the winning of this war. The controlling purpose of the Government of the United States is to do everything that is necessary and effective to win it. It wishes to co-operate in every practicable way with the Allied Governments, and to co-operate ungrudgingly; for it has no ends of its own to serve and believes that the war can be won only by common counsel and intimate concert of action. It has sought to study every proposed policy or action in which its co-operation has been asked in this spirit, and states the following conclusions in the confidence that, if it finds itself obliged to decline participation in any undertaking or course of action, it will be understood that it does so only because it deems itself precluded from participating by imperative considerations either of policy or of fact.

In full agreement with the Allied Governments and upon the unanimous advice of the Supreme War Council, the Government of the United States adopted upon its entrance into the war, a plan for taking part in the fighting on the western front into which all its resources of men and material were to be put, and put as rapidly as possible, and it has carried out that plan with energy and success, pressing its execution more and more rapidly forward and literally putting into it the entire energy and executive force of the nation. This was its response, its very willing and hearty response, to what was the unhesitating judgment alike of its own military advisers and of the advisers of the Allied Governments. It is now considering, at the suggestion of the Supreme War Council, the possibility of making very considerable additions even to this immense program which, if they should prove feasible at all, will tax the industrial processes of the United States and the shipping facilities of the whole group of associated nations to the utmost. It has thus concentrated all its plans and all its resources upon this single absolutely necessary object.

In such circumstances it feels it to be its duty to say that it cannot, so long as the military situation on the western front remains critical, consent to break or slacken the force of its present effort by diverting any part of its military force to other points or objectives. The United States is at a great distance from the field of action on the western front; it is at a much greater distance from any other field of action. The instrumentalities by which it is to handle its armies and its stores have at great cost and with great difficulty been created in France. They do not exist elsewhere. It is practicable for her to do a great deal in France : it is not practicable for her to do anything of importance or on a large scale upon any other field. The American Government, therefore, very respectfully requests its associates to accept its deliberate judgment that it should not dissipate its force by attempting important operations elsewhere.

It regards the Italian front as closely co-ordinated with the western front, however, and is willing to divert a portion of its military forces from France to Italy if it is the judgment and wish of the Supreme Command that it should do so. It wished to defer to the decision of the Commander-in-Chief in this matter, as it would wish to defer in all others, particularly because it considers these two fronts so closely related as to be practically but separate parts of a single line and because it would be necessary that any American troops sent to Italy should be subtracted from the number used in France and actually transported across French territory from the ports now used by the armies of the United States.

It is the clear and fixed judgment of the Government of the United States, arrived at after repeated and very searching reconsiderations of the whole situation in Russia, that military intervention there would add to the present sad confusion in Russia rather than cure it, injure her rather than help her, and that it would be of no advantage in the prosecution of our main design, to win the war against Germany. It cannot, therefore, take part in such intervention or sanction it in principle. Military intervention would, in its judgment, even supposing it to be efficacious in its immediate avowed object of delivering an attack upon Germany from the east, be merely a method of making use of Russia, not a method of serving her. Her people could not profit by it, if they profited by it at all, in time to save them from their present distresses, and their substance would be used to maintain foreign armies, not to reconstitute their own. Military action is admissible in Russia, as the Government of the United States sees the circumstances, only to help the Czecho-Slovaks consolidate their forces and get into successful co-operation with their Slavic kinsmen and to steady any efforts at self-government or self-defense in which the Russians themselves may be willing to accept assistance. Whether from Vladivostok or from Murmansk and Archangel, the only legitimate object for which American or Allied troops can be employed, it submits, is to guard military stores which may subsequently be needed by the Russian forces and to render such aid as may be acceptable to the Russians in the organization of their own self-defense. For helping the Czecho-Slovaks there is immediate necessity and sufficient justification. Recent developments have made it evident that that is in the interest of what the Russian people themselves desire, and the Government of the United States is glad to contribute the small force at its disposal for that purpose. It yields, also, to the judgment of Supreme Command in the matter of establishing a small force at Murmansk, to guard the military stores at Kola, and to make it safe for Russian forces to come together in organized bodies in the north. But it owes it to frank counsel to say that it can go no further than these modest and experimental plans. It is not in a position, and has no expectation of being in a position, to take part in organized intervention in adequate force from either Vladivostok or Murmansk and Archangel. It feels that it ought to add, also, that it will feel at liberty to use the few troops it can spare only for the purposes here stated and shall feel obliged to withdraw those forces, in order to add them to the forces at the western front, if the plans in whose execution it is now intended that they should co-operate should develop into others inconsistent with the policy to which the Government of the United States feels constrained to restrict itself.

At the same time the Government of the United States wishes to say with the utmost cordiality and good will that none of the conclusions here stated is meant to wear the least color of criticism of what the other governments associated against Germany may think it wise to undertake. It wishes in no way to embarrass their choices of policy. All that is intended here is a perfectly frank and definite statement of the policy which the United States feels obliged to adopt for herself and in the use of her own military forces. The Government of the United States does not wish it to be understood that in so restricting its own activities it is seeking, even by implication, to set limits to the action or to define the policies of its associates.

It hopes to carry out the plans for safeguarding the rear of the Czechoslovaks operating from Vladivostok in a way that will place it and keep it in close co-operation with a small military force like its own from Japan, and if necessary from the other Allies, and that will assure it of the cordial accord of all the Allied powers; and it proposes to ask all associated in this course of action to unite in assuring the people of Russia in the most public and solemn manner that none of the governments uniting in action either in Siberia or in northern Russia contemplates any interference of any kind with the political sovereignty of Russia, any intervention in her internal affairs, or any impairment of her territorial integrity either now or hereafter, but that each of the associated powers has the single object of affording such aid as shall be acceptable, and only such aid as shall be acceptable, to the Russian people in their endeavour to regain control of their own affairs, their own territory, and their own destiny.

It is the hope and purpose of the Government of the United States to take advantage of the earliest opportunity to send to Siberia a commission of merchants, agricultural experts, labor advisers, Red Cross representatives, and agents of the Young Men's Christian Association accustomed to organizing the best methods of spreading useful information and rendering educational help of a modest sort, in order in some systematic manner to relieve the immediate economic necessities of the people there in every way for which opportunity may open. The execution of this plan will follow and will not be permitted to embarrass the military assistance rendered in the rear of the westward-moving forces of the Czechoslovaks. —Washington, July 17, 1918. (From *Foreign Relations*, 1918, *Russia*, II, 287–90.)

CHAPTER V

SIBERIA TO THE CANADIAN
WITHDRAWAL

THE EFFECTS OF THE ARMISTICE ON THE
INTERVENTIONIST POWERS

The Armistice was signed on November 11, 1918, and on the 15th all the Allies in Vladivostok took part in a Victory Parade through the city streets, commencing at 11 o'clock. In a somewhat hollow show of solidarity, the contingent commanders still in Vladivostok, including General Graves and General Elmsley, shared the saluting base with the Commander-in-Chief, General Otani, who took the salute. The parade was followed by public dinners and receptions on the 16th and 18th.[1]

The cessation of hostilities and the utter collapse of the Central Powers—so unlooked for when intervention had been advocated—changed all Russian values and relations. Intervention had been undertaken as an operation of war, designed to draw the enemy from the Western to an eastern front, and to deny to the German armies the vast supplies of Russia. But the war was over; the German armies need no longer be feared. The subsidiary aim, to rescue the Czechs, was no longer valid; they had saved themselves. Therefore every military reason which had led to intervention had disappeared.

At the end of November, Lord Balfour, the Foreign Secretary, outlined the general lines of British policy towards the changed Russian situation. The original motive for the presence of British troops in Russia, he admitted, was no longer present, and it was not intended that they should now be committed to an offensive campaign against Bolshevism. 'It does not, however, follow that His Majesty's Government can forthwith disinterest themselves wholly from Russian affairs,' he went on.

'Recent events have created obligations which last beyond the occasions which gave them birth. The Czecho-Slovaks are our Allies and we must do what we can to help them. In the south-east corner of Russia in Europe, in territories adjacent to the White Sea and the Arctic Ocean, in Siberia, in Trans-Caucasia and in Trans-Caspia, new anti-Bolshevik administrations have grown up under the shelter of Allied forces for whose existence His Majesty's Government are responsible and whom they must endeavour to support. How far we can do this, and how such a policy will ultimately develop, we cannot yet say. It must largely depend on the course taken by the associated Powers who have far larger resources at their disposal than His Majesty's Government. For us no alternative is open at present than to use such troops as we possess to the best advantage; where we have no troops to supply arms and money; and in the case of the Baltic Provinces to protect as far as we can the nascent nationalities by the help of the fleet . . .'[2]

The British, it was clear, were not prepared to abandon their physical and moral commitments to the White Russians. In fact, as became apparent in a further statement of policy on 30th November, they not only agreed to abide by existing commitments but added new enterprises in the Caucasus and in South Russia. The plan would be:

'. . . to remain for the present in occupation of Murmansk and Archangel; to maintain the Siberian Expedition and to proceed with further arrangements connected with it as were contemplated prior to the Armistice; to try to persuade the Czechs to remain in Western Siberia; to occupy [with five British brigades] the Baku-Batum railway; to give General Denikin at Novorossisk all possible help in the way of military material; to supply the Baltic States with military material.'[3]

Militarily, the policy with regard to Siberia was simple and direct. Canadian and British troops would be used defensively to bolster up the Czech and Siberian troops and help them maintain their present front. Behind the lines, the organization and training of White Russian troops would proceed so as to enable offensive operations to be undertaken against the Bolsheviks by the Russians themselves.[4] With this policy, the French were in accord.

Something should be said at this juncture of the extended British commitments in South Russia. As early as December 23, 1917, an Anglo-French Convention had been held at Paris to regulate the future action of France and Britain in southern Russia; support of

Alexeiev and Denikin was then contemplated, and spheres of action of the two countries were apportioned on a geographical basis. The French, it was decided, would act in Bessarabia, the Ukraine, and the Crimea—that is, north of the Black Sea. The British sphere would be east of the Black Sea—in the Cossack territories, the Caucasus, Armenia, Georgia, and Kurdistan. This arrangement, immediately following the November Revolution, was designed as a precautionary measure to counteract, as far as might be possible, German exploitation of that part of Russia apportioned to the French by the Convention, and to prevent the Turks from penetrating into the other areas, which the British considered vital for the security of India.[5] The ports of northern Russia—Murmansk and Archangel—were later added to the British 'sphere'. At the time of the Convention, Clemenceau gave other reasons for the proposed action: 'The plan . . . of the Allies is to realize simultaneously the economic encirclement of the Bolsheviks and the organization of order by the Russian elements'; and it is significant that at the Peace Conference in 1919, Clemenceau, jointly with Foch, reiterated the same reasons.[6]

In November 1918, following the Armistice, the French and British reaffirmed their adherence to these spheres of interest; though Germany and Turkey had capitulated, it appeared equally important to prevent Bolshevik incursions into these regions. By the end of January 1919 the British occupied the great strategic line from Batum on the Black Sea to Baku on the Caspian, with naval forces in effective control of both these inland seas; supplies to Denikin were assured.[7] These events, however, properly belong in our account of South Russia, and will be considered in greater detail when we return to Denikin.

In an effort to strangle the Bolsheviks economically, a blockade was, in fact, applied. Although intervention in Siberia, in North Russia, and in the south, permitted a blockade to be enforced to some extent, there was no legal basis for it. No state of war between the Allies and the Soviets was ever declared, and without it Bolshevik Russia—as the Americans pointed out when participation by the United States was in question—could not be blockaded, for this would be an act of war. Despite this, the blockade continued until January 16, 1920, when it was officially terminated by the Supreme Economic Council.[8]

In Siberia, meanwhile, the United States had seized on the Armistice as an opportunity to bring pressure upon Japan to release her stranglehold on Eastern Siberia. On 19th November the British Foreign Secretary was advised by the American Chargé d'Affaires in London that his government had presented four points to the government of Japan. The first 'viewed with surprise' the large number of troops in North Manchuria and East Siberia, for which there seemed no 'warranted necessity'. The second declared that the United States was entirely opposed to any 'monopoly of control'; in the opinion of the Americans, the Siberian situation could only be dealt with in a spirit of frank and open co-operation. The vexed question of railway control came next—a settlement of this matter was imperative. Finally troops, as the Americans saw it, should be used to aid the Czechs, and for no other 'ulterior purpose'.[9]

The British, 'anxious for the active participation of American and Japanese troops in Siberia', let the Americans and Japanese know that they saw no reason for criticizing the mere presence of considerable bodies of Japanese troops on Russian territory; they failed, however, to understand the reason for their presence in Eastern Siberia or to what use it was proposed to put them. 'So far they seem to have made no serious effort either to help the Czechs or to protect friendly inhabitants against military aggression by the Bolsheviks—the real objects in which His Majesty's Government are chiefly interested.' With the second point, the British were in full agreement; there should be no monopoly of control either in Russia or in China.[10]

A settlement of the railway question was also deemed essential, for the British had viewed with 'much misgiving the rapid deterioration of all railway communication in Siberia; they believe that it is partly responsible for the extravagant prices which now rule in the Western part of that region, and they are of the opinion that the suffering thus occasioned is a potent cause of disorder'; they would accept any arrangement which the United States Government might come to with the Japanese about railway control. Finally, there was again full agreement with the last point. British troops were being retained in Siberia 'for no other objects but the relief of the Czechs and the safeguarding of the population who have loyally thrown in their lot with the associated Powers'. The British desired to support them, without using troops for any ulterior purpose; in this task they earnestly begged for American co-operation.[11] But owing in no small measure to the policy of General Graves, this was never forthcoming.

For Japan, the Armistice was a disaster. When war came in 1914 she had found ready markets in North and South America, Africa, the Malay States, India and China, all left open by European exporters whose products had been diverted to the war effort. The Japanese rapidly became the manufacturers for Eastern Asia; there was a favourable balance of trade and a growing surplus. In an effort to find raw materials near at home—the United States, Great Britain and others prohibited the export of iron, wool, raw cotton and chemicals to Japan because of war requirements—she had increased sharply her trade relations with Asiatic Russia. Now, with the end of the war, European and American manufacturers reappeared in the markets and trade declined.[12]

It was in anticipation of these developments that, since intervention, Japan had established herself in Eastern Siberia and forcefully created markets there with the possibility in mind, when in control of the railways, of invading the markets of Western Siberia and even of European Russia.[13] The Armistice, with the prospect of a League of Nations to establish the *status quo*, could only be a hindrance to Japan in fulfilling her aims of expansion—' a source of affliction', said a member of the Japanese Diet, 'to nations with limited areas that contemplate future development'.[14] The Americans, perhaps, were complacent about the fact that they themselves had no expansionist ambitions in Siberia. But it is hardly proof of higher ethics that a people who had not digested half the land they owned had in the main refrained from coveting territory or resources on other continents. There was, indeed, a body of American opinion which was well disposed to the expansion of Japan on the Asiatic mainland. A growing Japan, it was felt, must expand somewhere, and Siberia seemed the logical place in view of its proximity. Such views found expression in the *Detroit Free Press*, the *Review of Reviews*, and the *Boston Transcript*.[15] It was felt that American commercial penetration, which in Siberia could only lead to strained Japanese–American relations, should be directed instead towards Canada and Central and South America, when the Japanese, permitted to devote their energies to the development of Eastern Siberia, would look less enviously at the Philippines and Hawaii. General Elmsley, in Siberia, echoed these views. 'Japan's hostility would cease', he wrote, 'if her just claims in Siberia were recognized.'[16] But these were not the views of the American State Department.

Though the Armistice found Japan in a dominant position in East

Siberia, it was clear that the end of hostilities must affect her position. American troops, previously committed or in readiness for the Western Front, were now released for employment elsewhere if that should be necessary; already associations with Americans in Russia had pointed up the inferiority of Japanese weapons and equipment in comparison with those from the United States. The example of rapid build-up of forces, demonstrated by the American Expeditionary Force on the Western Front, had not been lost upon Japan.[17] Thus, when Secretary Lansing's four points were received a few days after the Armistice together with the statement of the British attitude, the climate was favourable for a reappraisal of Japanese policy in Siberia.

The immediate result of the American protest was the removal by Japan of some 50,000 troops from north Manchuria and Siberia. Then in January a railway agreement, which we shall study later, came into effect bringing with it some degree of order. Yet Semenov still received Japanese support and through him Japanese designs could still be fostered.[18]

Throughout Canada, in the wake of the Armistice, a wave of resentment against any further participation in Russian affairs swept the country. That the nature of Bolshevism was improperly understood becomes quite obvious from the tone of the many letters submitted to the government by Labour organizations from coast to coast, of which the following extract is a typical example: 'In view of the fact that the working class in Russia are fighting for a Real Democracy and a lasting peace, we the workers of Morricetown in Mass Meeting assembled, do hereby demand the withdrawal of the Canadian Siberian Expeditionary Force from Russia. An injury to one is an injury to all.'[19] Newspapers expressed similar views, stressing the fact that the Siberian force contained conscripts obtained for *the defence of Canada* under the Military Service Act, an unpopular measure which had split the country when introduced by Sir Robert Borden in 1917, and that these should be brought home now that the war was over.

A *Toronto Globe* editorial, for example, cited protests 'general throughout the country' against the continuance of the expedition which included men 'drafted under the Military Service Act, and in some cases from the Officers' Training Corps'. While the newspaper discounted reports which had appeared in other journals of 'something very like mutiny' on board a Siberia-bound troopship, it nevertheless believed that from 'sixty to seventy per cent of the men despatched to Siberia went unwillingly because they believed the expedition was one in which Canada had no right to be engaged'. It was a tribute to those men that they went 'without serious disturbance', but not very much of a tribute to the 'authorities at Ottawa who, under such conditions, have sent a considerable force of Canadian troops to take part in a faction fight in the heart of Russia, in which this country has no real interest'.[20] A letter in the same paper suggested that drafts at Vancouver not already despatched be kept there[21] while another demanded the 'return of every Canadian boy in Siberia' and that no others be sent.[22] Trades and Labour Councils, another newspaper reported, adopted resolutions demanding that 'Canadian troops now in Siberia and Western Russia be immediately withdrawn, also that all troops being mobilized in Canada to invade Russia be immediately demobilized'.[23]

Parliament was not in session in November, but an indication of what members felt about the Siberian expedition can be gained from questions asked early in 1919. 'What right', asked the member for Stanstead, 'has this country, with its enormous debt, to protect the interest of the United States, Great Britain, or France in Siberia? Why', he continued, 'should this country spend money on an expeditionary force to Siberia?'[24] The member for Brome insisted that the reasons for 'Canadian soldiers [in] Siberia, where they are fighting' should be given at the earliest possible moment. 'It would have been proper and fitting', he added, 'before this expedition was sent at all that Parliament should have been convened in order that the people's representatives might have been consulted. It has been suggested by someone that they are sent there for the purpose of promoting Canadian trade. I for one would rather that in all the future history of Canada we never sold a single mowing machine or any other article of manufacture or commerce there than that the blood of a single Canadian lad should be spilled in vain.'[25]

In November Sir Robert Borden was still in England. On the 14th, Sir Thomas White, the Acting Prime Minister, having tested the temper of the agitation, brought the concern which he and the government felt to the Prime Minister's attention. 'All our colleagues are of the opinion', he said in a cable to Borden through Sir Edward Kemp, the Overseas Minister, 'that public opinion here will not sustain us in continuing to send troops, many of whom are draftees under the Military Service Act and Order in Council, now that the war is ended. We are all of the opinion that no further troops should be sent and that Canadian forces in Siberia should, as soon as the situation will permit, be returned to Canada. Consider matter of serious importance.'[26] Only the advance party had as yet arrived at Vladivostok; thus White's proposal would mean that the main body of the force, then being assembled on the west coast, would not be sent but would, instead, remain in Canada for dispersal.

Borden's reply to White's telegram was made a week later. He had, in the meantime, conferred at the War Office and found out that it was not the intention to commit British or Canadian troops in an offensive campaign. Their presence in Siberia, it was believed, would have an important influence in stabilizing the situation, and they would assist in training the armies of the Siberian Government.[27] The British, despite equally strong public opinion, were adding to their force a battalion of the Hampshire Regiment—originally intended to relieve the Middlesex battalion—and planned to employ both units at Omsk. They urged that General Elmsley should immediately go forward with his staff to command these two battalions. The British appreciated that the main object was to prevent Siberia from lapsing into anarchy; the new government required a breathing space assured by armed force, and thus a first consideration would be to render the new Russian troops efficient. 'Experience has shown . . .', Borden was advised, 'that Russian troops will melt away if they have not the moral support and example of no matter how small an Allied contingent. . . . The presence of the small British, French and Italian forces has already had considerable effect. The advent of General Elmsley's Force will still further strengthen French and British plans and hearten the Russians. . . .'[28] Borden advocated, therefore, that Canadian troops should be retained until the spring and that 'the additional forces originally arranged for should proceed to Siberia for the purposes indicated, as well as for economic considerations which are manifest.'[29]

Privately, the Canadian Prime Minister assured the War Office that he attached the 'greatest importance to maintaining the British and Canadian troops we have already sent and reinforcing them to the full extent originally contemplated, in order to improve the general situation, to strengthen the hands of the Omsk Government and to assist in the organization of the Russian forces now being raised so as to enable them at the earliest possible moment to stand on their own legs and enable our forces to be withdrawn'.[30] He also cabled Ottawa suggesting that Elmsley should go forward at once to take command of the Middlesex battalion, and later of the Hampshire battalion which would proceed to Omsk on its arrival in Siberia at the end of November.[31]

Sir Thomas White, however, demurred. Many members of the Privy Council were opposed to any continuation; and it was not practicable to send only volunteers, as this would mean the breaking up of units ready to sail. The Minister of Militia went so far as to postpone the departure of further ships.[32] The Chief of the General Staff advised the War Office of these developments, concluding with the ominous news that ships, even those in readiness, would not sail for Vladivostok unless and until further direction was received from the Canadian Government.[33]

Borden, however, stood firm in his opinion that the expedition should continue. In a letter dated 22nd November he advised White:

'I think we must go on with this as we have agreed to do so and there seems some reason from our own standpoint as well as the common interest why the expedition should proceed. . . . [Our troops] will assist in stabilizing conditions and in giving needed aid to the recently organized Russian Government in training the newly organized formations of Russian troops. Then it will be of some distinction to have all British Forces in Siberia under the command of a Canadian Officer. Moreover the Economic Commission which we have sent over would otherwise be useless and would have to be recalled to our possible detriment in the future.'[34]

In another communication to White two days later he emphasized that a definite understanding had been made with the British Government, that 'they could reasonably hold us responsible for great inevitable delay in making other arrangements', and that Canada's 'present position' and 'prestige' (an obvious reference to the remarkable reputation earned by the Canadian Corps in France and Belgium) would be 'singularly impaired' by deliberate withdrawal from the undertaking. He left the matter, however, to the judgement of the Privy Council.[35]

The matter was considered by the Privy Council on the 27th. The same day Borden advised White that he had discussed the whole question with the Director of Military Operations (Major-General P. de B. Radcliffe, a former Brigadier-General, General Staff, of the Canadian Corps) at the War Office. The British attitude had been very reasonable. If the force must be withdrawn, it was hoped that General Elmsley, his staff, and fifty or a hundred instructors, would be permitted to remain. The question, said Borden, was now up to Council to decide.[36] Oddly enough, in view of the Government's preoccupation with public opinion, the British request for a mere handful of Canadian troops was rejected; the expedition would proceed as originally planned save that members would be permitted to return to Canada within one year of the signing of the Armistice if they so desired. The matter, reported the Privy Council, could now be considered closed.[37]

KOLCHAK BECOMES SUPREME RULER

Political events in Siberia had, in the meantime, moved swiftly. A week after the Armistice the Directory was overthrown and Admiral Kolchak, the War Minister, installed as dictator in its place. The first move in the overturn took place on the night of 17th November with the arrest of the Socialist Revolutionary members of the government; then, on the following day, the Council of Ministers, hitherto subordinate to the Directory, assumed all governmental power. The council promoted Kolchak from vice-admiral to admiral, and then offered to him as 'Supreme Ruler' all their governmental power for the time being. As well as this, he would have supreme command of all the armed forces of Russia. Any order by Kolchak, it was stipulated, would be subject to examination by the Council of Ministers; thus his power would be largely nominal.[38]

On the afternoon of 18th November, after some hesitation, Kolchak accepted supreme power and announced his reasons for doing so. Through the activities of the Socialist Revolutionary Party, he said, the same calamitous lack of discipline, which had ruined the old army eighteen months before, still existed. The only answer was to remove the Socialist Revolutionary faction from the government. His purpose would now be to create a disciplined army with which to overthrow the Bolsheviks, then, when the whole of Russia had come together, to call elections which would decide what form of government should replace his own temporary dictatorship.[39]

At this time, Alexander Kolchak was 45 years old. He has been described as a 'small, well-dressed, energetic man, moving about with quick, nervous gestures. His smooth-shaven face and smart appearance were more like that of a Western European officer than the traditional bearded and robust Russian soldier.' In manner, he was impetuous and excitable.[40] He had won distinction with the fleet both in the Russo-Japanese War and in the Great War, and on three scientific expeditions to the Arctic; he was greatly respected in naval circles in Great Britain and the United States, and had been received by President Wilson during October 1917, when visiting the United States. Following the March Revolution, mutineers had demanded his sword, but rather than surrender it, he had thrown it into the sea.[41] He was a man of the highest character, and a true patriot.

In the political and administrative fields, however, he had little experience. He made the formation of an efficient army his main goal, and left political and economic reforms for some successor government, whatever that might be. Unfortunately, in carrying out what he considered to be his main purpose—military success—such unpopular measures as drafting recruits and requisitioning supplies antagonized large sections of the population, and he dare not curb his military supporters by punishing their excesses. It should not be forgotten, however, that these excesses were at their worst in Eastern Siberia, carried out in Kolchak's name by such protégés of Japan as Semenov, who, although nominally a subordinate of Kolchak, obstructed his every effort to enforce authority east of Baikal.[42]

The Japanese, in fact, as we shall see, did all in their power to make Kolchak's régime weak and unpopular. The United States, which had welcomed the Revolution as the emergence of democracy in Russia, saw in Kolchak's title and régime the beginning of re-establishment of the monarchy. The British and the French welcomed the change, while Kolchak himself viewed intervention in this way: the interventionists could be regarded as two groups—the Anglo-French and the Japanese-American. The first was friendly to Russia and from them he could expect impartial assistance; the second was bent on economic conquest of the Far East and would not help him.[43] But the immediate effect of Kolchak's advent to power was on the Czechs.

THE ATTITUDE OF THE CZECHS

The Armistice found the Czechs in a happy mood. On 28th October, Czechoslovak independence had been proclaimed in Prague, and with the capitulation of the Austrians, Bohemia, Moravia, Slovakia, Silesia and Ruthenia had thrown off the Hapsburg rule. Czech soldiers in Russia were now citizens of a free country to which they were anxious to return; no longer were they branded with the opprobrious term—deserter.[44] Events in Siberia, however, soon changed this mood of exultation to one of discouragement. No statement of general Allied policy towards Russia had followed the Armistice, as they had expected. They were 'disheartened over the failure of Allied promises of support' which had never materialized, and more than that, through Japanese interference with railway communications, they were short of clothing and of ammunition.[45] Why then, should they continue to fight the Bolsheviks when the bulk of the Allied troops remained snug in Eastern Siberia, some three thousand miles from the battle line? Why risk their necks in faraway Russia for a cause which concerned them little when a new homeland beckoned from a region much more hospitable than this? If others could ignore the threat of Bolshevism, so could they. Then the Directory, formed largely at their instigation and regarded by them in a paternal light, was overthrown and subsequently replaced by Kolchak as Supreme Ruler. This was a crowning blow—the Czechs looked upon it as a retrograde step; as the quenching of a democracy by dictatorship. On 21st November the Czech National Council stated quite categorically that they regarded the *coup d'état* at Omsk as contrary to their ideas of government and the principles for which they were fighting; and that, as the representatives of the army bearing the brunt of the struggle with the Bolsheviks, they neither would assist nor sympathize with the changes at Omsk.[46] One exception was Gaida, who in these critical days favoured a move towards strong government. He offered his services to Kolchak and later commanded the northern wing of the Siberian armies.[47]

From November onwards the Czechs grew increasingly apathetic towards the White Russian cause, and at the middle of January, perhaps understandably, they withdrew from the front to claim their share of guarding the railway, as the Americans and Japanese were doing. There was no chance of their fighting again. 'As the Allies will not help by sending troops,' General Knox reported, 'as of now the whole fight with the Bolsheviks in the interests of the whole world devolves on the Russians whose Army is only in process of formation.'[48] With tangible Allied support at the front, it is probable that the Czechs would have remained; without it, the Allies were in no position to stand in their way. General Elmsley, as early as the end of November, advocated the despatch of the Canadian force to the front to support the Czechs, but in this, as we shall see, he was restrained by the Canadian Government. 'The Czechs' future attitude', Elmsley wrote, 'is the deciding factor. . . . If the Czechs withdraw their support, the Russian military, and possibly political, situation may collapse. If the Czechs stand fast with the co-operation of the Canadian forces, then the conditions enumerated by Sir Robert Borden will have a reasonable chance of being attained. As the Czechs' future attitude is very doubtful, it might have a beneficial influence if the Canadian Government could now guarantee them active support provided they continue their former policy of assistance to Russia.'[49] But his plea was of no avail.

THE WINTER OFFENSIVE

Kolchak, restless and uneasy about the Czech attitude, determined on a winter offensive, despite General Knox's view that the main task should be 'the raising of a small disciplined army, and that half-equipped levies should not be hustled to the front in the hope of gaining territory that could be conquered later on'.[50] The Supreme Ruler perhaps felt it incumbent on him to undertake some major military operation in justification of his policy and leadership. An attack on Perm, postponed in the autumn when the Bolsheviks advanced as we have seen, would be remounted, and this might achieve important results. If Perm could be captured, a continuation of the advance might bring about the fall of Kotlas and Viatka and achieve a link-up with the Allied and Russian forces which had pushed south from Archangel. In the absence of communications, Kolchak could not know that Ironside at the time was too hard pressed on the Archangel front to co-operate—when at last the Archangel force was reinforced in June, the northern wing of Kolchak's forces had been pushed back and the moment had passed.[51]

More cautious and competent counsel in Kolchak's military circle advocated instead a thrust towards the south to be carried out in the spring in an attempt to make junction with Denikin. But Kolchak was impatient of delay. The plan for the north-westerly attack on Perm had already been worked out by the Czechs and was ready for implementation; he had Gaida to lead it. He did, however, propose to link up his left flank with the Orenburg Cossacks under Dutov as a step towards union with Denikin in the south. In the face of Kolchak's determination to carry out an immediate offensive General Knox provided what British assistance he could. Train guards were furnished by the Middlesex battalion for troop and supply trains between Omsk and the front; Colonel Ward also asked if part of his Middlesex battalion might participate in the forthcoming offensive. He was permitted to do so with a few picked men.[52]

The Supreme Ruler had three semi-independent armies directly responsible to him: north, the newly recruited Northern Army under General Gaida based on Ekaterinburg; centre, the Western Army, formed around the nucleus of the army raised by the Constituent Assembly, based at Cheliabinsk under General Khanzhin; and, separated from the other two, the Southern Army south of Orenburg, made up largely of Cossack units, under General Dutov.[53]

Gaida's advance began on 18th December. He had requested the assistance of the 5th Czech Regiment, but the commander of the Czech Corps—General Syrovy—refused to co-operate. Despite this, owing to the unexpectedness of an offensive in the depths of winter and the state of the Bolshevik forces, the Northern Army under Gaida and his Russian associate, General Pepelieff, achieved a rapid and striking success.[54] The bridge over the Kama at Perm was taken intact; the town fell on December 24, 1918, yielding 30,000 prisoners and much booty, '4000 waggons, 260 locomotives, fifty guns and ten armoured cars'; the wagons were 'full of every conceivable domestic material stolen from shops and [from] the inhabitants loaded for evacuation by the Bolsheviks'.[55] Conditions at Perm revealed that, bad though life might be in Eastern Siberia, under the Bolsheviks it was far worse.

'From interviews with the local authorities and inhabitants, it would appear that the Bolsheviks subjected the inhabitants to horrible repressions and cruelties, especially after the attempt on Lenin's life. I have examined witnesses who found bodies of their relatives killed by bayonet wounds, the faces wearing the marks of boot nails; no bullet wounds were found on these bodies. Instruments used for torturing victims were also found. No data is

F

available regarding the number of people killed, but the number of intelligent people inquiring for missing male relatives is stated by the authorities as being very great. The intelligent population during the last three months has been practically starving, food allowances being given to people employed by the Bolsheviks only. The food supply of the Bolsheviks, however, is not great, one pound of bad bread being allowed daily for workmen.'[56]

Gaida now pressed forward, but he could achieve no more. The intense cold, combined with the failure of supplies, effectively stopped his advance. His troops were to hold Perm until Kolchak resumed the offensive in the spring.[57]

The second part of the plan—to join hands with Dutov—could not be carried out. The Bolsheviks, stirred into action by the loss of Perm, counter-attacked farther to the south and succeeded in taking Ufa on the last day of December. Though their hold on the town was only temporary, it succeeded for the moment in preventing a firm connection being made with General Dutov, for Ufa lay directly across the line of communications.[58]

CONDITIONS ON THE RAILWAY

It is not perhaps suprising that, due in large measure to lack of supplies, Gaida's offensive bogged down. During December, January, and early February, Semenov's activities at Chita effectively paralysed railway traffic. No sooner had Kolchak's offensive got under way than Semenov plugged the Baikal bottleneck and on 6th January we find the head of the British Railway Commission in Vladivostok reporting :

'It can now be said that transportation has completely broken down. No goods trains have left Vladivostok for the last ten days and the block on the Trans-Baikal is worse than before while twelve trains have now accumulated here. . . . Under existing conditions I am compelled to advise you that no further British troops should be sent west from Vladivostok until Allied control is established.'[59]

And as Allied personnel had priority for travel on the Trans-Siberian Railway, what of Russians and their supplies?

The situation grew worse throughout January, and at the beginning of February no fewer than forty-eight goods trains, including several munitions trains, were backed up on the Trans-Baikal section awaiting locomotives. Meanwhile Semenov, with a cynical disregard of Kolchak's needs, kept five locomotives—always in steam—attached to the armoured trains from which he and his men pillaged the countryside. He ordered two newly repaired locomotives and eight American cars to be prepared for further armoured trains and also stipulated that the next four locomotives to be repaired should be placed at his disposal. Additionally, his agents were annexing railway materials, in particular boiler steel for use as protective plate on these armoured trains. Work on engine boilers, in consequence, was completely stopped.[60] As early as December the Japanese had admitted to the British Representative, Irkutsk—quite openly—that they were helping Semenov with money, arms, and ammunition.[61] So it is hardly surprising that British protests concerning Semenov's railway activities should be addressed to the Japanese Agent; and though the Japanese agreed to curb him, there was little material result.[62]

Nor did the policies of General Graves facilitate the dispatch of supplies to Kolchak. With the bulk of American troops in Vladivostok for the winter, Graves had set them the task of guarding a stockpile of war materials which had been furnished by the Allies to the Imperial Government of Russia during the war years. These materials had, in fact, been one of the reasons given by the Allied governments for sending military forces into Siberia; it was deemed essential at the time to keep them out of German hands. We have a good description of the material which had accumulated.

'Estimates place this accumulation at 700,000 to 750,000 tons of goods. The stocks had originally been placed in warehouses. But, as the flow of war shipments to Vladivostok increased, the railway became more and more overburdened and less able to handle the materials flowing westward. They were then left piled on the docks and eventually newly received stocks had to be taken back toward the hills near the city and left in the open, frequently without any covering. At the time of the arrival of the American forces, in the fall of 1918, observers estimated the value of this vast accumulation at between 750,000,000 and 1,000,000,000 dollars. There was a hill of cotton, 37,000 railway truck wheels, a submarine, millions of rounds of ammunition, automobiles, shoes, tremendous quantities of barbed wire, agricultural implements, field guns, and other materials.'[63]

AMERICAN OBSTRUCTION

General Graves made up his mind that these stores should be inventoried and sealed, and they should be issued to no one until peace was restored. The British and French, on the other hand, knew that if immediate material support was to be given to the anti-Bolshevik movement, it would be in the form of munitions of war and here was a ready source. It was perhaps unfortunate that Graves' experience of Siberia was confined to the immediate environs of Vladivostok—he had never been west of Khabarovsk—where his impressions of White Russians were gained from the Japanese protégé Kalmykov, and of Semenov by repute. That the misdeeds of these White leaders were unparalleled in Siberia he could not know, nor had he seen by personal observation Bolshevik atrocities which, in turn, provoked and intensified retaliation by the Whites. That failure to release arms and munitions would deprive the administration at Omsk of the means to wage war must have been obvious to Graves, but by so doing he was satisfied in his own mind that he would also keep them out of the hands of the people he detested. He therefore determined on a policy of strict neutrality—no arms for anyone.[64]

He overlooked the fact that his decision would not affect Kalmykov and Semenov. Both these men could easily procure what they wanted from Japan, and in fact were doing so. Furthermore, his action could only drive such leaders even further into the arms of Japan and support the belief that he himself was a Bolshevik sympathizer, a charge which was often heard as the dreary intervention period wore on. All this was clear to General Knox, who, vitally interested in success at the front, opposed Graves and upset his plans. Knox claimed, quite categorically, that the supplies were of British origin, paid for by British loans to Russia, and he insisted on their release. Graves, convinced that some of the stores had been furnished by the United States, failed to produce acceptable proof, and as a result found himself guarding an ever shrinking stock amid general and growing animosity.[65] Even then, endless difficulties were made over every release. Finally, on June 12, 1919, when the American president and the State Department decided that the best hope for a unified and democratic Russia lay in Kolchak, Graves was at last ordered to release freely the stores at Vladivostok to the

Supreme Ruler, who would be given the opportunity to purchase more. But by then, even if Graves had facilitated deliveries, the time had passed for a successful offensive from Siberia by Kolchak—or anyone else.[66] Following the agreement made by President Wilson in June, rifles began to arrive for Kolchak at Vladivostok in September. On September 16, 1919, Graves refused a one million dollar payment for the weapons which he did not feel justified in delivering to Kolchak because he believed that Kalmykov and Semenov, amongst others, were planning to attack the Americans. An outcry in the Press—to which General Knox contributed—led to the rifles being delivered by the Americans to Kolchak's men at Irkutsk.[67]

ANGLO-FRENCH EFFORTS AT CONTROL

Failure of the supply service, caused by the depredations of Semenov along the Trans-Siberian Railway and American obstruction of releases, alarmed Kolchak's Anglo-French advisers. Even before Kolchak came to power, when Japanese and American intentions had become clear, the War Office had suggested that Knox should be *Directeur de l'Arrière* in Siberia, entrusted with the task of ensuring that the matériel for 200,000 Russian troops, supplied by the British, should reach the front. The French had agreed to the proposal, with the added stipulation that a French officer, General Maurice Janin (whom Clemenceau was sending out to command the Czechs), should be Commander-in-Chief of all troops—Russian and Allied—west of Baikal.[68] The British, convinced that a single front under one commander was the key to success, concurred.[69] It was decided at the middle of January to implement the two proposals.

Kolchak immediately objected to the appointment of a foreign commander. As General Dieterichs (Kolchak's Vice-Minister for Foreign Affairs) explained to General Knox, 'to hand over command to Janin would mean the break-up of the Russian Army'. Kolchak pointed out that the Czechs were being withdrawn from the front; the Allies were not helping by sending troops; thus the whole fight against the Bolsheviks devolved upon the Russians. 'The appointment of a foreign commander would shake the confidence of Russian conscripts in their officers and, above all, [the proposal] has already caused commotion among the officers who so far form the real fighting strength.'[70] Knox sympathized with Kolchak who, as he put it, 'has more grit, pluck, and honest patriotism than any Russian in

Siberia. . . . In Russia, you have to take what you can get and if you find an honest man with the courage of a lion he should be supported, although to Versailles he may not appear to have the wisdom of the serpent.'[71]

It is indeed true that Admiral Kolchak, a proud Russian patriot, was often compelled by force of circumstances 'to operate under conditions of humiliating dependence on the caprices of foreign interventionist powers',[72] but on this issue, at least, he stood firm. Agreement was reached on January 14, 1919, to the appointment of Janin as Commander-in-Chief of *Allied* forces west of Lake Baikal. Kolchak remained as Commander-in-Chief of the Russian forces, directing operations as before from Omsk. Dieterichs was to take temporary command of the front while the Czechs were withdrawing, and in order to assure unity of action, he would conform with general instructions to be issued by Janin as the representative of the Supreme Inter-Allied Command. General Knox assumed the position of *Directeur de l'Arrière* with the general role of organizing and instructing Russian troops in rear, and ensuring the arrival of material at the front.[73]

It was not felt necessary to obtain the prior consent of the Japanese or the approval of the Americans. Both General Graves and General Otani were advised after the event, however, as the functions of General Knox would apply in the territories east of Baikal. The move left the Americans indifferent. The Japanese made two stipulations : first, that Russian and Allied troops east of the lake should remain under Otani's command; and second, that any enterprise undertaken by General Knox east of Lake Baikal 'must previously and completely have been brought to the notice of General Otani'. They would then do everything possible 'to maintain free circulation on the Siberian railway', they would forbid 'Semenov to trespass on Kolchak's domain' and would also apply themselves with the 'utmost assiduity to arrive at a compromise between these two men'.[74] Agreement to the Japanese stipulations followed, and Semenov did in fact make a belated pledge of loyalty to the admiral. But his submission was never wholehearted.[75]

THE JAPANESE OFFER

The Japanese, at this juncture, were disturbed at developments in Western Siberia and were prepared to make concessions. Despite their disruptive tactics, Kolchak's rule appeared to be growing stronger rather than weaker. He had achieved some military success; with a proper organization and sufficient supplies it could be expected that he would achieve more. Further, White Russian groups outside Siberia were attaining unity. Krasnov in South Russia placed himself under Denikin's orders in January (though it was not before June 12, 1919, that Denikin subordinated himself to Kolchak), while General Yudenitch, who was operating against the Bolsheviks in Estonia, was working 'entirely harmoniously' with Omsk[76] Knox had already established—immediately after Kolchak's rise to power— an officers' school on an island near Vladivostok which was backed by the British with materials and instructors. The programme contemplated the complete rebuilding of the Russian army and aimed at the training of three thousand commissioned and non-commissioned officers; it was expected that the first group of five hundred officers, and an equal number of N.C.O.s, would graduate in February.[77]

What could not be achieved by fostering chaos and disorganization could perhaps be achieved by direct negotiation with Kolchak, and on the first day of February the Japanese Government offered the Russian Ambassador at Tokyo 'more friendly relations' and assistance in the training of Russian troops in Eastern Siberia.[78] Meanwhile, two Japanese generals proceeded to Omsk 'on a special embassy'[79] where they laid proposals before Kolchak that at least had the merit of being 'simple and direct'. They asked for 'the northern half of Saghalin [Sakhalin Island], part of Kamchatka, and control of the Manchurian [Chinese Eastern] Railway'. In return for these, they would send 'an army to Western Siberia which would crush the Bolsheviks in two months'.[80]

The offer must have been a tempting one. Had Kolchak possessed Lenin's sense of expediency he would no doubt have temporarily sacrificed any amount of territory, and then later, when the Bolshevik threat had been removed, sought American aid in restoring the *status quo*. But such methods were foreign to Kolchak's nature. He, like Denikin, was fighting for one Russia, 'great and undivided'; Russia had been entrusted to him, and he would not barter away its sacred soil. Now—as later, when the Finns, as the price for recognition of their independence offered to free Petrograd in conjunction with White Russian forces under General Yudenitch —he indignantly declined.

Japanese obstruction of a railway agreement, which they had used as a weapon to defeat Kolchak, was removed towards the end of January. A new plan called for general supervision of the railways by an Inter-Allied Railway Committee whose chairman would be Russian. Each Allied nation having troops in Siberia would have a representative on the Committee. The actual administration was to be carried out by a number of specialized agencies, the most important of which was the Technical Board. The technical operation of the railways was to be entrusted to the President of the Technical Board, and as it was understood that John Stevens would be named as president, the American State Department found the plan acceptable.[81] The Committee did not hold its first meeting, however, until March 5, 1919.[82]

The Chairman—a Russian— would obviously have to be someone connected with the leading political organization in Siberia, and that was the Omsk régime. Kolchak responded perfectly naturally by appointing Ostrugov, his Minister of Communications (formerly technical manager of the Chinese Eastern Railway), to the post. There can be no possible understanding of American approval of the agreement without the assumption that the State Department viewed the Kolchak government as at least the *de facto* government of Siberia. But Graves, acting in accordance with the *Aide Mémoire*, was still of the opinion that he was not to recognize the existence of any Russian government. At first he did not appreciate the full implications of the document; later, the American commander could not help thinking that it had been designed as a deliberate joke, and he protested in anger and pained surprise that it handed over the control of the railways to the admiral. In reply to his inquiries and protests, Graves received assurances from the War Department that he was to continue his own policy—clearly the activities of the State Department and the War Department were not co-ordinated.[83]

The orders of the Railway Commission could not be made effective without adequate guarding of the line, and to this end new sectors were assigned in April to the military forces of each nation, excluding the Canadians, east of Lake Baikal. The Chinese assumed responsibility for the Chinese Eastern Railway from Nikolsk-Ussuriisk (inclusive) to Manchuli (exclusive)—thus removing the Japanese from what had seemed almost permanent occupation—and for the branch line between Harbin and Kuan Cheng-tze as well as a section of the Ussuri line between Ussuri and Guberovo, a total of 1225 miles. The Japanese took over sectors between Nikolsk-Ussuriisk and Spassk, between Guberovo and Khabarovsk on the Ussuri line, between Khabarovsk and Karymskaia on the Amur line, and that running from Manchuli (inclusive) to Verkhne-Udinsk (exclusive) on the Trans-Baikal line, in all, a distance of 2500 miles. The remaining sectors, amounting to 316 miles of track, were taken over by the Americans. They guarded, for instance, the Ussuri lines from Vladivostok (where they had 2100 officers and men) to Nikolsk-Ussuriisk (exclusive) along with the branch line to Suchan, and the section running from Spassk to Ussuri. On the Trans-Baikal line they guarded the sector between Verkhne-Udinsk (inclusive) to Baikal (inclusive), using for the purpose some 2000 troops of the 27th Infantry Regiment under Colonel Morrow. In addition the Americans maintained a thousand-strong garrison at Harbin.[84]

West of Lake Baikal, General Janin placed a Russian force between the lake and Irkutsk, a Czechoslovak force between Irkutsk and Novonikolaievsk, and a Polish force west of that.[85]

General Graves, intent on carrying out the 'neutralist' policy which he had adopted from the beginning of American intervention despite the railway agreement, soon found himself in trouble. The orders for the guarding of the railroad issued by the Russian chairman of the committee specifically stated that no Bolsheviks would be allowed within ten miles of the line. Tracks and bridges, and even water supply stations, were particularly vulnerable to sudden attack by partisan bands, and any delay along the railway would play a major part in bringing about the defeat of Kolchak. Graves, however, contended that obedience of such an order would be contrary to his instructions, and he made it clear that American guards would fulfil their duties in the interests of the entire population 'irrespective of persons, nationality, religion or politics'.[86] Both to Kolchak and the representatives of the State Department in Siberia this seemed a most definite violation of the railway agreement signed in Tokyo, and the way in which it was to be implemented by the Russian chairman.[87] On May 9, 1919, an official of the State Department complained to Secretary of State Lansing that Graves was interpreting orders as though they required 'a rigid and aloof neutrality on his part'. 'The American command in Siberia', he went on, 'has always required a high degree of tact and large experience in affairs.

I cannot help thinking that, in spite of the narrow limitations set by his instructions, General Graves has proved lacking in both these qualifications.'[88] Consul General Harris at Irkutsk and Ambassador Francis in Tokyo both deplored Graves's actions, but nevertheless the general was supported completely by Baker, the Secretary of War, and even by President Wilson himself.[89]

Admiral Kolchak was stung by the attitude of General Graves into an indictment of American policy: 'But since the beginning of American intervention . . . they have left a bitter after-taste by supporting, at times very strongly, the Bolshevik Government.'[90] So intensely did the Kolchak Government resent American actions that they lodged a strong protest over the guarding by American troops of the vital Baikal sector of the railway (which was extremely vulnerable to sabotage because of the many tunnels) where, it was contended, they would have 'further opportunities for spreading their Bolshevistic ideas and protecting Bolsheviks'.[91]

It was, however, impossible for Graves to maintain consistently an attitude of strict neutrality, despite his own wishes. He had had definite proof that the State Department was committed to a policy differing from his own interpretation of the *Aide Mémoire*, which was that the Bolsheviks were one of many Russian factions, and nothing more. It must have been obvious to him now, after the Railway Agreement had been signed, that there was war, although undeclared, against the Soviet régime.[92] In carrying out guard duties in the sectors assigned to them, American troops were compelled to expedite trains through their areas without checking on the contents of the trains or the identities of the passengers. It was, of course, well known that trains carried troops and supplies for Admiral Kolchak. This led to accusations from the Bolsheviks and the Social Revolutionaries that the Americans were actively interfering on the side of Kolchak, and as a result small bands of partisans began to attack trains as they passed through the American sectors. Skirmishes ensued, in the course of which thirty-six Americans lost their lives in widely scattered areas.[93]

AMERICAN-JAPANESE FRICTION

During this period further friction arose between the Americans and the Japanese. A Bolshevik named Mukhin, who had sought sanctuary in China, crossed the border into Russia in February 1919, placed himself at the head of Bolshevik irregulars, and carried out a series of operations against Japanese railway detachments in the neighbourhood of Blagoveschensk. The Japanese, outnumbered, appealed to the American detachment at Harborovsk for military assistance. The Americans ignored the appeal, and in consequence the Japanese suffered heavy casualties before their reinforcements could restore the situation. Graves explained the matter; he was not convinced that Mukhin and his band were Bolsheviks, and in fact believed they were harmless citizens goaded into revolt by the arbitrary acts of the Kolchak Government. The Japanese, nevertheless, considered it a disloyal act, as did the Russians and the other Allies.[94]

A similar incident occurred on 13th April at Shkotova, which lay about thirty miles from Vladivostok on the branch railway line to the Suchan mines fifteen miles from the main Trans-Siberian line from Vladivostok to Omsk. There, a small Russian garrison guarding Bolshevik prisoners was surrounded by an insurgent force and Shkotova itself was in danger of falling into their hands. The loss of this place would cut off all railway communication with the Suchan mines and also endanger the safety of the main line to Omsk. General Otani accordingly called upon the Allies to suppress the insurgents. All (including the Canadians) complied, with the exception of the Americans, who refused on the same grounds as before. Despite the reasons given for the refusal, the Americans of their own accord sent a battalion into the same area a month later to clear Bolsheviks who had fired on a train, killing or wounding some of the passengers.[95]

It is hardly suprising that Graves, through his policy and actions, was marked down in Allied and Russian circles as a 'sympathizer with Bolshevism'.[96] General Elmsley, who saw much of Graves in Vladivostok, dismissed the accusations levelled at the Americans. 'Americans here, although officially opposed to interference in Russian affairs, are privately convinced that intervention would be an act of liberation and not suppression.'[97] But there is overwhelming evidence that Graves gave no real support to Kolchak; he was an idle and often a hostile bystander in so far as any material aid to the admiral was concerned. The American commander, who had proof of autocracy and militarism in the area in which he was situated, never looked beyond these things. The Kolchak Government was, at least, understood by the majority of Russians who had had no experience in self-government. Any attempts to establish a constitutional government would have been fruitless; it could not be representative of Russia when so many of the larger population centres were in the hands of the Bolsheviks. The overthrow of the Bolsheviks, to which Kolchak was dedicated, was therefore a first step on the road to democracy. In his own words, with the end of Bolshevism, 'steps can be taken for the establishment of a proper Russian Government . . . an election would follow . . . when these preliminaries have been carried out I will be willing to lay down the reins and never appear in public life again'.[98] And yet, to overthrow the Bolsheviks, swift military success was essential, and lack of support by the Allies with most troops in Siberia militated against this.

American and Japanese aloofness from the real issue—active support of the White Army—heartened the Bolshevik leaders. They, 'able to resist or to vanquish only when they have to deal with like or less disciplined troops than themselves', were perfectly aware that they would never be able to withstand an offensive carried out by a 'well-organized army such as the Allied'. Trotsky declared openly, 'When the Allies manage to act unanimously and to undertake a compaign against us, we shall be lost', but added immediately that this would 'absolutely not occur'. Lenin agreed; on the contrary, he expected Bolshevism to infect the Allies too. Meanwhile, Trotsky supplied the secret Bolshevik societies in Siberia with 150 'organizers and agitators' and 76,000,000 roubles with which to foment unrest.[99]

CANADIAN DOUBTS

Not only was there no unanimity between the Allies in Siberia; between Canada and Great Britain a divergence in policy also became evident a week after Canada had decided to proceed with the Siberian expedition as originally planned. Sir Robert Borden had informed the British of the decision taken by the Canadian Government, and the information had been received with much satisfaction. The War Office, hopeful that something would now be salvaged out of the Siberian muddle, suggested that the Canadians be moved to Cheliabinsk to act as a stimulus and example to the Russian troops in training.[100] General Elmsley, who foresaw the withdrawal of the Czechs from the front if they should be denied Allied support much longer, suggested the direct co-operation of his force with the Czechs to prevent such eventuality.[101] He had already been in touch with

Colonel John Lash (sent to Siberia by the Minister of Militia to be his personal representative at Allied Headquarters at Omsk) with a view to finding accommodation for his force at Omsk, which would be his Advanced Base, and at some railhead west of there to support his future forward positions.[102] He had also requested the War Office to cancel the orders placing him under the command of General Otani, 'as the latter disclaims responsibility west of Baikal'.[103] During the first week in December, Elmsley despatched one of his officers, Lieut.-Colonel T. S. Morrisey, and a party of forty-four all ranks to administer the Hampshire and Middlesex battalions at Omsk; Morrisey was instructed to report to 'Janin as Allied Commander-in-Chief and arrange accommodation for the Canadian Force at Omsk and its subsequent suggested disposition'.[104]

But all Elmseley's efforts were to no purpose, as indeed were those of Sir Robert Borden. Though the Prime Minister had had his way about the continuation of the Siberian expedition, the cabinet now decided to place restrictions on the use of Canadian troops in Siberia. Early in December, Borden received advice from White of a telegram which had been addressed by the C.G.S. to the War Office with the knowledge of General Mewburn. The general situation in Siberia was reported to be disturbed : among the Allies there was no general agreement; the Americans were inactive; and the Japanese, bent on commercial penetration, were said to be subsidizing insurgent elements.[105] Indeed, as early as August the President of the Privy Council had requested Borden to define the exact relationship of the Canadian force to the Americans and the Japanese. Conflict between the last two seemed not unlikely, and Canadian sentiment would almost certainly align itself on the side of the Americans. The British, on the other hand, bound by the Anglo-Japanese Alliance and traditionally more friendly to Japan than either America or Canada, might request Canadian neutrality.[106] It was therefore stated that, though the dispatch of troops would continue, they would not move inland pending clarification of British policy. Further, it might be necessary to withdraw them altogether unless their mission was made clear.[107]

Borden, justifiably exasperated at this late development, recounted the circumstances which had led to his assurances to the British. In his reply he explained that some few days before the British had practically understood that Canadians would withdraw, and at that time they had been amenable. Then had come the decision of Council to proceed wholeheartedly with the expedition as originally planned, and on the strength of that he had so advised the British Government. He would no longer allow himself to be placed in the position of a vacillating intermediary. Members of the Council were armed with details of the political and economic conditions in Siberia; they were aware of the military situation. They, then, should judge, and with that he virtually washed his hands of the matter.[108] He had sent in what he hoped were the final messages concerning the Siberian Expedition.[109]

White, seizing the opportunity afforded by Borden's communication, wrote General Mewburn without delay '. . . we should at once cancel further sailings and arrange for the return of our forces at as early a date as possible . . .'.[110] It was, however, decided by Council that troops would remain until the spring. The War Office was notified and, at the same time, informed of restrictions placed on the employment of Canadians : 'Meanwhile the Dominion Government cannot permit them to engage in military operations, nor, without its express consent, to move up country; and Elmsley should not leave Base until [Brig.-General H. C.] Bickford, his infantry brigadier, reaches Vladivostok . . .'.[111]

This, to the War Office, was the last straw. For all the good the Canadians would be at Vladivostok, they might as well be on the moon. Elmsley was even forbidden, until the arrival of the main body of Canadians under Bickford, to move forward to Omsk to take direct command of the two British battalions as had always been contemplated. These two units would have to remain for all practical purposes under General Knox, who, as *Directeur de l'Arrière*, had quite enough to do as it was. The War Office, having realistically weighed the implications, sent off a forthright message to the C.G.S. in Ottawa :

'. . . We note that 1800 other ranks for Vladivostok have now sailed. In view, however, of the decision of the Canadian Government not to allow their troops to proceed inland and other factors, we have been obliged to recommend to the War Cabinet :

(1) That the two British battalions should be withdrawn to Vladivostok.

(2) That the Canadian forces should be returned to Canada . . . We suggest therefore :

(1) That at any rate no more troops should be sent.

(2) That if there is no chance of the Canadian Government re-
considering its decision, even those en route mentioned above
might be recalled by wireless. . . .'[112]

The distribution of the Canadian Expeditionary Force (Siberia) at
the time was as follows: in Siberia, 1100; at sea, 2700 (not 1800 as
the War Office thought); and in Canada, 1200.[113] Those at sea were
not recalled by wireless, nor were troops in Siberia returned at this
juncture as the Canadian Government was prepared to 'let matters
stand as they are now provided that there is any hope of a very early
decision respecting the Siberian problem on the part of the Allied
and Associated Powers'.[114] Further sailings, however, were can-
celled, largely through the 'increasing popular opposition to the
despatch of Canadian Expeditionary Force'.[115]

The men on the spot—Sir Charles Eliot (the British High Commissioner), General Elmsley, Colonel Lash, and Lieut.-Colonel Morrisey—all protested most vigorously against any withdrawal. Elliot
was 'dismayed by the proposal to recall the Canadians, and to withdraw the British battalions to Vladivostok'. The consequences of such
a retirement, he said, must be judged not by the real reduction in
military efficiency but by the impression which would be produced
on an emotional people by the apparent abandonment of them at a
critical moment. 'The withdrawal of our troops will certainly be
interpreted as meaning that we have ceased to support the anti-
Bolshevik cause'; no explanation would be of any use. 'I cannot fore-
cast the result, and do not wish to exaggerate it, but it is probable
that there will be serious trouble among the Czechs and that a considerable number of Russian troops at the front will join the Bolsheviks. The Kolchak Government may be overthrown and anarchy
prevail . . .'. On the other hand, he went on, the Bolsheviks in
Siberia and neighbourhood were not a formidable adversary from
the strictly military point of view for even a small force, if well
organized, and if the Canadians garrisoned towns west of Irkustsk
they would be doing useful work and not running much more risk
than by remaining at Vladivostok.[116]

Elmsley considered that Canadian withdrawal might have 'disastrous effect' on the situation,[117] while Lash at Omsk, impressed by
'the enormous effect produced by even a small number of British
troops', felt that to pull back the British battalions would be taken as
'desertion' by the anti-Bolsheviks, and cause 'attendant encourage-

ment to the Bolsheviks'.[118] In Morrisey's view, 'relatively small forces of well-trained Allied troops would be sufficient to . . . ensure success to the Siberian Army if sent this spring'.[119] Nevertheless, the Canadian force did not leave Vladivostok. The British battalions, however, were allowed to remain at Omsk.

Hamstrung as he was, Elmsley could do little with his troops. 'Home or Fight!' was now their sentiment. Friction developed between General Knox and the Canadian commander, for Knox considered that Elmsley should have moved west before restrictions had been placed upon him. There was little point in doing so then, however, for the Canadian advance party consisted mostly of administrative services, and Elmsley was of the opinion that he would be of more use forward with some of his fighting troops (Force Headquarters, one squadron of cavalry, one section of artillery, and one infantry battalion) when these arrived in January; the remainder of his force could be sent up as it disembarked.[120] Later, when Knox continued to press for the move to Omsk, Elmsley could in no way comply. There was much exasperated correspondence between the two, of which the following excerpt from one of Knox's letters is an example: 'I still hope they [the Canadian Government] will send troops to go the whole hog. If they only think of playing the American-Japanese sitting game in the Far East, I honestly don't see much use in their coming at all.'[121]

The climate at Vladivostok, where all Canadians were concentrated with the exception of the small staff which left for Omsk in December, was reminiscent of Eastern Canada and not unpleasant; voluntary societies, working with the Canadian Red Cross, provided some amenities.[122] In camp, every effort was made to provide entertainment for the troops. Concert parties, utilizing artists of many nationalities drawn from the refugee population of the town, were frequent. In addition units furnished their own talent, one act which brought the house down being an Egyptian belly-dance performed by a young gunner officer named Raymond Massey.[123] There was boxing as well as sports events between Canadians and Americans.[124]

By now Canadians had become familiar with conditions in Vladivostok. This city, set on the hillsides overlooking the harbour, should have been beautiful, but at the time it was badly run down. It had become an end-of-the-road haven for hordes of refugees of many nationalities; a population of 40,000 had suddenly risen to almost four times that number. At the terminal of the Trans-Siberian, in the waiting rooms of the bullet-scarred station, a cross-section of this heterogeneous mass could always be observed, gorgeous White Russian women muffled in furs, Mongolians with running sores, ragged children, and crippled beggars. The streets surged with crammed humanity, some in uniforms of many hues and styles, some in civilian clothing, many wearing anything they could procure. Troops and refugees predominated, but in addition the scum of the Orient had assembled; Vladivostok was a centre of corruption and vice.[125]

With the arrival of the main body—2700 all ranks—on January 15, 1919,[126] training began in earnest in an attempt to occupy the men. Company training in January was succeeded by battalion exercises in February.[127] Route marches were common, and in March a reconnaissance of a line of approach to Vladivostok over high ground behind Force Headquarters was carried out.[128] Only one operational task was ever given to Canadians—when a contingent was supplied at General Otani's request, as we have seen, to suppress insurgents at Shkotova during April.

Shkotova was a village situated about thirty miles north of Vladivostok at the head of the Ussuri inlet, on the branch railway line from the main Trans-Siberian line to the Suchan mines. The mines themselves were guarded by an American detachment. On 12th April a small Russian garrison guarding Bolshevik prisoners at Shkotova was surrounded by a Bolshevik force and there was a danger of the village itself falling into their hands. As this would cut off rail communication to the mines and endanger the main Trans-Siberian line, Otani called upon the Allies to furnish detachments to suppress the insurgents. Elmsley sent a company of the 259th Battalion on the 13th, but it was not before the 19th that the total force had assembled, deployed in three groups, and prepared to attack. By then the Bolsheviks had evacuated the area. The Canadian company returned to Vladivostok on 21st April without having fired a shot, but disappointment was tempered somewhat by the issue, on Otani's instructions, of ninety-six bottles of wine, eighteen bottles of whisky and three casks of sake.[129]

Meanwhile Elmsley kept in close touch with the overall situation. He received copies of British diplomatic reports as well as material from the War Office and Canada, and was fully aware that public hostility to the retention of his troops in Siberia might bring about a withdrawal. To prevent this, if at all possible, he forwarded back to Canada the views of such men as Sir Charles Eliot and General

Knox, and added his own urgent representations that public opinion in Canada could be silenced if the government would explain the reasons for the presence of troops in Siberia. This, he suggested, could be done on these lines:

'(1) Majority of soldiers here has made no sacrifice in this war compared to their comrades in France.

(2) They represent the whole of Entente interests, both military and economic.

(3) No interference in Russia's internal affairs is intended except to ensure continuance of peace in Europe and Turkestan covering India, which Bolsheviks admittedly are attempting to destroy.

(4) Without firing a shot, presence of C.E.F. ensures protection of lives of thousands innocent people and millions of pounds Allied stores.

(5) Premature withdrawal might wreck whole Entente policy and leave America and Japan dominating all economic interests; further, it would encourage Bolshevism and precipitate repetition atrocities under their rule, most appalling of which is the nationalization of women for purpose of sexual intercourse.'*[132]

THE PRINKIPO PROPOSAL

By this time, however, the Prime Minister had undergone a complete *volte face*; he bowed to pressure from home and no longer supported Canadian participation in the Siberian venture. It had become obvious to him that the economic motives which had been a major reason for the dispatch of the force were no longer valid. Canada could reap no advantages under the chaotic conditions which prevailed in Siberia. On December 30, 1918, at a meeting of the Imperial War Cabinet, he broke the long impasse which existed between himself and the cabinet in Ottawa by recommending a new departure in

* Elmsley is referring here to a proclamation, captured at Saratov, which came into his possession. The proclamation followed a decision of the Soviet of Peasants', Soldiers', and Workmen's Deputies at Kronstadt to abolish the 'private ownership of women'. Thereafter, each man wishing to use 'a piece of public property' bore a certificate from a Factories Committee or a Workman's, Soldier's, and Peasant's Council certifying that he belonged to the working-class; he then had the right to use one woman not more than three times a week for three hours. Elaborate rules were set up covering fees, health, and the bringing up of children resulting from such unions by the State.[130]

The President of the Privy Council, in an indictment of Bolshevism, also referred to this subject in the Canadian House of Commons.[131]

Russian policy. He suggested, instead of keeping troops in Russia, an invitation to the Russian governments, both White and Red, to declare an armistice and send representatives to Paris for a conference with the Allied and associated nations. Pressure could then be brought to bear to control aggression in Russia and to bring about conditions of stable government.[133] This unrealistic suggestion has been described as a 'futile, almost childish, attempt to stop one of the bloodiest and most determined of civil wars ever fought'.[134]

Borden's proposal, however, was made shortly before the time when the Allied leaders at the Peace Conference, full of uncertainty as to the right course to follow, grappled with the Russian problem. Winston Churchill believed Russia to be the key to the whole peace settlement; it must be made a partner in the League of Nations and a friend of the Allied powers, or there would be 'neither peace nor victory'.[135] To this end, he said, a peace treaty with Turkey must be made that would show her that England was her friend and enable the Batum-Baku venture in the Caucasus to be wound up. Pledges to anti-Bolshevik forces would be faithfully discharged by arming and equipping them from Britain's surplus of munitions and by helping them to train efficient armies of their own; and hand in hand with this, all the border states hostile to Bolshevism would be combined into one system to take the offensive against the Soviets. It was a matter of contracting commitments and selecting obligations which must be backed to the full by all the Allies and associated powers in order to make a success of them.[136] Foch, at the Supreme War Council, contemplated forming a considerable army (consisting largely of American troops together with Poles and Russians) to protect Poland and crush the Bolsheviks.[137] Lloyd George, at the Paris Peace Conference, outlined three possible solutions: the first, like that proposed by Foch, was to declare the Bolsheviks a danger to civilization and destroy them by military force; the second, to enforce a strict blockade which, however, would have the unfortunate result of bringing famine and death to the general population; and third, Borden's suggested conference between the various Russian governments.[138] President Wilson would have no part of the first two suggestions, but found the third agreeable.[139] The statesmen, accordingly, 'took refuge in platitude'.[140]

On January 21, 1919, it was decided that the United States should draft the invitations, and this was done by Wilson. Paris, the place of meeting suggested by Borden, was however changed to the island of Prinkipo in the Sea of Marmora. One of the first tasks of the 'Great Friendly Powers', Wilson wrote, would be to bring about peace in Russia, 'to reconcile conflicting nations under it, and peoples both in Russia and in adjacent states and territories, and to bring succor to suffering populations'. Pending decisions that would be taken at the meeting, 'Great Friendly Powers call upon all the governments, parties and peoples in States and territories in question to abstain from further aggressions, hostilities and reprisals and require them to keep peace both at home and with their neighbors'. The invitation concluded with a statement that the great powers were prepared to enter discussions with the representatives of any faction which had suspended hostilities.[141] The invitation set 15th February as the date for the conference, at which Sir Robert Borden would be the chief British delegate.[142]

Lenin, who had foreseen that the end of the war would bring increased danger to his régime—as well as enhanced possibilities for revolution—had obviously decided that the proper Soviet policy under the circumstances was to play for time and to offer peace under any conditions to avoid provoking the Allies. Between November and the beginning of February the Bolsheviks addressed seven peace proposals, extremely conciliatory, to America, Britain, and France, clearly designed to ward off effective military intervention and stop the flow of munitions on which the White Russians were dependent. If Lenin could do this, there was little doubt that the Soviets would come out of the civil war victorious, when 'glittering revolutionary prospects' would offer themselves for exploitation in the 'war-weary European countries'. After all, Brest-Litovsk had been annulled eight months after signature—an unfavourable peace with the Allies could well vanish in much the same way in a flood of social revolution.[143]

On 4th February the Soviet Government accepted Wilson's invitation, though they did not cease fighting nor give any concrete promise to do so. They did, however, make striking concessions. They would recognize all Russian financial obligations, they would repay interest on loans with raw materials and permit the exploitation of mines and forests by the Allies; they would even consider conceding territory.[144] Churchill repudiated the suggestion that such objects 'have influenced . . . intervention in Russia. The supreme desire of the Allies is to see peace restored in Russia and the establishment of a Government based upon the will of the broad mass of the

Russian people',[145] and neither Wilson nor Lloyd George were impressed by this crude attempt to buy off the Allied powers.[146] The uncertain wind of public opinion, both in Britain and France, now veered round to blow against any negotiations with the Bolsheviks.[147]

But the proposal really foundered when the leading Russian Whites—Kolchak and Denikin—indignantly rejected the invitation. Moral considerations did not permit them to 'confer on an equal basis with traitors, murderers, and robbers'.[148] Even at home, in the Canadian parliament, the member for North Essex* deplored the initiative of the 'Earl of Prinkipo' (Borden) who had placed himself in the position of 'opening communications with [the Bolsheviks] and inviting them to meet decent people'.[149]

The invitation to Prinkipo, though it came to nothing, did incalculable harm to Kolchak's cause. It gave credence to widespread reports that an armistice and an agreement with the Bolsheviks were in contemplation, and that these would be followed by the withdrawal of Allied support. 'Bolshevik influence in the army and elsewhere became stronger.'[150] The admiral regarded the invitation as 'a hostile act', and 'the impression that he no longer has the support of the Powers is spreading and weakening his authority'.[151] It was now darkly predicted that the Siberian Army was 'not likely to be successful against the Bolsheviks unless supported by foreign troops . . . which need not necessarily be large . . .', and the fall of Omsk to the Bolsheviks in the spring was for the first time envisaged.[152] Kolchak himself was 'nervous and depressed' and now stated quite openly that his Government was in danger.[153] The withdrawal of Canadian troops shortly afterwards—the predecessor of other withdrawals—did nothing to lighten his burden.

Borden, though his idea for a conference had not borne fruit, acted in the spirit of his proposal. At the end of January he suggested that the Canadian Government demobilize troops awaiting shipment in British Columbia.[154] This was done quietly, as it was thought desirable not to encourage the Soviet Government unduly. Early in February the Canadian Prime Minister informed Lloyd George of an intention to withdraw troops from Siberia about April; there was no protest.[155] The Russian situation was discussed at the Peace Conference in Paris between 13th and 17th February, when Sir Robert 'adhered absolutely to [his] determination that Canadian troops must be withdrawn in April' despite considerations of the conse-

* William C. Kennedy.

quences of withdrawing troops placed before him by Lord Balfour
and Mr Churchill. These were : firstly, the Bolsheviks would overrun and control all Russia; secondly, if the present Allied forces were
to remain in Russia for some months, Bolshevik power would probably crumble. Borden replied that such considerations 'would not
carry the judgement of Canadian people in favour of further military
effort' and 'moreover, Bolshevist policy and action are becoming
more moderate'.[156] The British Government 'in view of the very
decided attitude taken up by Canada' had no option but to acquiesce
as it was felt 'impossible to continue to urge the Dominion Government to share, against its will, in a task of much difficulty and
anxiety'.[157]

KOLCHAK'S SPRING OFFENSIVE

Kolchak turned from these depressing events to a continuation of his
winter offensive. It had of necessity to be prepared under ill-starred
auspices, for the railway agreement had not yet become effective—
even when it did it came too late and was too much of a compromise
to allow Stevens ever to create an efficient service—and the Japanese
and Semenov were still astride his vital communications with Vladivostok. As an indication of what this could mean, during April 1919
the Russian commander of the engineers' company of the Ninth
Siberian Division requested American assistance in reaching the
front. Twice, he said, he had been ordered to the front, but had been
prevented from doing so by Semenov on both occasions. By May,
with American assistance, the Siberian unit had reached Verkhneu-
dinsk when Semenov again stepped in and refused to furnish onward
transportation.[158] Despite shiploads of supplies from England, Russian troops at the front were ill-equipped and poorly armed, through
interference with the railway system.

The plan of campaign was substantially the same as that followed
for the winter offensive. On the right, the Northern Army under
Gaida would again strike in the direction of Viatka, threatening a
junction with the Archangel force under Ironside. The Western
Army, on the left, was to press towards Samara with the object of
gaining the line of the Volga as a prelude to linking up with Denikin. Meanwhile, a thrust would also be made in the centre towards
Kazan.[159]

It may be doubted if this plan, which entailed an advance on a broad front of 700 miles with a total strength estimated at 100,000 men, was the right one to adopt. Rivalry between the Northern and Western Armies led to a continual struggle for the limited supplies available, and to a complete lack of military co-operation. Success at Perm in the winter had encouraged an unfortunate concentration on the right wing, whereas correct strategy favoured weight on the left where the advance would lead to more populous and milder regions and more certain union with General Denikin. A sound plan would undoubtedly have grounded the northern and central thrusts, and devoted every resource towards the south.[160]

Be that as it may, Kolchak adhered to his plan and, early in March, his offensive was under way. His armies everywhere met with early and substantial success. On the right, Gaida swept across the Bolshevik line which had been established along the river Kungur, forcing the enemy to evacuate the Kama river basin, and captured Glazov, midway between Perm and Viatka, after a total advance of 140 miles. Thereafter, having outrun his creaking supply train, he could do no more. In the centre, General Khanzhin's army broke the Soviet front, to be joined immediately afterwards by two Red battalions which defected to what seemed to be the winning side. Ufa, which had been lost to the Reds at the end of 1918, fell on 13th March; Sterlitamak, some sixty miles south of Ufa, on 4th April; and at the end of April Khanzhin's force had penetrated to within 100 miles of the important Volga town of Kazan—a forward movement of some 250 miles. On the left, success was even more spectacular; Uralsk, Nikolsk, both fell swiftly, until the White Forces finally captured Yerskov, some thirty-five miles from the Volga, from which place they could threaten both Samara and Saratov.[161]

These victories marked the high-water mark of Kolchak's military success. At the end of April his line ran from north to south as follows: west of Glazov and Urzhum, along the line of the river Viatka (a hundred miles east of Kazan) to west of Bugulma, Buguruslan, Buzuluk, Uralsk, Nikolsk, to Yershov. A great bulging pocket had been carved out of Soviet-held territory in European Russia, and this, coupled with the success of Denikin's Volunteer Army, which smashed four Bolshevik armies in May, caused Lenin to tell his Revolutionary Military Council, 'if we don't conquer the Urals before winter, I think the destruction of the Revolution is inevitable'.[162]

But Kolchak's victory was more apparent than real. It was due not so much to the strength of the Russian forces as to the weakness of

their opponents. The Fifth Red Army, which held the sector covering the line of advance on Ufa and later Samara, was under strength.
Furthermore, its communications were threatened, and sometimes
cut, by a peasant uprising in the Syzran and Sengilei districts of the
Middle Volga brought on by Bolshevik seizure of the last reserves
of village grain. It is notable that it was in this sector that the White
Russians achieved their greatest advance.[163] British and French ap-
preciations compiled in 1918, which had predicted that even one
Allied division properly supported by artillery and reserves would
have been able to advance irresistibly, were not, it would appear, far
short of the mark.

Kolchak, however, had no reserves, save untrained ones, and thus
found it impossible to reinforce his extended front which would become extremely vulnerable if the Bolsheviks could effect a concentration, and the White advance had proved sufficiently alarming to
call forth a vigorous mobilization behind the Red Lines.[164] His line
of supply, precarious even before the advance, was now stretched out
to breaking point, whereas the Bolsheviks had been driven back on
internal lines. Worse, defections of White troops, short of food and
clothing, had already begun, and the competence of Kolchak as
Commander-in-Chief was in question. As Baron Budberg, his War
Minister, commented: 'The Admiral understands nothing in land
warfare and easily yields to advice and suggestions . . . in the whole
staff there is not one man with the least serious military and staff
experience.'[165]

THE 'BIG FIVE' SUPPORT KOLCHAK

Such was Kolchak's position when, in May, the Supreme Council of
the Allies turned to the question of his recognition. Clemenceau,
Lloyd George, Wilson, Orlando, and Saionji, the Japanese delegate,
anxious to 'restore peace within Russia by enabling the Russian
people to resume control of their own affairs through the instru-
mentality of a freely elected constituent assembly', were 'convinced
by their experience of the last twelve months that it is not possible to
attain these ends by dealing with the Soviet Government of Moscow'.
They were disposed, therefore, 'to assist the Government of Admiral
Kolchak and his associates with munitions, supplies and food and
the help of such as may volunteer for their service, to establish themselves as the government of all Russia provided they receive from

them definite guarantees that their policy has the same end in view as the Allied and Associated Powers'.[166] In a note to Kolchak they listed points on which the Allies desired assurance which included the summoning of a Constituent Assembly on reaching Moscow, the holding of free elections, abstaining from restoring to power any régime overthrown by the Revolution, recognition of the national debt, and the willingness of Russia to join the League of Nations.[167] Kolchak, in a reply dated 4th June, answered satisfactorily all the questions put before him, whereupon the Council of Five, on 12th June, expressed their willingness 'to extend to Admiral Kolchak and his Associates the support set forth in their original letter', amounting to *de facto* recognition.[168] On the same day Denikin placed himself unreservedly under the admiral's command.[169]

If, as Churchill observes, this decision was wise in June, would it not have been more so in January? There had been little change in the overall situation during those six months, save that half the power available in January had gone by June. 'Six months of degeneration and uncertainty had chilled the Siberian Armies and wasted the slender authority of the Omsk Government.' It had given the Bolsheviks the opportunity to muster forces, and intervention, at best irritating occupation, 'had provided enough opposition to stimulate and not enough to overcome' the sources of Bolshevik strength. 'The moment chosen by the Supreme Council for their declaration was almost exactly the moment when that declaration was certainly too late.'[170]

It might be supposed that the decision to support Kolchak ended doubts and vacillation, but such was not the case. The powers which had aided him with munitions and diplomacy, Britain and France, continued to do so; had all done the same, there might still have been a good result. But General Graves, as we have already seen over the question of releasing munitions on payment to Kolchak, continued his 'neutralist' tactics. Even when Ambassador Morris told him point-blank that the State Department, and not the War Department, was now responsible for American policy in Siberia, Graves retorted that the State Department was not running him! But he was not removed.[171]

'Their decisions to support Kolchak', wrote Churchill, referring to the 'Big Five', '. . . represented only half a mind. The other half had always been, and was throughout the summer of 1919, uncertain of itself, sceptical about the prospects of the anti-Bolsheviks

[and] ill-informed about the true nature of the Soviet Government. . . .'[172] But there were reasons for this, as we have seen, in the battle between America and Japan.

THE CANADIANS WITHDRAW

To return to the Canadians, it was during this successful period that withdrawal and the move back to Canada was made. The first party embarked on April 21, 1919, and the last went on board on 5th June.[173] There was one last appeal from the British Secretary of State for War to the Canadian Prime Minister. Churchill, on 1st May, reviewed the successes of Kolchak's forces and appealed for volunteers in these terms:

'I cannot help being sorry that Canada has not been able a little to help us in bringing about these good results. I of course agreed to your wish to withdraw the Canadians from Vladivostock. If they were not allowed to go beyond Vladivostock, there was not much use in their taking up the limited accommodation available. But is it not possible for us to have a few volunteers from the Canadian Forces to cooperate with the volunteer detachments which compose our various missions to the loyal Russian armies? . . . I am sure there would be a good response. More men have volunteered exclusively for service in Russia during the last three weeks than for the whole of the rest of the Regular Army together. . . .'[174]

The 1st Canadian Tank Battalion, then awaiting shipment in England for demobilization in Canada, had indeed volunteered for service in Siberia,[175] but it was not sent,[176] and though a few volunteers from Canadian units in Siberia remained with the British, there are no records of any major contribution.[177]

The British also hoped that Canadian administrative details would remain in Siberia to administer the two British battalions after the C.E.F. had left, but this proposal was rejected by the Canadian Government.[178] Having lost Canadian administrative support, and without hope of reinforcements, the British battalions were also withdrawn. The Middlesex sailed from Vladivostok for England on September 8, 1919, followed by the Hampshire on 1st November.[179] We shall examine the sequel later, but it might be noted here that withdrawal of the symbols of British support—which had been consistent—together with the retreat of his forces which began in the summer, consummated the ruin of Admiral Kolchak.

CHAPTER VI

NORTH RUSSIA TO WITHDRAWAL

With the Armistice of November 11, 1918, the original aims of the Allied expeditions to Northern Russia, as in Siberia, disappeared. It might be expected that a new declaration of Allied policy would have been made to suit the changed conditions, but niether Maynard nor Ironside received any instructions. Were the Allies to withdraw from Murmansk now that the tasks set at the outset of the expedition, and so well achieved, had become no longer valid? Were troops in the Archangel theatre to continue fighting an enemy with whom they were not at war? In the absence of any clear orders both commanders were forced to review the situation and formulate policies of their own.

The British General Staff appreciation of June 1918, which advocated Allied intervention in Siberia, considered also Northern Russia. It was stated at that time that 'the chances of securing the co-operation of the Czecho-Slovak Corps at Archangel appear to be rapidly diminishing' and that 'the fact must be faced that the small forces now at or on their way to the White Sea ports are inadequate even to provide for their own safety'. Unless there was a reasonable chance of immediate Allied intervention in Siberia, the appreciation continued, the North Russian detachments 'should be withdrawn as soon as they have completed the removal of what stores may still remain at the ports and the removal or destruction of as much rolling stock as can be seized on the railways.'[1]

Thus the retention of forces in North Russia would depend on the progress of intervention in the east. That, too, was clearly foreseen in the British appreciation:

'The only valid reason for the occupation of the White Sea ports is to keep open communication with the pro-ally and patriotic elements in Russia *pending the intervention of Allied forces from the East. Only on the assumption that such intervention is imminent and that it will be carried through with the utmost energy and* *determination is it permissible to risk the small forces that have been despatched to Archangel and Murmansk*—and the risk, be it noted, is a serious one.'*[2]

But Allied intervention in Siberia, as we have seen, did take place. Allied troops had already reached that theatre before the Armistice. Consequently it was clear that present British policy would be to keep the troops in North Russia until the outcome in Siberia had become clear.

By November, ice had sealed in the force at Archangel which in any case must remain there until the spring break-up. The question of withdrawal did not arise immediately and in the meantime the outcome of intervention in the Siberian theatre would determine future policy in the North. In March 1919 it seemed to the British Government that there was little likelihood of decisive operations from Siberia—Allied intervention there hindered Kolchak more than it helped him—and though there was still no Allied declaration of policy towards Northern Russia the War Office (with Cabinet authority) informed both Maynard and Ironside that 'in all probability, Archangel and Murmansk would be evacuated during the coming summer'.[3]

Meanwhile the only course open to Ironside was to turn to the defensive and to try to maintain his present positions. If that meant fighting, it would have to be accepted. Obviously there could be no evacuation until the spring and he was not going to be driven out of his winterized blockhouses if he could help it. Maynard, however, had an ice-free port at his back, and thus the War Office could exercise some choice as to the disposal of his force. But he was certain that his troops would not be recalled immediately, whatever the final Allied decision might be. With Ironside locked in at Archangel, the Allied grip on Murmansk would continue to be an obvious military necessity. Whether the awaited policy favoured evacuation as soon as circumstances permitted, or provided for intervention on a larger scale, it could not alter the present position to any marked degree. A state of war with the Bolsheviks—though still not declared —did in fact exist and must continue, it seemed, as long as the Allies remained on Russian territory.[4]

'Up to the present, such action as I had taken against them had been solely with a view to preventing them from hampering my

* Italics supplied.

operations against von der Goltz; now, unless our own safety were endangered, I should fight them only in order to assist the loyalists in their endeavour to establish themselves more firmly in the Murman Area; but fight them I must, if occasion demanded, just as I had fought them previously.'[5]

These considerations left Maynard clear as to his course of action : 'I must consider the interests of the anti-Soviet movement in my own area as my chief concern, and do my best to enable it to stand alone as speedily as possible'.[6] and this entailed a movement southwards, pushing back the Bolsheviks as it went. A Russian army capable of standing on its own was needed; for this there would have to be men, and men could only be found in sufficient numbers by extending the recruiting ground to the south. But an immediate start was not possible; time was required to effect new dispositions, to organize transport, and to complete training. Maynard expected to be ready by the middle of February 1919; he contemplated no move before then unless forced to do so by enemy action.[7]

CANADIANS IN THE MURMAN AREA

The Canadian party under Lieut.-Colonel Leckie, as we have seen, reached Murmansk towards the end of September, and Maynard decided to disperse its members for use in the units of a special mobile force being formed from Allied contingents and local levies. They were all 'adventurers of the deepest dye', who had volunteered, when volunteering was out of fashion, to go on an expedition to an unknown destination where the one important qualification was to be unmarried and without dependents.[8]

Immediately on arrival the Canadians were ordered to Maynard's main defensive position at Kola, where log huts were being built by Russian carpenters who used the axe and adze with equal skill. At that time most of the Expeditionary Force was at Kola. It consisted of General Maynard and his staff (which included Sir Ernest Shackleton of Antarctic fame), detachments of Royal Engineers, the 11th Royal Sussex, two batteries of British field artillery, a general hospital (which moved to Murmansk later), a machine gun company, a Serbian infantry battalion and two companies of Italian infantry.[9]

Later in the year, a detachment of about 180 husky dogs, under a Canadian officer, arrived at Kola, but the dogs were not a success.

Apart from their mournful howling, which they kept up every night, they were unaccustomed to reindeer, and the end of the huskies as suitable transport came the first time the dogs met reindeer on the same trail. 'The herd was a large one, and the melee that followed . . . [made] Headquarters decide quickly and absolutely that the dogs must go.'[10] A party of two officers and six men, all Canadians, went up the Tulomar river in October to cut birch logs for sleigh runners. The return journey which called for the negotiation of rapids in overladen boats was especially hazardous. Sleighs were constructed and Lapp reindeer teams mobilized for the transport of troops and supplies throughout the country.[11] Seven mobile columns, each about 200 strong, were in process of formation; Maynard called upon the Canadians to train them in the use of weapons, skis and snowshoes.[12]

Meanwhile, in an effort to enrol more Russians, the North Russian Government ordered general mobilization. The Slavo-British Legion (Russian) at Murmansk numbered only about 400 men. Throughout the whole occupied area there were few able-bodied Russians not employed in one or other of the various local civilian services. The mobilization scheme—'far less unpopular than most of us anticipated'—did, however, reveal a superfluity in one or other of the civilian services, so that the area between Murmansk and Soroki in all yielded about 3500 recruits. The paucity of numbers indicated still further the need for a southerly advance.[13] Soroki, the most southerly Allied garrison, would be the jumping-off point for this, and on November 12, 1918, the Canadian contingent was transferred there from the defence-line at Kola. Lieut.-Colonel Leckie assumed command of all Allied troops at Soroki on arrival, and was promoted colonel.[14]

The Bolsheviks forced Maynard to act before February, as he had planned. In January they concentrated south of Soroki, more with the object of spreading propaganda and securing adherents than as a threat against Soroki. In this area the Allies themselves hoped to gain recruits, and thus it was against their interests to allow the Red Army movement to continue. The most important villages in the area were Undozero and Rugozerski, both west of the railway, the latter (a Bolshevik advanced headquarters) being sixty miles west-south-west of Soroki. A mobile force of 200 Karelians, under Canadian command, was ordered forward with the object of reconnaissance, and the clearing of Rugozerski at the discretion of the commander (Captain R. D. Adams) after he had assessed the strength of the opposing troops. Rugozerski could not be left in Red occupation during the projected move down the railway in February with the capture of Segeja as its object; if not attended to now, the village must be cleared as part of the Segeja operations—a complication Maynard was anxious to avoid.[15]

Local information gave the Bolshevik strength at Rugozerski as about 150. The Allied force surrounded the place on January 16, 1919, and attacked, killing or capturing the whole garrison at a cost of six wounded. 'All their headquarters papers fell into our hands, and these were found to shed a very considerable light on the situation on our front.' The village was retained under Karelian garrison. For this exploit, Adams won the M.C. becoming the first Canadian to be decorated in this theatre.[16]

ARCHANGEL—WINTER FIGHTING AND THE LOSS OF SHENKURSK

The situation at Archangel at this time caused concern, and it is necessary to review events in that theatre since Ironside had taken over from General Poole.

We have seen that an American attack mounted to reach Pleset-skaya at the end of September had not been successful.

At the middle of October, Ironside ordered another attempt to be made. Plesetskaya would not only deprive the Reds of their advanced base; it would give the Allied troops plenty of shelter for the winter and make their position more secure by removing the threat of a Soviet flanking movement along the road from Plesetskaya to Seletski.

The attack would take place in two phases. In the first, the Yemtsa River Column supported by the Seletski detachment of the 68th Canadian Field Battery would ferry across the Yemtsa north of Kodish and take the village. This, it was hoped, would distract the attention of the Bolsheviks while a party from the Railway Column was infiltrating through the forest to cut the tracks behind the Bolshevik armoured train, and while the main column moved frontally against the train. Phase two would be an advance of both columns against Plesetskaya.[17]

At first light on 14 October the Yemtsa column, having ferried the river during the night, attacked and seized Kodish:[18]

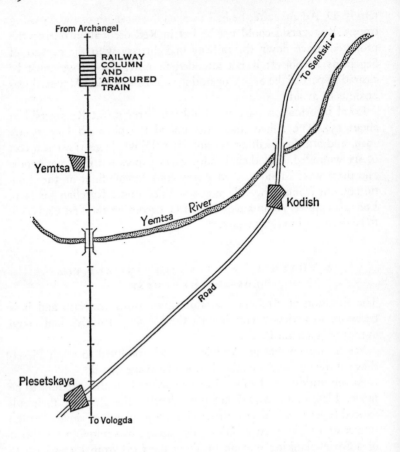

'The Canadian gunners here first showed the Americans what valuable allies they could be: their shelling of the enemy positions was beautifully accurate, and was without doubt largely responsible for the Reds' abandonment of Kodish without having put up much of a struggle.'[19]

But on the main railway front little progress was made. The Allied detachment (two platoons of French infantry and two platoons of Americans) creeping in to cut the tracks with guncotton was spotted by the Reds, who at once despatched a party to cut them off. Before the French and Americans could fight their way through to the railway the armoured train steamed south and the most that could be done was to spray it with bullets. Fighting continued until 17th October, resulting in a slight overall advance. The Canadian gunners manning the British armoured train did excellent work. '. . . the armoured train went forward and fired with open sights on Bolo [Bolshevik] parties . . . we kept the Bolo on the run for three days. The train did very effective work in driving back the Bolo trains and direct hits were reported.'[20] But with the bridges destroyed and the enemy armoured train still uncaptured, Plesetskaya could not be taken.[21]

At Kodish the enemy counter-attacked in force at the end of October, forcing the river column to give up the village and retreat to the north bank of the Yemtsa,[22] so that the only gain from these operations was a few miles' advance by the Railway Column which still found itself in open country.

Ironside refused to accept the situation. He realized that a major advance in winter was out of the question, but he saw no reason why Plesetskaya, with its abundant winter accommodation, should not be taken. Reports that the Allies had constructed winter lines at the present positions would have reached the Bolsheviks, so a renewed attack would come as a complete suprprise. His plan, much the same as that for the previous attack in October, would be carried out at the end of December. Again he would cross the Yemtsa river and attack Kodish with American, British and Russian troops, supported as before by two sections of the Canadian 68th Battery. The capture of Kodish would be followed up by a direct advance on Plesetskaya by road. Meanwhile, on the main railway front, Allied troops would once more infiltrate behind the Bolshevik column, this time to strike at the village of Yemtsa, some ten miles south. The troops chosen for this outflanking movement were the Russian volunteers of the French Foreign Legion, recruited in Archangel and trained by a French Canadian (Captain Barbateau)* in the use of snowshoes. Barbateau, who was extremely proud of his men, referred to them as 'Les Coureurs de Bois'. With Yemtsa cleared, the main column moving down the railway should have little difficulty in pressing through to Plesetskaya which would then be under the combined attack of both the road and railway columns.[24]

The attack, in 20° – below weather, went in at dawn on 30th December. Kodish fell, but otherwise the operation was not successful. Two American companies, supported by Canadian artillery,

* A French reserve officer, and not a member of the Canadian contingent.[23]

G

evicted the enemy from the village and surrounding defences against stiff resistance, but a British machine gun company, assigned the task of sitting astride the Plesetskaya road to cut up the Red retreat from Kodish, failed to open fire through the commander having, to quote Ironside, 'succumbed to the festivities of the season'.[25] This neglect was matched by the failure of the 1st Archangel Regiment (Russian troops) which had the job of pursuing the Reds to Plesetskaya. This unit made no appearance, its Russian commander having deemed the day unpropitious for attack! The left jaw of the pincers, there-fore, closed only as far as Kodish,[26] while the right jaw never budged at all.

The 'Coureurs de Bois', faced with high drifts of light, powdery snow on the right flank and hampered by heavy clothing, arms, and extra rations, were late in reaching Yemtsa. The Bolsheviks, mean-while, appreciating correctly that the thrust of Kodish was just one part of a two-pronged attack, began to shell the front of the Railway Column so that the commander, Colonel Lucas,* called off his frontal blow.

Ironside, in conference with Lucas later in the day, examined the reasons for failure on the spot: he found that the French column commander had not co-ordinated the attacks, as ordered. Both Lucas and the Russian commander were reprimanded and the delinquent British commander was relieved.[27]

There was now no course open other than to establish the winter defensive line where it was, and Ironside visited Kodish to see to this. He spent the night with an American company commander in a blockhouse which was attacked by a Red ski patrol. The attackers were thrown back by machine gun and mortar fire, and the British general and his American host went out into the snow to see things for themselves. Six bodies, camouflaged in white capes and already frozen stiff, were found just beyond the wire. Two had suffered only minor leg wounds, but in that temperature had expired within minutes of being hit. 'This little attack showed me once more the strength of the defensive in a Russian winter', remarked Ironside, and despite the failure to take Plesetskaya he returned to Archangel reassured.[28]

Thereafter, both the Yemtsa and the Vologda Railway Columns settled in for the winter, constructing blockhouses connected by de-fensive wire which, when snow-covered, formed an effective barrier.

* An officer of the French contingent.

In addition to these, boxcars on the railway front were converted to domestic use, and this column undoubtedly spent a much more comfortable winter than any of the others. Daily trains brought rations and supplies and evacuated the sick and wounded, though there were few of these since the winter fighting for this column amounted to no more than artillery duels. It was with regret that the Canadian gunners, in January 1919, left their cosy quarters on the railway to rejoin the 68th Battery which, with the exception of the Seletski (Yemtsa River) detachment, was stationed around Shenkursk.[29]

With Ironside's arrival at the middle of October, the emphasis was placed on defence. Only in the case of the Railway Column was he interested in further advance, and that, as we have seen, to gain more comfortable winter quarters. Then came November—and winter. The days grew remarkably short, and the troops saw the weak arctic sun riding low over the dark forests to the south for briefer and briefer periods each day as the month wore on. Heavy snow fell fitfully, burying the defensive wire and completely concealing it from view so that it seemed impossible for the enemy to reconnoitre such positions. The indefatigable American engineers, spurred on by the first snowfalls, worked tirelessly with the infantry in constructing log blockhouses, billets, dugouts, and machine gun emplacements. 'The problem was to dig in, hang on, and live out the winter.'[30] Only the American 2nd Battalion, which had remained as the security force in Archangel, viewed the prospect with any kind of equanimity; even there fire-fighting apparatus had to be set up and guarded and the city constantly patrolled. Incendiary activities by Bolshevik agents against a city of wood in the depths of winter would nullify the efforts of the defensive fronts and would be disastrous.

The withdrawal of naval gunboats, as we have seen, led to the Bolshevik attack against the Dvina Column at Tulgas; it came within an ace of success. It was quite obvious that winter conditions would not bring a cessation of hostilities. Shenkursk was extremely vulnerable, since progress of the Dvina and Vologda Railway Columns had not kept pace with that on the Vaga; thus there was no flank protection for Shenkursk from the time of its capture onward, and there seemed little hope that any could be provided after the failure of the Allied attack on Plesetskaya at the end of December. Shenkursk, in fact, lay outside the area originally decided on for winter defence, but the Provisional Government at Archangel insisted on its retention as a conscription area; already, by December, 400 townsmen had been called up in the local Russian forces and were working well. It was, however, the most likely place for a Bolshevik attack.[31]

For that reason General Ironside visited the Shenkursk area in December, arriving at Colonel Sharman's headquarters near Bereznik on the 14th; there he received a warm welcome from his old friends of the Canadian Corps in France. He was able to say a word to the drivers who had shown 'such bravery' in the Dvina fighting.[32] Ironside found Brigadier-General Finlayson, the commander on the Dvina, to be in ill-health, and on the advice of his medical officer, was obliged to send him back on leave. The Dvina command was by far the most important and the Commander-in-Chief was most concerned to find a replacement for Finlayson. He decided on Sharman, who was an experienced artillery commander, but as he had never handled other arms, the command would be temporary.[33]

Colonel Sharman, who, after his visit to Tulgas when the Bolshevik attack went in, described himself as 'a harbinger of ill luck', happened to be in Shenkursk with the 68th Battery when the Reds mounted a massive attack in January.[34]

On the morning of January 19, 1919, at about 7.30 a.m., a preliminary attack was launched against the outer defences of Shenkursk around the village of Ust Padenga, one day's march south of the city, when the temperature was forty-five degrees below zero. Mixed American and Russian infantry, numbering about a hundred men supported by two 18-pounders at Visorka Gora (a village some 1100 yards in rear), attempted to stem the enemy attack. The two field guns, manned by Russians, had been detached from the column artillery, consisting of a motley assortment of guns and howitzers held by three subsections of the 68th Battery and by the personnel of the 1st Russian Light Battery. The 18-pounders were the armament of the Russian battery, all the Canadian guns having been left at Bereznik. Russians and Canadians alternated in manning the forward guns, and when the Red attack developed, it was the Russians' turn. A message soon reached Shenkursk that the American commander of the outer defences would feel happier if Canadian gunners could be sent. Accordingly Lieutenant Douglas Winslow, one N.C.O. and eight gunners went forward, reaching Visorka Gora on the night of the 19th. Meanwhile, under strong Bolshevik attack, the Americans and Russians had withdrawn from Ust Padenga into blockhouses near the guns, the Americans having lost seventeen men.[35]

Throughout the 20th and 21st the Bolsheviks launched attack after attack covered by artillery fire, but 'the Canadian gunners were in full swing, and their shrapnel was horribly effective against the Soviet soldiers attempting to cross the open valley below. At fantastic cost in dead and wounded the Communists succeeded in occupying the deserted houses of Ust Padenga, but they made no headway against Visorka Gora.'[36] On the evening of the 22nd, however, a message from Shenkursk ordered the village to be abandoned; intelligence reports indicated a large enemy envelopment of Shenkursk itself. The outpost had to be withdrawn by stages, obstructing the enemy as much as possible. Russian drivers found it impossible to manage horses half-crazed by shellfire, and abandoned their guns. Winslow, however, with the few men at his disposal, managed with great difficulty to pull out one gun to the next line of defence; the other, lying on its side in a ditch, he destroyed.[37] Winslow was not allowed to stay at Spasskoe, the next village to be defended. Instead, he was ordered directly back to Shenkursk with his tired men while Captain O. A. Mowat, with one gun at Spasskoe, covered the withdrawal of the Ust Padenga garrison. The enemy followed up the retirement quickly, and at 10 o'clock on the morning of the 24th launched about 700 men, supported by three guns and two howitzers, against the village. Mowat used the church tower as an observation post from which to direct the fire of his gun, but for once the enemy went to ground and relied mainly on bombardment—possibly because the Canadians had achieved 'a vicious reputation among the Bolsheviks for the calm skill with which they used shrapnel as a short-range weapon against foot soldiers'.[38]

Mowat certainly was calm, as is demonstrated by this account:

'A piece of flying steel clanged against the church bell, and in the momentary silence that followed Mowat's clear voice could be heard, intoning with the accent of a spieler at a country fair: "One cigar!" It broke the tension, and the skirmish line collapsed in a short but therapeutic fit of laughter.'[39]

For his gallantry at Spasskoe, Mowat received the M.C. But it cost him his life. From the outset, the enemy directed his artillery fire on the single gun position; and in the afternoon, when the Canadian officer was encouraging the men at the gun, a Soviet shell found its mark. A gunner was killed, the American commander was cut in the neck, and Mowat was so badly wounded that he died later in the hospital at Shenkursk.[40]

The gun was knocked out, and without artillery it was useless to try to hold the position. The gallant Americans, exhausted after five days of almost superhuman effort, pulled back to Shenkursk that evening accompanied by the gunners who had first taken the precaution of removing sights and breech block from the abandoned gun.[41]

Even then there was little rest. Intelligence reports of the encircle-ment of Shenkursk had proved well founded, and in addition the Reds had moved up their heaviest artillery which the Allies could not match. Shells were being lobbed into the town from all points of the compass, including the line of retreat along the main road to Berez-nik and Archangel north of the town. It was a question of breaking through, and that very soon, or remaining to be destroyed by the Soviet guns. All units, accordingly, were ordered to be ready to move off by 11 o'clock that night, the 24th. Nothing would be taken by individuals, apart from weapons and three days' rations, and inten-tions to withdraw could not be revealed to the enemy by destroying what was left by explosives or by fire. If needed, the bayonet only would be used; no shot was to give the game away.[42]

Mounted Russian scouts were sent out to probe the roads leading from the city. They reported, incredibly enough, that one road—if it could be called that—appeared to have been overlooked by the Reds. It was a rough, little-used logging trail across the river from Shen-kursk, leading into the forest, and then rejoining the main Bereznik road twelves miles north of Shenkursk. This, then, was the route to take.[43]

The city streets saw no sleep that night. Troops hurriedly prepared for the long march; the wounded were taken out of hospital and muffled on to sleighs; and to add to the confusion, civilians who had no wish to stay loaded their families and household possessions be-hind the same spirited horses which had pranced so gaily on the way to gala evenings such a short time before.[44]

Not before 2.30 on the morning of the 25th did the column actu-ally move off. The Canadians had no thought of abandoning the field guns, Russian though they were, and they moved ahead of the main body to blast a way through if necessary. Behind the guns came ninety hospital sleighs, then the foot soldiers, and last of all the civilian sleighs carrying some five hundred persons. In all, there were about two thousand in the column covering more than a mile when stretched out along the trail. There was no wind, and the snow squeaked drily in the icy night. Men wearing clumsy Shackleton boots* slipped and fell in deep ruts, staggered to their feet, and somehow kept moving. But the Russian scouts had done an excellent job. Not a single Red soldier was encountered, and after what seemed hours in the sombre forest, the main road was reached without mishap. Behind them, enemy shells were still bursting in Shenkursk.[45]

Canadian-manned guns were then detailed to cover the retirement of the column back across the river and north along the main Bereznik road to the intermediate village of Kitsa. It was well that this was done, for though no enemy was met on the next three days, strong enemy patrols caught up with the column on the morning of 29th January, but they were 'soon scattered with a few rounds from the 18-pounders'.[46] Once again, the Canadians proved their 'incalculable value to the expedition, thoroughly discouraging the vanguard of the Soviet pursuit with some splendid open-sight marksmanship'.[47]

Under the cover of Canadian guns, firm defensive positions were established at Kitsa, some twenty miles from Bereznik and hence easily reinforced from there; these were approximately in line with the Dvina defences still holding out at Tulgas. The long retreat was over. Colonel Graham, the British officer who had commanded at Shenkursk while Sharman had the Dvina column, now assumed command of both the Vaga and Dvina columns in view of their proximity, and was promoted Brigadier-General. The hospital sleighs and civilians meanwhile, no longer harassed by pursuit, moved on to Bereznik and later to Archangel.[48]

The retreat from Shenkursk, despite its successful outcome, was nevertheless a major setback. There is little doubt that the occupation of Perm on 24th December by Gaida's Siberian force had inspired the Bolshevik attack, and for it Trotsky had committed the Sixth Red Army. A union of Gaida's troops, then 150 miles from Viatka (about 400 miles from the nearest outpost on the Dvina), and the Allied force in North Russia would have been disastrous from the Soviet point of view, and to forestall it Trotsky had driven Ironside back towards Archangel.[49]

* Designed by Sir Ernest Shackleton for use in North Russia.

IRONSIDE IS REINFORCED FROM MURMANSK

Reports of the loss of Shenkursk caused considerable alarm in London. Archangel itself appeared in danger. Reinforcements were obviously necessary, and these could come from only one place—Murmansk. The War Office called upon Maynard for troops which would have to be sent by the overland route, Soroki–Onega–Archangel.

Maynard had to comply. In all, two British battalions (the 6th and 13th Yorkshire) and the 280th Machine Gun Company were sent. With a February offensive already planned he deplored the loss, but there was no alternative. 'Out of the 5000 Britishers shipped to me originally, 1000 only would remain in my theatre,* half of whom were claimed at the time by Petchenga.' Reindeer could not be used for the move as these animals subsisted on moss and there was none on the route from Soroki to Onega. Horse-drawn sledges were therefore employed, but as few were available, men could be sent in parties of 300 only, so that time was unavoidably lost whilst the horses made return journeys to Soroki. Fortunately, Maynard's responsibility for transportation ended halfway along the route, where Ironside took over. Under the Arctic conditions prevailing, a 'due share of credit for its success [was apportioned] to the officers of the Canadian Contingent' whose experience proved invaluable.[52] This depletion in the strength of the Murmansk force called for a further redistribution of troops; the men of the 11th Royal Sussex left the Petchenga garrison during March for the southern sector, making the first leg of the journey to Murmansk by reindeer sleigh.[53]

MAYNARD'S SUCCESSFUL FEBRUARY OFFENSIVE

The weakening of the Murmansk force did not cancel the February offensive. 'By February my preparations were complete, and I was as well placed to commence my movement then as I should be in March or April'.[54] In fact, Maynard turned the reinforcing of Archangel to his own advantage; the offensive, to be successful, must depend on surprise, and rumours were deliberately fostered that pre-

---

* Of the reinforcements from England which reached Murmansk in the autumn, one battalion of the Liverpools and a battery had already been transferred to Archangel.[50] The battery reached the Kitsa Front on 4th February—too late to be of use at Shenkursk.[51]

paratory concentrations of troops and transport at Soroki were again occasioned by reinforcement of the Archangel sector.[55] The Bolsheviks, far from expecting an offensive, were proclaiming that they would soon drive the Allies into the sea.[56] Though vital to the Allies that the new anti-Bolshevik Russian force should be expanded, there were other compelling reasons to drive southwards. In the first place, it was important not to lose the initiative to the Bolsheviks; and secondly, Maynard was anxious to test his preparations and training for winter mobile work on the enemy, counting on the mobility of his troops to outwit the Bolsheviks.[57]

The enemy's main forward garrison (numbering about 400) was at Segeja, on the railway some seventy miles south of Soroki. The intermediate villages were Olimpi, Onda, and Nadvoitskaya, the Bolsheviks having detachments at the two latter places. The bridges between Olimpi and Onda had been destroyed during the earlier Bolshevik withdrawal; but those between Lake Onega and Soroki were intact, so that the Bolsheviks—unlike the Allies—could bring up reinforcements rapidly by train from Maselskaya and other points on the railway north of the lake. Surprise was thus essential.[58]

The Allied plan called for four columns. One was to operate right of the railway from Soroki, and one left (with Sumski Posad, a village twenty miles east of Soroki on the White Sea, as its jumping-off place); both columns to capture Segeja. Two smaller columns were to capture Nadvoitskaya and Onda respectively. The total Allied force numbered 600, of whom 200 were in reserve. Canadians took a major part in the operations; Colonel Leckie was in command; Major L. H. Mackenzie led the Segeja column jumping-off from Soroki; Major Alfred Eastham commanded the Nadvoitskaya column; Captain J. W. Hunter was in charge of transport arrangements at Soroki, and Captain Adams, of those at Sumski Posad. Finally, other Canadian officers and N.C.O.s were sprinkled throughout all columns consisting of British, French, Russians, and Serbians.[59]

Major Mackenzie had the most difficult role. It was important that a 400-foot bridge at Segeja should be captured intact—and if a frontal attack were made at Onda it was feared that the Bolsheviks would withdraw and destroy it. Segeja, Onda and Nadvoitskaya would therefore be captured simultaneously, which meant sending Mackenzie's column more than a hundred miles through unmapped forests, over frozen lakes and snow-covered trackless tundra, in weather that was 'pitilessly cold, the temperature dropping to over forty degrees below zero, with a biting wind and heavy snow-squalls'.[60]

Leckie made his first move on February 15, 1919, with the column from Soroki to Sumski Posad, the remaining columns following at prearranged intervals. Moving cross-country to carry out simultaneous attacks was extremely difficult under the prevailing conditions. The attack on Onda failed to materialize. 'With skis deep sunk in newly fallen snow, and in face of the tearing blizzard, the Serbians . . . struggled gamely on, but were forced to abandon the attempt when still some miles from their goal.' Eastham, however, captured Nadvoitskaya on schedule; and the Onda garrison, hearing shots to its rear, withdrew hurriedly down the line into the hands of his waiting troops. Segeja fell the same day—18th February—with its bridge intact, and half the defenders killed or captured. Before the attack, a Russian patrol breached the railway south of the town, covering the dismantled track with machine guns. A trainload of Bolshevik reinforcements from Maselskaya, forced to halt at this place, met a hail of small-arms fire and pulled back hastily. The Allies repulsed a Bolshevik counter-attack next day, and no further Bolshevik effort developed here. Known enemy losses—those in the train were not assessed, but few could have escaped—were 200 killed and captured at a cost to the Allies of one killed and ten wounded. 'The recruiting area had been extended by over 3000 square miles; the Reds had been taught a most salutary lesson . . .'; the newly-enlisted Russians had emerged with high credit; and the feasibility of winter operations had been amply demonstrated.* Furthermore, the captured bridge was of great importance in view of a possible continued advance later. For these operations both column commanders, Mackenzie and Eastham, were awarded the D.S.O.[62]

POLITICAL DIFFICULTIES IN THE MURMAN AREA

February brought political problems with the Karelians and the Finns. Briefly, the Karelians, having tasted independence, wanted more of it. Accordingly, they submitted a case for 'self-determination' to the Allied Commander-in-Chief at Murmansk, who in turn

* It was, however, found that 'machine guns in this weather are only fit to be used in strong points where they can be kept warm'. Dog sleighs were employed operationally for the first time, and proved useful for messages.[61]

referred the matter to the representative of the North Russian Government. The official attitude displayed no sympathy with Karelian aspirations—Karelia was an integral part of Russia, and such it should remain. The Karelians received refusal sullenly; they would discourage recruiting, and they would not serve under Russian officers. This latter threat was disturbing, as Maynard proposed to extend the force under Russian administration before the Allies should withdraw. A compromise was arrived at whereby Russian officers would be gradually introduced; the regiments as a whole would remain under British control, with a British commanding officer for each battalion. Thus the matter reached a temporary settlement, but it left a feeling of discontent and gave rise to future disaffection.[63]

The Finn Legion, on the other hand, composed as it was of Bolshevik Finns, had been useless to Maynard since the Armistice. It could not be employed against the Soviets and there was the possibility that at any time it could constitute a real danger. The Legion was anxious to return to Finland. Maynard was equally anxious to see it go—he had insufficient troops to disarm the men— but he first required guarantees from the Finnish Government that there would be no reprisals against them. Negotiations with Finland were protracted and unsatisfactory. The Legion planned to mutiny early in April, destroy two bridges at Kandalaksha, and then move south to join the Russian Bolsheviks; Maynard, forewarned, mustered a force of British infantry and Marines and arrested the ringleaders. Unexpectedly, no punishment was meted out: the offenders were instead granted safe passage to join the Soviets. This magnanimity, with a promise to send an Allied delegation from Murmansk to Helsingfors to help speed repatriation, kept the Legion quiet until it finally returned to Finland on September 1, 1919. The Canadian commander of the Legion, Lieut.-Colonel Burton, accompanied his troops and was present in Finland as 'prisoner's friend' at a form of court-martial before which every legionnaire appeared. A few were given prison terms, but the majority, thanks to Burton's representations, proceeded to their homes in peace.[64]

ARCHANGEL—A CRITICAL PERIOD

In the Archangel theatre, the fall of Shenkursk brought a comparative lull in the fighting. Attacks on the 27th and 31st of January against the Tulgas positions on the Dvina were beaten back. 'We were heavily engaged for seven hours,' the 67th Battery laconically reported of the first attack, 'the enemy being eventually driven off.'[65] A third attempt to take Tulgas was thwarted by a round from a newly arrived howitzer of the British 41st Howitzer Battery. The attack never matured. 'We found out from prisoners taken after that we had disturbed them by dropping a 4·5 with a 106 fuse in their midst, just as they were preparing to debouch from the woods for the attack. A Soldiers' and Sailors' Council had been immediately called, decided that they had had quite sufficient in their last two attempts, and they returned home.[66] Thereafter during February, though troops were continuously in touch with the enemy, little of importance happened.

Owing to the capture of Shenkursk, however, the Red morale was high while that of the Allies was correspondingly lowered. It was generally known that Americans had suffered in the fighting there, and rumour in the other U.S. units exaggerated the casualties:

'In the bitter cold and what seemed like perpetual darkness, they sat in their blockhouses and pondered still the tiresome question that had irked them from the beginning: what was it all about? And now, to many, another question arose like a specter: would they ever get out of it alive?'[67]

Though conditions favoured the defensive—no attack could be long, and cover must be secured at the end of it—it was difficult to keep up the spirits of the men if they were never to leave the security of the blockhouses. 'We had to sit passively awaiting attack . . . which is never satisfactory for any troops,' said Ironside. The Canadians took advantage of the respite to carry out tests on the guns under the most severe conditions. The old oil buffers were filled with ordinary issue non-freezing buffer oil and the guns were then fired in temperatures of thirty-five below zero, the ammunition being at the same temperature. In spite of the cold, they got perfect results after making normal corrections for temperature and ranges, 'the guns recoiling and running up without any jar'.[68]

In the blockhouses the manipulation of arms was easy; in the open it was a different matter. 'Woollen gloves with a separate compartment for the trigger finger were essential. When the fingers became numbed, there were gauntlets strung round the soldier's neck, into which they could be thrust until the circulation came back. To touch metal with the bare hand was like grasping a piece of red-hot iron. . . . If a machine gun jammed, the only way of getting it going was by taking it apart and boiling it. This precluded their use in the open.'[69] The hours of darkness, twenty out of twenty-four, were telling on the men, but above all it was the seeming purposelessness of their mission in Northern Russia which affected and dispirited the troops.

The disaffection of the troops revealed itself in mutinies. On 26th February, one of the British battalions (the 13th Yorkshire) sent from Murmansk to reinforce Ironside's force refused to proceed to the front. The trouble was quickly suppressed, the battalion marching the same day. A company of French Colonials refused to go to the front at the beginning of March, and this incident was followed at the end of the month by the refusal of one section of the Canadian Field Brigade to obey orders, and the refusal of an American company to return to the forward posts.[70]

Ironside began to count the days to the thaw which would cause hostilities to cease for about a month. 'We were drawing terribly near to the end of our tether as an efficient fighting force,' he confessed.[71] President Chaikovsky had left for Paris to join the White Russian Council in January, and his successor, Zoubov, did no more than Chaikovsky to counter the Bolshevik propaganda reaching Archangel and its surroundings, which had doubled after Shenkursk. He did little to bring information to the peasants of the real issues of the struggle, and the British general, when talking to villagers on his visits to the various fronts, found that they knew absolutely nothing of the Provisional Government. They thought the fighting was a private quarrel between the Allies and the Bolsheviks. 'Any idea that they were helping themselves was completely absent,' said Ironside. 'The Provisional Government seemed to be out of touch with the people they were governing.'[72] Zoubov's main concern seemed to be for the continuing support of the Allies. Neither he nor his ministers revealed any qualities of leadership whatever :

'They had no confidence in themselves, and there was not one of them who showed any white-hot patriotism to win through, such as the Bolshevik leaders seemed to possess in so large a measure. Not one of them had been out in the country making touch with the peasants.'[73]

In Archangel itself, discipline was at a low ebb. It had become a haven for officers and men whose morale did not fit them for the front but who could not be shipped home. The liquor factory of the Provisional Government produced vodka for sale at a shilling a bottle (20 cents as the exchange was then) and there was far too much drink about. Dance-halls, cafés, and places of entertainment were always crowded. General Ironside called Archangel 'a sink' which needed cleaning out at frequent intervals—a task almost impossible with 'so many nationalities and jurisdictions involved'.[74]

GENERAL MILLER EXPANDS THE RUSSIAN FORCES

The only cheering event during this depressing period was the arrival of General Eugene K. Miller at the middle of January to take over the post of Governor-General from Marushevsky. As his functions included that of commander-in-chief of the North Russian forces, the personality and capabilities of this man were of great interest to Ironside. He was fifty-one years old, of middle height, with a long, fair, cavalry-type moustache and kindly blue eyes. He had a fine record, both on the staff and as an army commander.[75] His appointment was to Ironside extremely reassuring, and thereafter his relations with the Provisional Government became much easier. Like Kolchak and Denikin, the new commander insisted that Russia must be regarded as one and indivisible. Ironside put it to him that the Whites 'would do well to acknowledge the freedom of the Poles, Finns, Lithuanians, Latvians and Esthonians' and that his theory 'might be a calamitous one for the White cause', but Miller 'merely shrugged his shoulders. We shook hands as we agreed that these matters were not for us to settle, and that we both knew what we had to do in Archangel.'[76] Miller, who was calmly optimistic as to the outcome of the struggle against the Bolsheviks, saw the need for a stronger Russian force in North Russia and quietly went about the mobilization of troops. From a total of about 6000 at the end of January, he doubled this figure by the end of February. At the beginning of March, Ironside was able to withdraw the Pinega Column and hand over that area completely to Miller's new Russian troops.[77]

At the end of January the Prinkipo proposal (Sir Robert Borden's idea of a conference between the Bolsheviks and the Whites to arbitrate the Civil War) reached the Provisional Government of the Northern Region from President Wilson. The government unanimously rejected the proposal and gave Miller the job of answering the Great Powers. There is little doubt that the apparent willingness on the part of the Allies to treat with the Bolsheviks undermined General Miller's efforts to build an anti-Bolshevik army. There were rumours that the Allies were preparing to evacuate North Russia, and a report that 'the mass of the people is turning back to Bolshevism'. Bolshevik agents, detecting signs of weakness, moved on to bolder action, planting the seeds of sedition which ripened in the form of desertions and, later in the year, in mutinies.[78]

WINTER PROBLEMS IN THE MURMAN AREA

As at Archangel, and for the same reasons, the morale of even Allied contingents at Murmansk suffered during the first three months of 1919. 'The Great War was over, and others were being demobilized, and according to the men's views, snapping up the best civil billets, whilst they, banished in a forsaken wilderness, were risking their lives for a cause not directly concerned, so far as they could see, with the welfare of their country.'[79] The prevailing atmosphere of disorder, dissatisfaction, and lawlessness in Northern Russia at that time did not, however, affect the Canadians adversely:

'never had our men been more contented with life. Compare the lot of the average citizen of a country during times of peace, whether he be a city clerk or a country farmer, with a soldier under conditions such as existed with us at this time. My heart pounds as I write, in fact it is this comparison and the memory of those joyous adventurous days which prompts me to tell those who care to read these lines that to join a gentlemanly conducted campaign of this sort surpasses all other occupations for a young man of normal health and spirits.'[80]

With the coming of March it began to seem that the trials of winter, and their effect upon most of the troops, had nearly passed. The temperature rose above freezing point for the first time in three months. But before spring arrived to cheer the troops, one further anxiety had to be contended with. Bolshevik agents, judging the time propitious for a *coup d'état*, planned simultaneous risings at Murmansk and other centres; the Finns and Karelians would mutiny and, in concert with these events, an attack would be launched from the south. The Allied intelligence system was by now working efficiently. On 23rd March the Russian authorities—Allied troops were not to lend active assistance unless called on—pounced on the known leaders. Deprived of leadership, the insurrection and mutinies fizzled out. The military attack became 'a half-hearted endeavour to drive us from Segeja, made on April 7th, and frustrated with ease'.[81]

MAYNARD RESUMES THE OFFENSIVE

In April the Allies resumed the offensive in the form of an attack on Urosozero, a village on the railway some twenty miles south of the southernmost Allied garrison, Segeja. A Canadian (Major Peter Anderson) commanded the latter. He knew that the Bolsheviks had received considerable reinforcements, and that concentrations were starting to arrive at Urosozero with a view to capturing his post following the abortive attack on the 7th. Faced with this threat, Anderson decided on a bold course. Judging that every hour was of importance, he himself attacked on 11th April, using his armoured train, and a total force of less than 100 including men of the new Russian army. Though heavily outnumbered, the assailants achieved complete success, killing fifty of the enemy and capturing forty with much booty (including two field guns), at a cost of one killed and five wounded. The Commander-in-Chief, himself a man of vigour and determination, did not reprove Anderson for launching the enterprise without consent; instead, Anderson was promoted Lieut.-Colonel and awarded the D.S.O.[82] In accordance with the policy of never withdrawing from any territory once it had been won, Urosozero was garrisoned. Neighbouring hamlets now had to be cleared of Bolsheviks to protect the approach to the village; this the newly raised Russian Rifle Regiment successfully accomplished.[83]

The advances of February and April had extended the recruiting ground, but not sufficiently if the Russian armies were to stand alone with any prospect of success after the Allied withdrawal. The regions acquired were still bleak tundra, sparsely populated. Further south cultivated soil supported a sturdy peasant class. An advance of another fifty miles might produce several thousand recruits who would welcome the chance of turning against their Bolshevik oppressors, and events proved these hopes well founded. It would secure other advantages. The occupation of Medvyejya Gora and the adjacent town of Povyenets (both on Lake Onega) would block the only avenues of approach to the north; the front would be shortened owing to the proximity of the Finnish border on this line; and finally, the offensive might relieve enemy pressure on the Archangel sector. The internal situation in the Murman area was now quiet. Up-country garrisons could be reduced. Furthermore two British infantry companies (one of the King's Royal Rifle Corps and one of the Middlesex Regiment), which had been sent out in response to Maynard's appeal when the mutiny of the Finn Legion seemed inevitable, reached Murmansk on 17th April. Two companies of American railway troops had arrived on 25th March, relieving all anxiety for the maintenance of the railway system. In all, Maynard could count on three thousand troops for the operation—1000 British, 700 French, Serbians, and Italians, 1000 Russians, and about 500 Karelians and Russians in composite units. The War Office, though having decided in March that withdrawal of the Allies would take place that year and thus reluctant to permit any further offensive action, sanctioned the undertaking in view of the highly beneficial results to be achieved.[84]

On 1st May the advance began in three columns, moving on a front of sixty miles, and was to be carried out in two bounds—from Urosozero to Maselskaya and from Maselskaya to Medvyejya Gora. The right column, consisting of the Olonetz Regiment (a Russo-Karelian unit) had the task of clearing the western and southern shores of Lake Segezero, acting as a flanking guard. The centre column in which Colonel Leckie commanded a group of 100 British Marines, 100 Russians, thirty Americans, thirty Canadians and sections of British and French artillery, was to advance rapidly down the railway. Meanwhile the left column (Russian) would follow the Vojmosalmi–Povyenets road. The centre column captured Maselskaya on 3rd May after forty-eight hours' continuous fighting. The enemy, whose communications on the west of Lake Segozero were now threatened, withdrew rapidly, pursued by the right column. The left column, after stiff opposition, reached a point twenty miles east of Maselga. A pause to repair the railway and replenish stores was broken on 11th May by an unsuccessful Bolshevik attack on the right column.[85]

On 15th May the advance continued on a frontage reduced to thirty-five miles. The entire centre column came into action at once against a strong covering party, which it dislodged. Next day the same column encountered a series of trenches which, because marshy ground precluded turning movements, it had to attack frontally. The Middlesex Regiment and the K.R.R.C. companies, supported by fire from railway trucks, carried the position. By 19th May the column was within five miles of Medvyejya Gora; but enemy resistance was strong, including greatly increased artillery fire. A captured order later revealed that Trotsky had forbidden any retirement. Enemy gunfire, though heavy, was inaccurate. Our own guns, firing from the railway, proved more effective and enabled the columns to continue forward. Medvyejya Gora fell on 21st May; three days earlier the eastern column had entered Povyenets. The final objectives gained, positions were consolidated.[86]

These operations had been undertaken during the spring thaw, under conditions totally unfavourable to the advance. A postponement, however, would have brought an enemy lake flotilla into open water ready to act in co-operation with the Red land forces, thus making the Allied task more difficult. Having arrived at the port while the lake was still ice-bound. Maynard had time to organize artillery defence and construct bases both for vessels and seaplanes (expected at the end of May) without disturbance, which tasks he pushed forward. Six motor-boats and two steam-launches brought down by rail had been launched by the first week in June; by that time seaplanes had arrived. At the end of May, following a limited advance of eight miles, artillery to guard the entrance to the bay was in position—none too soon, for on 8th June a Bolshevik flotilla approached the port. The Allied flotilla, covered by coastal guns and aided by seaplanes, dispersed it, converting what might have been a reverse into a victory which had a tonic effect upon morale.[87]

As we have seen, there was still no Allied declaration of policy towards Northern Russia although the War Office (with Cabinet authority) informed both Maynard and Ironside that 'in all probability' Archangel and Murmansk would be evacuated.[88] It was then March, and with the date of probable evacuation given as some time during the summer, there might be but three months left for White Russian forces to prepare to stand alone. An increase in fighting strength was necessary.[89] By early July, with the addition of the newly gained recruiting ground, the Russian army had doubled to a strength of 5000 men.[90] A Russian officer (General Skobeltsin) arrived from Archangel on 6th June, 1919, to take over command of all Russian troops in the Murman area.[91]

KARELIAN AND FINNISH PROBLEMS

During April, May, and June, the tangled skein of local politics again caused Maynard anxiety. Reports reaching the Allied commander at the end of March indicated that on 10th April the Karelians would rise in arms, demanding separation from Russia and incorporation with Finland.* It appeared that Finland was prepared to give the Karelians active assistance. 'The whole position was kaleidoscopic. Six months previously my Karelians had opposed the White Finns strenuously and had served me well. . . .' Now it appeared that the Allies must reopen operations against the Finns, with the Karelians their allies, in the interests of the North Russian Government. Finnish incursions began early in April, armed parties crossing the frontier west of Lake Onega, south of the Allied line. Synchronized with this penetration by Finns was an epidemic of desertions from the Karelian Regiment, the deserters carrying arms and disappearing in the direction of the Finnish frontier. On 26th April the situation became clear. Five thousand Finns (reportedly volunteers), assisted by local Karelians, began to advance on the Bolsheviks at Olonetz and Petrozavodsk, some 100 miles south of the Allied front. This was by no means distasteful. Instead of a rising against the North Russian Government—and therefore against the Allies—it seemed that an unexpeceed ally had been acquired against the Bolsheviks. The latter, however, checked the Finnish advance. The Finns then made overtures for the Allies to co-ordinate movements with them, but in view of North Russian suspicions, Maynard—though he personally welcomed the suggestion—requested assurances from the War Office concerning Karelia's future; provided these were given, certain stipulations must be met as to how the Finns would be employed. The reply, received on 26th June, came in the form of a message from the Finn commander. He would co-operate with Maynard in any way, but all Russian troops should be withdrawn. Finnish intentions were obvious: the omission of Russians from forthcoming operations could have only one interpretation —Karelia was to come under Finland, and Russians must have no part in driving out Bolsheviks. Maynard could not co-operate under

* Karelia had belonged to Finland until annexed by Peter the Great. Though Karelia desired complete independence, there seemed little likelihood of this. Incorporation with Finland was a second choice, but offered a better prospect of fulfilment, as it would meet with Finnish support.

such terms : Russian troops must play a part in any further advance. He replied to this effect, expressing the hope, nevertheless, 'that our respective forces would work in friendly conjunction'.[92]

The Allies did in fact advance from Medvyejya Gora. Finnish troops found in some of the outlying villages caused Maynard unending trouble until 'Bolshevik successes drove the whole volunteer rabble back into its own country'. The troubles of which he complained were efforts to undermine the loyalty of Karelians to the North Russian Government and terrorizing villagers who failed to be moved, combined with looting. During the first week in July the entire volunteer force had withdrawn. 'The Bolshevik army had shown itself the less inefficient of the two.'[93]

On 2nd July the Finnish Government approached the Allied commander openly. It had been decided to replace volunteers with regular troops—could Maynard join them west of Petrozavodsk within a fortnight? This might now be feasible, as Finland had waived her claims to Karelia pending future settlement by plebiscite. Such a plebiscite, it seemed to Maynard, could only take place after Allied withdrawal; he could do nothing to prevent it. His immediate interest lay in co-operation with the Finns. 'I should have felt bound to fall in with the proposal had it been within the bounds of practicability.' But it was not. War Office instructions restricted any further advance to Russian troops only and these were 'not yet ready for a move on so large a scale'.[94]

The Finnish regulars, if ever sent, accomplished nothing. The Finns ceased to be a factor in the military situation. But the three-month episode had one important effect—the doubtful attitude of the Karelian Regiment, through widespread desertion, compelled Maynard to disband it. This was done on 20th May, its members being offered other employment; a Labour Battalion (unarmed) and Frontier Guard were well to the fore in popularity.[95]

MURMAN: SUMMER OPERATIONS

In July Maynard received definite orders for the evacuation of all Allied troops from Murmansk before winter set in, but the withdrawal began long before this. All French troops left at the beginning of June. Orders arrived on the 7th to hold all Royal Marines in readiness for embarkation. Two days later, the immediate return of the Canadian contingent was called for but it remained, however, until August;* both companies of American railway troops left at the middle of July; and finally, all British troops who had arrived at Murmansk before February 1, 1919, were placed under orders to leave before the end of August—an order affecting the original infantry and machine gun companies, and a large part of the administrative services.[98]

Meanwhile, following the capture of Medvyejya Gora, the line was consolidated, while the building-up of Russian forces proceeded. Colonel Leckie had assumed command of Allied troops at Povyenets, which was undamaged, and its whole garrison was billeted very comfortably. Both towns were within the fringe of an agricultural district and, thanks to Maynard's foresight, green vegetable seeds had been obtained from England. 'Our main crops were lettuces and mustard and cress. These grew fast and well, and enabled an occasional all-round issue to be made'—a welcome change for men with whom 'green food has been, for months on end, nothing more than a tantalizing dream'.[99]

On 3rd June the relative quiet was broken by an uprising of the inhabitants of the northern part of the Shunga Peninsula (some twenty miles due south of Povyenets across the lake, and forty miles south-east of Medvyejya Gora by land) against the Bolsheviks, and an appeal for assistance and arms. Russian troops at Medvyejya Gora —advanced positions had been established across the railway eight miles south—were not yet organized. Maynard decided to ship 400 Russians from Povyenets with rifles and ammunition for the local people. The risks were great. Bolsheviks had superior naval force; the rising might be quelled, necessitating an opposed landing; and even if a foothold was successfully gained, future supplies could be sent only by boat in the absence of land communications. 'Once again however the future interests of the Russian army swung the scale in favour of the enterprise'—the Shunga Peninsula promised to be a fruitful recruiting ground, and indeed so proved. The Povyenets force landed without opposition on 4th June and won a small victory which began a growing anti-Bolshevik movement which was important for subsequent operations; two thousand men were recruited for the North Russian army.[100]

* Maynard protested against the withdrawal of Canadians at this juncture, stating that their departure would jeopardize the safety of British and Allied troops. He promised to release them as soon as possible.[96] The next day the Canadian Government agreed to their retention.[97]

This operation resulted in another, again entrusted to local forces
—the opening up of communications with Shunga by land, which
entailed an advance of from ten to fifteen miles. The plan called for
an attack by newly raised Russians on Siding 10, the next place of
importance down the railway between Medvyejya Gora and Kyapeselga, supported by the well-tried Olonetz Regiment on the right.
The latter did well, but the new Russian troops, who bolted under
fire, failed to take their objective. It seemed to Maynard that this
'contemptible show' might shape the whole future of the new Russian army. Victory could not be left with the Bolsheviks; confidence
must be restored. Allied infantry would have to be used, but this
could not be helped, despite War Office instructions to the contrary.
This time three columns were used : the Olonetz Regiment on the
right, reinforced by British and Serbs : a railway column, almost
entirely British; and on the left, another column, largely Russian
under Canadian leadership, with orders to gain touch with the
Shunga force. On 13th June Maynard launched the attack. Siding 10
fell without Allied loss, largely due to the accuracy of artillery fire.
Both the right and left columns made good progress, but land communications were not yet assured as enemy guns at Dianova Gora
commanded the coast road. Accordingly, Maynard determined to
press south along the whole line west of the lake. On 20th June the
right column captured Kartashi; the railway column arrived at the
outskirts of Kyapeselga on 4th July; and the left column, linking up
with the Shunga force on 25th June, had gone on to capture Dianova
Gora and Unitsa on the 28th.[101] Leckie infiltrated a party of seventy
men, under a Canadian officer, to the rear of the Bolshevik positions.
'When Colonel Leckie developed his attack, the garrison of Dianova
Gora retired, and as they came down the road in two's and three's
some of them dragging machine guns on wheel mountings . . .
[we] captured them all and had a pretty gang of Bolsheviks and
equipment to hand over. . . . In the afternoon with motorcycle
mounted machine guns and a few men we captured Unitza, another
village to the south-west.'[102] On the night of 5th–6th July, the three
columns combined to attack Kyapeselga, from which the Bolsheviks
were driven in confusion. The reaching of the Kyapeselga line
enabled communications with the Shunga Peninsula to be fully
established by land.[103]

Russian interests now dictated the course of action. The present
line, blocking all main approaches from the south, was excellent.

Maynard decided to hold it firmly; to continue the Russian offensive in the Shunga Peninsula, thereby increasing the flow of recruits; and finally to break up Bolshevik preparations for a northward advance by bold and frequent raids by land, air, and water.[104]

Fighting continued on the peninsula for many weeks. The Bolsheviks employed Red Finns, who proved to be tenacious opponents. With the establishment of land communications, however, Allied guns were brought in and soon neutralized the fire of enemy ships. Throughout July the North Russians held their own; in August the tide turned in their favour. Tolvoya, the main town on the peninsula, fell on 3rd August to a combined attack by North Russians and the Allied lake flotilla, now strengthened by the addition of six submarine-chasers.[105]

Raids, made by small parties behind the enemy lines, were effective. One, which took five days from 18th July, succeeded in destroying the railway bridge across the Suna river near its mouth, thirty-five miles south of the Allied line. Another resulted in the capture of the commander of an enemy brigade, his staff, fifty other prisoners, and the breech block of a 3-inch gun. Planes attacked the docks and rail centre at Petrozavodsk, and also enemy vessels on the lake in conjunction with the Allied flotilla. In July and August the total enemy losses in ships amounted to four sunk, either by bombs or gunfire, and three captured—

(i) The 300-ton twin-screwed steamer *Silni* with an armament of two 3-inch guns, one 3-pounder, and six colts.

(ii) A small armoured destroyer mounting two 3-inch guns and two machine-guns in revolving turrets.

(iii) An armed tug. . . .[106]

This, besides being a period of continuous fighting, was also one of preparation for Maynard's withdrawal from the theatre. Recruits were flowing in; training, both operational and administrative, proceeded so as to make them self-supporting in all branches.

'It is hardly too much to say that the eviction of the Reds from the Shunga Peninsula and its occupation by Allied troops were mainly responsible for raising the loyal Russian forces to a strength sufficient to enable them to undertake single handed, with a reasonable prospect of success, the defence of the territory already won by them with Allied assistance.'[107]

A disturbing incident occurred on July 20, 1919, when Russian troops holding the Onega section of the Archangel front mutinied and handed over the entire district to the Bolsheviks. Not only did this threaten Maynard's extended communications from Murmansk to the south; it also drove an effective wedge between the Murmansk and Archangel forces, severing all land communications. Maynard dispatched two small forces to bar incursions against his vital railway. One, based on Sumski Posad, advanced to Nyukhotskoe on the White Sea in the direction of Onega, and the second concentrated at Povyenets and Vojmosalmi (the latter place about midway between Povyenets and Nyukhotskoe) with strong patrols forward. Additional troops were found for Soroki by evacuating Petchenga on 25th July. An attempt to recapture Onega, made on 1st August by Ironside, failed and the town remained in Bolshevik hands throughout August. The date fixed for evacuation of Allied troops was drawing close, and the North Russian Government insisted that the port should be regained before the Allies left. Another attack on Onega on 30th August, again from Archangel, failed to intimidate the Bolsheviks into immediate withdrawal, though eight days later they did withdraw, leaving the town in flames. On 10th September Russian forces from Archangel marched in unopposed.[108]

ARCHANGEL—THE ALLIES WIN THROUGH TO SUMMER

In the Archangel theatre neither the 67th nor the 68th Battery had any serious engagements in February, but March was a trying month. The 68th Battery on the Vaga was the first to be engaged. Early in the morning of 1st March the Bolsheviks launched strong attacks, moving infantry supported by artillery against Vistavka and Yevievskaya, outposts of Kitsa, and at the same time attempted to outflank the main position by an encircling movement on the right. All these attacks were broken up by artillery and were not remounted immediately, though a week of skirmishing followed as the prelude to a 'grand attack' on 9th March. Shelling started early in the morning of that day on all the positions, ten guns being concentrated on Vistavka alone. After a two-hour bombardment attack after attack developed, pushed home with maximum determination until nightfall. But the infantry stood firm and, in the words of the battery report, 'after all the shouting was over our positions were still intact', but it was touch and go. 'Had he, at any time, summoned up sufficient courage to rush any position, weight of numbers would have carried him to victory.' As it was, the enemy established himself in proximity to the Vistavka outpost, in view of which the forward guns there were moved back to the vicinity of Kitsa. At the same time, the British howitzers were ordered back to Bereznik where elaborate defences were established as reserve positions in case of need.[109]

For the next few days, log blockhouses were taken down, the pieces numbered, and reassembled in concealed locations at the rate of about five a day. 'This system saved many a casualty, for the old village sites were in every case systematically shelled flat.'[110] Typical diary entries up to the end of the month read laconically as follows:

> March 26th. Bolo commenced shelling 10 a.m. Infantry advanced in skirmishing order driving in our outposts. Fired 140 rounds. Attack broken up.

> March 27th. Fired 198 rounds . . . on Bolo parties. No attack made on our positions.[111]

Then, on 3rd April, three of the long-promised 60-pounder guns arrived at Bereznik, two going to the 68th Battery and one to the 67th. Their movement from Archangel by Canadian Artillery personnel—using a total of 118 horses to pull the enormous weight of even the dismantled parts—is an epic in itself,[112] as is the passage of the ammunition ship through the White Sea ice. 'Every ice-breaker in the country was used', said Colonel Sharman, 'and after three weeks' strenuous battle, the *Wardown* staggered into port almost in a sinking condition.'[113] The arrival of the guns and ammunition in the nick of time before the thaw, when the headwaters of the Dvina would become clear of ice, permitting Bolshevik naval forces to operate before the Royal Navy could sail up the still frozen lower reaches of the river, eased the situation and brought reassurance to Ironside. To the Canadian gunners they were a godsend. 'At last we had range supremacy and could "talk back" however weakly, a thing we had not as yet been able to do.'[114] Ten days later the Yemtsa River detachment rejoined its parent unit, so that the battery was complete once more,[115] and on the 18th, in anticipation of strong Bolshevik action with the river thaw, Kitsa was abandoned. The whole of the Vaga Column now moved back to strong positions at Bereznik with the 60-pounder covering the withdrawal.[116]

On the Dvina, meanwhile, the 67th Battery had found the month

of March to be fraught with uncertainty. The repeated attacks on
the Vaga front bred rumours that the whole column would withdraw to Beneznik, and twice during the period the gunners were
packed ready to move.[117] On 1st April these fears were laid to rest:
the column would hold the present line until the arrival of the Navy.
By this time General Miller had 14,000 Russians under arms, half
of whom were already in the line. There was now a complete Russian field battery on the Dvina, and some 800 infantry of the 2nd
Battalion, 3rd North Russian Rifle Regiment who pressed for an
independent command of their own. They were given the Tulgas
side of the river; all our men (including the 68th Battery) were withdrawn to Kurgomen, a village on the opposite bank.[118]

In the early hours of 25th April the Russian battalion mutinied,
murdering seven of their officers, and three hundred men made off
to join a Bolshevik force waiting in the woods. Together, the mutineers and the enemy turned to attack Tulgas, now manned by the
machine guns and some riflemen who had stood firm, as well as by
the Russian gunners. The river was virtually impassable at the time,
the ice having started to shift, and communications on the Tulgas
side had been destroyed. The Canadian battery, seeing guns firing at
point-blank range on the other bank, 'decided to put a light box
barrage about the whole situation so as to keep any person from getting in or out of the position if possible', and then a Russian artillery
officer arrived by small boat after a perilous journey through the
moving ice to request close support. Under Canadian supporting fire,
the Russian battery and loyal riflemen managed to withdraw.[119]

'One of the proudest things on which the 67th Battery can look
back [is] that the Russian Battery, which they had "mothered" and
trained by precept and example during the winter, should stand firm
when their own Infantry mutinied and remained true to their traditions and teaching although completely surrounded,' reported
Colonel Sharman.[120] Nevertheless, the loss of Tulgas created a most
precarious position for the Dvina force at Kurgomen. The Bolsheviks
were only 2500 yards away across the river, and they controlled the
other bank for ten miles behind the Allied positions. The ground
was higher, so that they could see the Canadian gun positions without difficulty. For the next four days Red frontal attacks, supported
by artillery fire from the opposite bank, were held off. Then, on
30th April the enemy flotilla appeared—twenty-nine river craft
ranging from large boats mounting 6-inch naval guns to smaller

craft armed with 4·1-inch guns. On the Tulgas bank the Bolsheviks massed 2500 troops, eight guns and 'two heavier pieces', while on the Kurgomen side the Allies were directly faced by 3000 infantry and 'some twelve land guns—all of which outranged our 18-pounders'. The Allies had only 550 all ranks (including seventy-five Russians, 160 British infantry, and 140 Canadians), supported by two 60-pounders, four 18-pounders, and one Russian field gun.[121]

On the face of it, the position looked hopeless when, at 2 a.m. on the 1st May, the enemy opened a preliminary bombardment from both banks and the river, followed by a frontal infantry attack. His artillery pinned down the crews of the field guns so that they were unable to retaliate, but the 60-pounders came into action against the flotilla with excellent effect, causing it to hesitate. 'It was then that he made his big mistake. He lifted the fire of his Tulgas guns from the 18-pounders to the 60-pounders. It was no sooner done than the 18-pounders popped out of their pits, and in three minutes Tulgas was silent.' The situation changed from that moment. 'The 60's drove the navy back, his infantry was forced to retire; . . . by 3.30 a.m., the situation was ours. . . .'[122]

Nevertheless, for the first five days in May the overall situation remained critical. Infantry attacks were frustrated time and again by gunfire, 'the guns getting them before they came to close quarters'. But only the 60-pounders could hold off his rivercraft. 'Had we been silenced for the space of half an hour . . . it meant a fight to a finish with odds against us, as there was no way out, his whole twenty-nine armed ships waiting to rush our positions.' Notwithstanding the fact that several heavy shells broke the lips of the 60-pounder pits, covering the crews with earth, not a man was scratched. By a miracle, it seemed, the guns survived.[123]

On 6th May, by dynamiting the ice down river, the first Royal Navy monitor nosed its way through swirling waters which bore huts and even enemy dead downstream. Next day two gunboats (6-inch guns) came up, placing the Bolsheviks on the defensive. Joint efforts on land and water forced the Bolsheviks back, and Tulgas was recaptured on 18th May.[124]

THE CANADIAN GUNNERS WITHDRAW

On that day the Canadian Prime Minister (Sir Robert Borden) addressed the British Secretary of State for War (Mr Churchill) insisting that the Canadians should be withdrawn from Northern Russia immediately. Two previous requests in March had elicited the information that this could not be possible before the early summer because of ice. In his letter Borden emphasized that the 'demobilization of the Canadian Corps and the withdrawal of Canadian troops from Siberia render any further continuance of our forces at Archangel absolutely impracticable', and pointed out that the port of Archangel was now open to navigation. The same day Borden wrote to the British Prime Minister, Lloyd George, enclosing a copy of his letter to Churchill, and emphasizing his request.[125]

His wishes were at once complied with in the case of the 16th Field Brigade, which was relieved in little over two weeks. This was possible through the arrival from England of a relieving force of two brigades, each with a battery of howitzers, on 27th May and 5th June respectively, and by putting further Russian forces in the line. The Provisional Government was enlisting men more quickly. Numbers grew from a monthly total of seventy in September 1918, to 1894 in October, and by the end of April in the following year General Miller, the Russian Governor-General, had organized a force of 16,000 men.[126] There were mutinies, notably of the Dyer battalion of the Slavo-British Legion on 7th July, followed by the Onega mutiny. Otherwise the Russians fought steadily and well and there was hope they would hold Northern Russia for the anti-Bolsheviks after the evacuation of the Allies.[127]

On 11th June, at Archangel, General Miller inspected a farewell parade of the artillery brigade. He addressed the troops and, in the words of Colonel Sharman,

'informed them that his heartfelt thanks went out to the Government of Canada for the magnificent work of their troops. Although four of the officers had been awarded Russian Decorations during the winter, he stated that he would not allow a single officer of the Brigade to leave Russia without some mark of appreciation from his Government. All officers not previously decorated were then awarded the Order of St. Anne or the Order of St Stanislaus. The Governor-General also presented to the Brigade ten St. George's Crosses and ten St. George's Medals (The Russian equivalent to the Victoria Cross and D.C.M. respectively). These were given to the men in recognition of their splendid work and following the Russian custom, the men of each Battery chose the ten bravest.
. . .'[128]

Ironside also addressed the men; the Canadian commander went on to say that 'General Ironside, the Commander-in-Chief . . . told them . . . what the Canadian Artillery had meant to him during the winter. Over and over again the C.F.A. had saved the force from destruction and the highest traditions of the Canadian Corps had been fully maintained.'[129] It was no more than the sober truth.

The brigade embarked 11th June for England, thus ending a unique experience in the history of the Canadian armed forces.[130] Its casualties in the campaign had been surprisingly light: five killed in action, one died of wounds, and one natural death.[131]

CHURCHILL'S EFFORTS TO ACHIEVE A SUCCESSFUL OUTCOME

The story of the arrival of the British relieving force, considerably more powerful than the old contingent, is a curious one. Winston Churchill had succeeded Lord Milner as Secretary of State for War in January 1919, and one of his first concerns was to try to obtain some policy at the Peace Conference with regard to Russia. To that end, he journeyed to Paris in February, faced the American President, and bluntly demanded a statement of Allied aims. Churchill was convinced that if the Bolsheviks were to be crushed it must be within the next few weeks, and it was his passionate conviction that if Russia was not restored to the Allied ranks as a democratic power there would be 'neither peace nor victory'.

Woodrow Wilson favoured withdrawal; but Churchill at once pointed out that the result of that would be the complete destruction of all the anti-Bolshevik forces in Russia. 'There would be no further armed resistance to the Bolsheviks in Russia, and an interminable vista of violence and misery was all that remained for the whole of Russia.'[132] With a statement by Wilson that not one of Allies was prepared to reinforce its troops, Churchill did not agree. He conceded that to conscript troops for Russia was out of the question, but volunteers could be obtained and war materials sent in greater quantity.

Wilson's uncertainty is revealed in his reply. Some of the war materials would reach 'reactionaries', yet on the other hand, he himself felt guilty because he had sent insufficient forces to Russia. He could not, however, send more, and the whole situation placed him in a 'cruel dilemma'. On being further pressed by Churchill for a positive decision, he said that if Prinkipo came to nothing, he would do his share with the other Allies 'in any military measures which they considered necessary and practicable to help the Russian armies now in the field'. And with that he left Paris for New York.[133]

Next day, Churchill did his utmost, with all the eloquence at his command, to carry the Allies along with him. The Prinkipo offer had in fact come to nothing, and he proposed that it be revived in a more definite form. An Allied Council should be set up, including a military section, to draw up a concerted military plan of action against the Bolsheviks; the Bolsheviks should then be requested to cease all military hostilities within five days. If they refused the Allies would then be in a position to decide definitely whether to adopt the plan, or clear out altogether.[134] This was an offer the Bolsheviks could hardly accept, as Churchill must have realized; but if they did not it would be, unlike Prinkipo, a propaganda victory for the Allies and would put the Bolsheviks in the wrong. Thus the way would then be open for concerted Allied action.

Clemenceau gruffly agreed, but Churchill's proposal foundered when Wilson, on the *George Washington*, was apprised of it by radio. On February 19th he replied as follows:

'Greatly surprised by Churchill's Russian suggestion. I distinctly understood Lloyd George to say that there would be no thought of military action there and what I said at the hurried meeting Friday afternoon was meant only to convey the idea that I would not take any hasty separate action myself, but would not be in favor of any course contrary to that which may mean the earliest practicable withdrawal of military forces. It would be fatal to be led further into the Russian chaos.'[135]

The American President had in fact made up his mind to withdraw U.S. troops from North Russia. As early as 20th February, the day following his communication to the Peace Conference, American troops in the Archangel sector heard by radio the first reports that they would withdraw.[136] Though De Witt Clinton Poole, the American Chargé d'Affaires in Russia after the departure of the U.S. ambassador, pleaded against withdrawal and bemoaned 'since the Prinkipo invitation, an uncertainty in the American attitude toward the Bolsheviks';[137] nevertheless, by the end of May, American troops had been concentrated in Archangel itself, or its vicinity, ready for embarkation. Having fought tenaciously and well throughout the bitter winter, they sailed in June in the returning ships which had brought the first British relief brigade.

Churchill, fully cognizant of the threat posed by Communism for the future, left the Peace Conference determined to do alone whatever could be done to crush the Soviets while a little time still remained. On March 3, 1919, he deliberately painted the picture in North Russia blacker than it really was, sounding a warning that it might be necessary to send reinforcements to that theatre to ensure the safe withdrawal of the tired troops. Newspapers took up the call, silencing for the present public agitation to 'bring the boys back home'. A call then went out from the War Office for volunteers, and the response was tremendous. Eight thousand men were accepted to be formed into two brigades equipped with the latest equipment. 'The British had definitely decided now to evacuate North Russia by the autumn of 1919; but to do this hardly called for a "rescue" force eight thousand strong.' Ironside himself had no qualms. His lines were much the same as when winter had started and White Russian strength was growing. 'With a superior flotilla on the river I did not believe that anything could stop us from getting out.'[138] There seemed little doubt that the new force was to be put into North Russia as soon as ice conditions would permit for a last throw against the Bolsheviks.

The fortunes of Kolchak's Siberian armies were the key to success. It was known that Gaida was at Perm and thus within striking distance of Viatka. From Viatka the Trans-Siberian branch railway led to Kotlas, 200 miles away. Ironside was not the man to go marching into the interior of Russia in pursuit of a chimera, but, 'If there were in truth a chance of junction with Kolchak, I could without danger be more bold in my thrusts.'[139] On 21st March, Russian troops of the Pinega column made contact with patrols from Gaida's army on the northern wing of Kolchak's front. 'A detachment sent by Captain Alashev has contacted Siberian troops near the village of Ustkozhva. All territory along Petchora and farther toward Perm is free from Bolsheviks.'[140] There was hope of the rapid formation of a single front against the Reds. General Miller had previously proposed that anti-Bolshevik forces should be unified by North Russian recognition of Admiral Kolchak as supreme leader; the North Russian Government finally accepted this on April 30, 1919. Kolchak appointed Miller the Governor-General and Commander-in-Chief of all Rus-

sian forces on the Northern front—in other words, a military dictator in the Northern region.[141]

On 22nd May, Ironside received from the War Office news which
had come from General Knox in Siberia. It confirmed that Kazan
and Viatka were to be occupied by the Siberian army, a detachment
being sent north to join the Archangel forces. The British commander drew up plans, with War Office approval, to utilize the
British brigades then being sent in a drive down the Dvina with
Kotlas as its final aim.[142] The first brigade under Brigadier-General
G. W. St. G. Grogan arrived at Archangel on May 26th (in ships
with specially reinforced hulls to batter through the ice) just as the
ice was being finally carried away by the Dvina; on 6th June, the
second brigade under Brigadier-General L. W. de V. Sadleir-Jackson
arrived. The Canadians, when turning over their positions to the
new arrivals, referred to them as 'extravagantly decorated'[143]—
Grogan himself had the V.C.—and as Ironside watched them disem-
bark, he felt that 'they could walk through anything in North
Russia'.[144] They received the tumultuous welcome of cheering people
and peal after peal of bells.[145]

On the 20th June, Grogan launched a limited offensive using one
battalion of Hampshires in conjunction with Russian troops. The
objectives were the villages of Topsa and Troitsa, south of Tulgas
on the Dvina. The Russian attack was a success and the whole
offensive would have been more so if the Hampshires had participated. The reason for their not doing so lies with the C.O. and becomes clear from a letter written by him later (after he had been
relieved of his command and sent back to England) and published in
the London *Daily Express*.

'I volunteered for service with the North Russian Relief Force in
the sincere belief that relief was urgently needed in order to make
possible the withdrawal of low category troops, in the last stages of
exhaustion, due to the fierce fighting amid the rigours of an Arctic
winter. . . .

'Immediately on arrival . . . I received the impression that the
policy of the authorities was not what it was stated to be . . .
troops . . . which we were told had been sent out purely for
defensive purposes were being used for offensive purposes on a
large scale and far in the interior. . . .'[146]

For that reason, he had held back his battalion.

Nevertheless, enemy positions in front had been destroyed, and for ten miles south no organized resistance was encountered.[147] Ironside, who had previously decided that he would be able to attack in strength from 1st July onwards[148] saw no reason to change his plans, and hurried Sadlier-Jackson's brigade to the Dvina front.[149]

FAILURE IN SIBERIA FORCES EVACUATION

Then, on 1st July, came catastrophic news from the War Office— Gaida had lost Perm, Kungur and Krasnoufimsk in June. The prospects of a junction were unfavourable; any advance on Kotlas, therefore, was out of the question and the only course now was withdrawal. On the 2nd, the British general saw Miller and told him the news—'hardly a muscle of his face moved. I could only see in his pale blue eyes how desperately tired he was.'[150]

A few days later further symptoms of a hopeless situation appeared. On the 7th, Dyer's battalion of the Slavo-British Legion mutinied, killed three British officers and mortally wounded two more, as well as killing four Russian officers and wounding a fifth. In all, a hundred men deserted to the enemy. It was obvious that the efforts of both Ironside and Miller to create a dependable Russian army had failed.[151] Then, on 20th July, came the mutiny of the 5th Russian Infantry Regiment at Onega which, as we have seen, surrendered the whole front to the Bolsheviks. The same day, a similar revolt was attempted on the front of the Railway Column by the 6th Russian Infantry Regiment; but while some positions were surrendered to the Bolsheviks, Australian, French and Polish troops restored the situation. Still another unit, the 7th Russian Infantry Regiment at Seletski, planned revolt, but the fact became known and it was suppressed.[152] These events convinced Ironside that evacuation was indeed the only course to follow, and he advised London that he was drawing up plans to that end.[153]

To facilitate disengagement Ironside planned one last, hard blow against the Bolsheviks. The date for this was set for 10th August, the date chosen to make public the fact that the Allies were about to evacuate North Russia completely.

Meanwhile, on 1st August, it was announced in London that General Lord Rawlinson, a former commander of a British Army on the Western Front, had been appointed to co-ordinate the Allied evacuation of the two separate commands at Archangel and Mur-

H

mansk.[154] Rawlinson had further reinforcements from Britain at his disposition which went to Murmansk: three additional infantry battalions; one Marine battalion, one machine-gun battalion; two batteries of artillery; a field company of engineers, and five tanks. Powerful naval forces, including monitors which could ascend the Dvina river, also came, and ample shipping.[155]

Ironside had no need of additional troops. On 10th August, as planned, the British force that Ironside had slated for the drive to Kotlas (Sadleir-Jackson's brigade with Russian troops) struck the Bolsheviks on the Dvina. The objectives were limited, but the power of the stroke was not restricted in any way. 'The plan was a bold one. About a quarter of [the force] in a frontal attack and the remaining three-quarters in an attack from the flanks and rear. Each body of men was to attack and attack and go on attacking till there was nothing left to deal with.'[156]

The operations were planned in detail. Communications by wireless were arranged between the command post, naval flotilla, ground troops, and artillery. Barrages and the use of smoke were carefully timed.[157] The operations were completely successful. British and Russian troops smashed through the Soviet resistance like a hammer through glass. The whole Bolshevik front was enveloped and destroyed. The better part of six Soviet battalions were killed or wounded and more than 3000 prisoners taken. Also captured were eighteen field guns, 2000 rifles, machine guns and ammunition, and two crippled gunboats; a third gunboat was sunk, all at a cost of 145 killed and wounded.[158] Russian troops took over the advanced line.

'The enemy having been temporarily paralysed, a swift and unmolested withdrawal was made' first to the inner defences which Ironside had established around Archangel during the previous winter, thence to the ships. Food and arms were left with General Miller and his Russian troops. The British evacuated by sea 6000 refugees who had elected to go. By 27th September the evacuation of Archangel was completed. 'Those who remained to continue the civil war did so of their own free will. . . . Safety was provided for every Russian man, woman and child who wished to leave,' said Churchill. Many of those who stayed faced firing parties in the not too distant future. The responsibility for their predicament rested, continued Churchill, 'upon the mighty and resplendent nations who had won the war, but left their task unfinished'.[159]

The reinforcements brought by Rawlinson to Murmansk meant

no gain in Allied numerical strength in that theatre; the entire Italian contingent of 1200 as well as the original British expeditionary force sailed for England on 10th August. In compliance with a War Office order directing that all British troops who had arrived in North Russia prior to February 1919 were to be returned to England before the end of August, the Canadian contingent left Murmansk on August 22, 1919. The local Russian army, however, now totalled between six and seven thousand (exclusive of Karelians), with two field batteries and engineer units. Russians manned half the boats of the flotilla, and the training of air pilots was well advanced. 'It had become', said Maynard, 'a force with which the Bolsheviks would have to reckon seriously.'[160]

Rawlinson, on 11th August, urged the North Russian Government to abandon Archangel and to concentrate all Russian forces on the Murmansk front, where they could threaten Petrograd, and would have at their backs an ice-free port. Maynard, doubting the possibility of a successful fight on both fronts, agreed. Political reasons led the government to reject the proposal—no victories gained along the Murmansk–Petrograd railway would compensate for the loss of Archangel.[161]

Maynard's evacuation plan consisted of an offensive to gain the line of the Suna river, some twenty miles from Petrozavodsk, immediately prior to withdrawal, and until this could be mounted he would exploit success in the Shunga. The latter resulted in the whole peninsula being cleared of Bolshevik forces by the end of August. This not only gave a fresh impetus to recruiting; it also rendered the left flank secure for the projected offensive to the Suna. The timing of this was left to Rawlinson. The withdrawal from Murmansk could not precede that from Archangel, now set at the last week in September. The final decision was that the Suna offensive would start at the middle of September, and that Murmansk would be evacuated in the first week of October.[162]

The offensive entailed an advance of thirty-five miles. No Allied troops, Rawlinson stipulated, should operate south of the Nurmis river, some ten miles from the final objective. The object of the advance was twofold—first to strike a blow which would facilitate the handing over the front to anti-Bolshevik Russians and which would prevent the enemy from interfering with Allied withdrawal, and secondly to inflict such casualties as would render the Bolsheviks incapable of an early resumption of the offensive. Surprise, however, was lacking. Allied evacuation had been proclaimed in newspapers. The blow at Archangel, with similar objects, having already fallen, the Bolshevik commander opposing Maynard could reasonably assume that he, too, would shortly face attack. Thus, preliminary operations designed to outflank Bolshevik garrisons failed, and there was no time to organize other attempts. Accordingly, on 14th September, the final offensive was launched along the whole front with a strength of 9000, two-thirds of whom were Russians. On the 18th, British troops occupied the line of the Nurmis—'beyond which no Allied units were permitted to operate'—and Skobeltsin, the Russian commander, decided to postpone further offensive action until he was firmly established here.

> 'The Bolsheviks had been hustled and hammered for three days, and their casualties had been extremely heavy. . . . In prisoners alone they had lost 1000, besides large quantities of supplies, rolling stock and war material. . . . In addition the Nurmis afforded a satisfactory line of defence. . . . By the 25th the transfer of the flotilla, of R.A.F. machines, and of all war material in the forward zone had been completed, and Skobeltsin and his army stood alone to champion the cause of loyal Russia.'[163]

The evacuation of Allied troops ended on 12th October, when the last troopship cast off her moorings and swung into the tide of the Kola Inlet.[164]

The sequel to Allied intervention in North Russia was dismal, and may be told briefly. Anti-Bolshevik resistance crumbled soon after Allied departure. Russian forces finally collapsed at Archangel on February 19, 1920, followed by those at Murmansk two days later. Soviet rule, accompanied by its customary excesses, was then re-established over the whole of the White Sea region. Though General Miller escaped, mass executions of officers and leaders quenched the last hopes of anti-Bolshevik life and freedom in Northern Russia.

Miller himself, a member of his staff* testifies, left by icebreaker for Norway at the very last moment. He had done everything possible to stabilize his front and undoubtedly saved the lives of over a thousand White Russians (including that of the staff officer himself), who were taken off with him. In 1936 Miller was kidnapped in Paris, removed to an unknown destination, and has never been heard from since.

---

* Captain John Hundevad, now Editor-in-Chief of the Canadian *Legionary*.

CONCLUSION

As a strategic move against Germany, intervention in North Russia was successful—more so in the Murmansk sector than in Archangel—and amply justified. Subsequent embroilment with the Bolsheviks grew out of it and must be regarded as a thing apart. At the outset, Moscow raised no objection to the enterprise and even sanctioned it for the defence of Murmansk. It was in the Allies' interests that there should be no break in relations with the Bolsheviks, since the main object was to prosecute the war against Germany. That the rupture occurred was solely the responsibility of the Bolshevik leaders. The question remains whether it was politic, after this rupture, to continue operations against the Bolsheviks following the overthrow of Germany.

The Allied forces in North Russia were largely British, under British command, and though the record reveals no clear statement of Allied policy, that of Britain is revealed by steady support of Kolchak in the East and of Denikin in the South in their efforts to overthrow the Bolsheviks. Consequently the North Russian force held that area against the Bolsheviks long after the war with Germany was over in an attempt to protect free Russians in a given locality and to complete the encirclement of the Communists until such time as decisive force should be applied from Siberia, which was always regarded by the British as the decisive theatre. Thus the continued presence of Allied troops in North Russia after the Armistice with Germany was always consistent with British policy.

The course of intervention and Kolchak's efforts in Siberia have been studied. It is sufficient to say that of Kolchak's semi-independent armies only Gaida's had the objective of junction with the Allies at Archangel. The others pursued different objectives; as a result, despite success on all fronts up to the middle of 1919, all failed eventually and had to retreat. Gaida, as early as December 1918, had advanced to within 400 miles of Ironside's nearest posts on the Dvina, but at that time no help could be extended by the slender Allied forces which had been diverted from the Western Front and which were fighting desperately to hold their positions in the depths of winter. Churchill saw to it that a strong force reached Archangel at the first opportunity after the melting of the ice, but when Archangel was open and fresh troops were arriving, Gaida was pulling back to the Urals, never to advance again. There was then no more reason to retain Allied troops in North Russia, and evacuation was sanctioned.

One thing that the fighting in North Russia revealed quite sharply was the weakness of the Bolshevik armies. To advance from Archangel, the British War Office had considered one or two divisions necessary. With a fraction of that strength, largely made up of British infantry of low medical category and Americans reported by the Canadians to be 'new, untried, [and] very green troops',[165] the Allies made a deep advance over unfamiliar ground into the interior of Russia at a time when the Bolsheviks had many times the men and superior river craft and guns. Only against troops of a very low calibre could such an advance have been made.

There is considerable evidence as to the inferior quality of Red Army troops in 1918. In an account based on contemporary American reports we read this:

'. . . although there was no lack of Bolshevik troops on this front, most of them were hopelessly untrained and used their weapons as effectively as so many baboons. Almost invariably they fired far too high. They were, in short, the epitome of what General Poole had hoped the entire Red army might turn out to be: ragged peasants with no notion of how to conduct a military operation. Unfortunately, this was by no means true everywhere in North Russia. nor was it a condition that remained long unchanged under Trotsky's driving leadership of the Bolshevik forces. But for the time being [the] young Americans were, relatively, in the desirable military posture of crack combat troops facing greenhorns—this as the surprising result of a few weeks of assault training and target shooting at Fort Custer, Michigan.'[166]

Of his first Russians in the line, Ironside said: 'They were not highly trained, but they were better than anything the Bolsheviks could produce'; and in May 1919, when Tulgas had been wrested back from the enemy, hundreds of enemy deserters crossed over to the Allied side:

'They were all in miserable condition, badly fed and clothed, and all indescribably dirty. They had the same tale to tell. They had been conscripted in South Russia and brought up to what was to them virtually a foreign country. Here they were thrown into a fight without any training. They had no desire to fight any more on either side, and they did not understand why they had been made to do so. . . . Their condition was certainly an indication of the poor quality of some of the enemy troops opposed to us. I had little doubt that we could break the enemy lines whenever we wished to.'[167]

Maynard, in describing the withdrawal of the White Finnish 'volunteer rabble' in July 1919, puts it much more simply : 'The Bolshevik army had shown itself the less inefficient of the two.'[168]

To sum up, judging by the North Russian experience, the claim of General Knox in Siberia that one properly equipped division of Allied troops could have taken Moscow if employed before the Armistice would not appear unrealistic.

Finally, why did American troops take such an active part in North Russia when, in the main intervention sphere, their stand was 'neutral'? Both forces were governed by the same *Aide Mémoire* from the pen of President Wilson. It might have been expected that military action in either theatre would have been similar. The answer lies in the vagueness of language, the very ambiguity of Wilson's document, and in the different personalities of those responsible for its interpretation. In Siberia, Graves read into it one thing, and in so doing found himself at loggerheads with American officials of the State Department. Colonel Stewart, who commanded the American contingent at Archangel, unlike Graves, placed himself under the wing of David R. Francis, the American ambassador, and looked to him for guidance; and Francis did not place the same interpretation on Wilson's instructions as did Graves. Both Francis and his successor, De Witt Clinton Poole, were firm opponents of Bolshevism. The former saw it as 'a foul monster', favoured intervention in considerable force, and never relinquished his views; the latter argued that the more resolutely the Allies intervened in Russia the more enthusiastically the population would rally against the Communists.[169]

Had such American sentiment prevailed in Siberia, the advance from that theatre might have gone much further than it did, the ordeal of the North Russian troops might not have been in vain, and the course of world history might well have been changed.

CHAPTER VII

COLLAPSE OF THE WHITE ARMIES

SIBERIA

Kolchak had staked everything on military victory, and his spring offensive had resulted in a spectacular and reassuring advance. The northern wing of the Siberian armies was midway between Perm and Viatka; the centre within 100 miles of Kazan and only 500 miles from Moscow; while the southern wing, thirty-five miles from the Volga, threatened both Samara and Saratov. But the very size of the captured regions combined with insufficiency of supplies made it almost impossible to consolidate the newly won ground into a solid front. The Whites had now penetrated from the wooded Urals into populous steppe country and here they tried to augment their forces by mobilizations in towns and villages. Recruits obtained in this way, however, were of little value; lack of equipment and instructors meant that they could not be counted upon as soldiers, and it was soon found that they had a predilection to return to their homes at the first reverse.[1]

The Reds, on this vital front, were able to field dedicated and therefore much more reliable troops, by decreeing special levies from members of the Communist Party itself or from trade unions which were under Communist control. Thus the Penza Executive Committee furnished a regiment of shock troops, the Novgorod Provincial Committee mobilized half its members, and in the end twenty-two provinces sent troops to Samara, Simbirsk, Kazan and Viatka, the four main concentration points behind the Red lines.[2]

With the coming of the spring thaw, Kolchak's men should have found the task of defence an easy one. Streams swelled into torrents; the ground softened into almost impassable mud. These conditions had already come to the aid of the Bolsheviks who now held the line firmly while waiting for their strength to grow.

The Reds struck at Kolchak's centre during the last week in April. A strong Red Army force, which had been concentrated facing Buzuluk on the Samara–Orenburg railway, attacked the left flank of

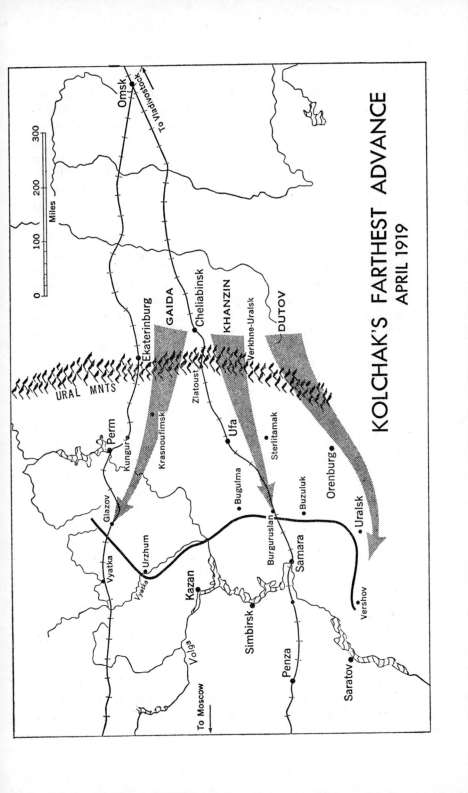

KOLCHAK'S FARTHEST ADVANCE
APRIL 1919

General Khanzin's Western Army spread out too thinly over too wide a front. A breakthrough was achieved, whereupon a British-equipped regiment of Ukrainian troops which was holding Buguruslan on the right, and whose desire to return home proved stronger than loyalty to Kolchak,[3] killed its officers and passed over to the enemy. Red troops poured into the gap between Buguluk and Buguruslan, driving a wedge into the centre of the Siberian armies. Gaida's Northern Army, convinced perhaps that the line of the river Belaya between the broken front and Ufa would be held, ignored the threat and continued to advance on Glazov, the intermediate town on the Trans-Siberian Railway between Perm and Viatka.[4]

The river line, however, could not be held. Khanzin's troops, insufficient in numbers, exhausted by long marches during the advance, and dispirited by lack of supplies, threw down their arms or were hustled back towards the Urals. The Reds forced the Belaya on 6th June, and three days later captured Ufa, the starting-point of the White offensive.[5] The loss of Ufa marked the end of White success in this theatre. From then on they relinquished ground steadily to the advancing Reds.

A Bolshevik offensive now developed in a north-easterly direction on Krasnoufimsk, between Perm and Cheliabinsk. The capture of this town would threaten Ekaterinburg and compel Gaida, whose supply lines would otherwise be cut, to pull back his forces from Glazov at least to Perm. Two subsidiary offensives were also mounted; in the centre from Sterlitamak and Verkhne-Uralsk on Cheliabinsk; and in the south towards Uralsk and Orenburg. The latter thrust would not only prevent Denikin from uniting with Kolchak, it would also enable junction to be made with Red forces hitherto isolated in Turkestan.[6]

These plans had been arrived at only after a sharp difference of opinion as to the right course to follow among the Soviet leaders. Trotsky, the War Commissar, and his Commander-in-Chief, Vatzetis, saw in Denikin's army, whose advance assumed considerable proportions in May and June, the main threat to Soviet Russia. Both men advocated, therefore, a halt on the river Belaya and a transfer of forces to the south to counter the onward progress of the Volunteer Army.

Lenin insisted that the Ural Territory was the vital theatre, and his will finally prevailed. In consequence, Vatzetis resigned, to be replaced by Kamenev (Trotsky, who wished to do the same, was persuaded to remain in office), and the Bolshevik offensives continued after the fall of Ufa.[7]

In the face of Soviet pressure towards Krasnoufimsk, Gaida's Northern Army was forced to begin a retreat which turned into a disorderly rout as his troops scrambled back from their exposed positions. There was now no longer any possibility of linking up with Ironside's Archangel force, which, reinforced in June, was then ready to march on Kotlas. In the centre the Red forces also made good progress, while towards the south, in the Ural and Orenburg Cossack regions, White forces met one defeat after another until finally a considerable part of their army was trapped between the advancing Red Army from the west and the Red group moving northwards from Turkestan; it was forced to surrender. At the end of June, the completely disorganized White troops had been pushed back to a line which ran from Perm through Kingur–Krasnoufimsk–Sterlitamak to Orenburg.[8]

The defence line connecting Ekaterinburg and Cheliabinsk advocated by the French in the late summer of 1918 would have assumed some importance at this juncture, had it been established. The suggested reserve at Omsk could have been brought forward, while behind it Kolchak's shattered forces would have been able to reorganize and recuperate. But no such line existed, nor was there any appreciable reserve. Red Army thrusts developed as the French had foreseen along the two branches of the Trans-Siberian Railway in the direction Perm–Ekaterinburg and from Ufa towards Cheliabinsk through the intermediate town of Zlatoust, key to the wooded range of the Ural Mountains which formed a natural barrier.[9] Perm fell on 3rd July, and eleven days later the victorious Red troops entered Ekaterinburg, the capital of the Ural Territory. On the 13th, the Ural barrier was forced by the capture of Zlatoust, and the Bolsheviks pressed on towards Cheliabinsk.[10] The demoralized White armies, with no defended line behind which to rally, were displaying all the signs of break-up. Desertion and voluntary surrender to the Reds were widespread.

Kolchak, by now thoroughly alarmed, sought a remedy by a change in leadership. On 12th July he dismissed General Gaida, who had been particularly bitter about absence of direction and lack of supplies and reinforcements, and appointed Dieterichs in his place. Gaida left for Vladivostok, which he reached on 8th August.[11] Dieterichs saw no hope of any stand in the Urals, but between the fleeing armies and Omsk lay three rivers, the Tobol, the Ishim, and the Irtish; a stand, he considered, would be possible behind any one of these rivers which formed natural lines of defence in Western Siberia.[12] But Lebedeff, 'the young Chief of Staff . . . whose cock-sure blunders had already exerted an unfavourable effect on the course of the campaign', prevailed upon Kolchak to try another plan. Lebedeff proposed that the Reds should be allowed to occupy Chelia-binsk; he would then outflank them from high ground west of the town, cut them off, and destroy them. Unfortunately, the suggested counter-stroke lacked simplicity; it called instead for a complicated movement, feasible only with skilled leaders and seasoned troops. In the absence of these, the attempt could only fail. For the sake of it, however, Kolchak, at the end of July and at the beginning of August, committed his last reserves. His troops were routed and 15,000 prisoners were taken by the Reds. The whole of the Ural industrial region had now been lost; Siberia alone remained.[13]

Dieterichs, who perhaps understandably replaced Lebedeff as Chief of Staff, had the thankless task of defending Siberia with what few troops were left—not more, it was estimated, than 50,000. His first move was to pull back the remnants of the White forces behind the Tobol river, some 350 miles west of Omsk, where he reformed them into three 'armies' under General Pepelaieff, General Lokhvit-sky, and General Sakharoff. A more orderly withdrawal was then made to the Ishim river where a defensive line was established. During August and September the new front remained relatively stable, as the Bolsheviks—preoccupied with the advance of Denikin —were unable to muster sufficient forces to continue their drive on Kolchak's capital, now only 160 miles away.[14]

It was during this lull that General Graves was ordered to visit Omsk in the company of Roland Morris, the American Ambassador to Japan. He had never previously ventured west of Khabarovsk and apparently had no wish to do so since receiving instructions that no American assistance was to be given to the Czechoslovaks beyond Lake Baikal. His policy had always been to remain aloof from de-velopments under Kolchak in the main part of Siberia, and he had no direct communication with Omsk; he had avoided any so as not to be accused of interfering in Russian affairs. Even now he pro-tested to the War Department against the visit, but on this occasion, at any rate, he was overruled.[15]

Ambassador Morris was making the journey as a result of the

readiness of the Supreme Council in Versailles to help Kolchak establish himself as the government of all Russia. He left Vladivostok with General Graves, a few interpreters, and a military guard on 11th July and travelled by the shortest route—the Chinese Eastern Railway—arriving at Omsk at the end of the month. Short stops were made at all the important towns on the way, which included a visit to the 27th Infantry Regiment at Verkhne-Udinsk, and at these places Morris became convinced of the failure of the Russian military officials and the Social Revolutionaries to sink their differences and work towards a common goal. The general population also, it seemed, after eight months of Kolchak's government, were no more willing to rally to the anti-Bolshevik cause than at the beginning. Disintegration, however, was worst in Omsk itself.[16]

The Admiral and a few supporters were struggling against overwhelming odds. Frantic efforts were being made in the surrounding areas to recruit men for the army, but only apathy was met; to draft them would only antagonize them, producing ready deserters who would cross over to the Reds with all their arms and equipment at the first opportunity. Their only wish was to remain on their land undisturbed; they were indifferent to the ultimate outcome of the war. Officers there were in plenty. Omsk was crowded with them, 'tens of thousands . . . loudly protesting their willingness to serve but unwilling to take any post below that which they had formerly held',[17] and though General Dieterichs did at last try to organize units from surplus officers, the time had passed for them to be effective. Small wonder that natural barriers such as the Ural Mountains could not be held at various stages of the war—either by Whites or Reds—when defended by such generally apathetic troops. It was a war of no real battles conducted in vast areas which changed hands with comparative ease. 'A war', said Churchill, 'of few casualties and unnumbered executions.'[18]

Graves visited the front near Petropavlovsk while Morris discussed the situation with the Russian leaders. He was not impressed. There was disorder everywhere, and the same lack of supplies, though General Dieterichs had already put in hand reforms which enabled him to attack the Bolsheviks with success in this sector some weeks later. Morris, meanwhile, made it clear to Kolchak that a successful stand by his armies might bring for him full recognition; but he realized that a tremendous change in spirit at Omsk would be necessary to bring this about. A fresh contingent of 24,000 American troops, Morris concluded, and a liberal loan of money would save the situation; but while the Americans might now consider that a small price to pay, Congress in 1919 most definitely would not approve such measures.[19] The proposal, in any case, came far too late. On 6th September Ambassador Morris, having seen the situation and reported to his government what in his opinion would be required to bolster up Admiral Kolchak, returned to Vladivostok with General Graves.

During the last days of September, Dieterichs had rallied his troops sufficiently to launch a counter-offensive.[20] Storming forward from their defences on the river Ishin, the White troops in a last desperate effort recovered a hundred miles of railway from the Reds, and drove them back over the Tobol river. But success was shortlived. Dieterich's field commander, General Sakharoff, short of supplies and reinforcements, could not maintain the attack, and by mid-October the Red Army, now reinforced, was on the march once more. Petropavlovsk, the starting-point of this last White attempt, fell on 30th October, and Kolchak's troops scattered headlong, broke up, and ceased to be a factor in the military situation.[21]

There was nothing now between the Reds and Omsk, and the question of holding the Siberian capital arose. Dieterichs considered that any attempt to defend it even for the obvious psychological advantages would be folly; General Sakharoff, on the other hand, claimed that he could do so, and was appointed Chief of Staff to make good his claim. At the cost of the last garrison troops and trainloads of supplies captured in the sidings at Omsk, it was found that Dieterichs was right. Thereafter refugees and demoralized troops streamed eastwards to escape the retribution of the Reds. The sight of several *de luxe* trains waiting with steam up to carry away the various Allied missions did nothing to uplift their flagging spirits.[22] The horrors of a retreat of more than a thousand miles to Lake Baikal in the Siberian winter along the choked railway and roads, harried by partisan bands which now ventured forth with impunity, will not be dwelt on here. It is estimated that of Kolchak's troops, numbering half a million at their peak, less than 20,000 reached Trans-Baikal. No total of men, women, and children who perished on the way from hostile action, exposure, starvation or disease was ever arrived at. The Red Army entered Omsk triumphantly on 14th November, and on this occasion Kolchak appealed once more to the United States. Mass flights showed the fear in which the Bolsheviks were held by the general masses. He was fighting, he said, for the rest of the world as well as for Russia.[23]

On January 15, 1920, Kolchak arrived at Irkutsk, where a new government had been formed ten days earlier. The disintegration of the Admiral's régime had permitted another authority to be set up, a coalition drawn from various parties, including the anti-Kolchak Socialist Revolutionaries, known as the Political Centre. Additionally, the collapse of Kolchak gave the Social Revolutionaries opportunities to revolt and assert themselves in the various towns between Omsk and Irkutsk, but their programmes amounted to little more than empty words; they could solve none of the pressing problems. In an ostentatious show of democracy, or perhaps of expediency in view of the advancing Red Army, the Bolshevik minority was recognized and permitted to occupy posts from which they could easily undermine the new administrations. In town after town, Bolshevik members overthrew these inefficient structures in readiness for the approaching Reds.[24]

The fate of Kolchak was decided at Irkutsk. From Omsk eastwards there had been indescribable confusion along the railway, for the Czechoslovaks had decided that it was now a question of escaping or perishing, and their cars clogged the tracks. The progress of Kolchak's train, with a second train carrying the Imperial Russian treasure which had been captured at Kazan, was painfully slow. At Nizhne-Udinsk, 800 miles from Irkutsk, General Janin (who was still the commander of the Czechs) offered the Admiral Czech protection for himself and the gold in view of the activities of partisan bands along the railway and political disturbances in Irkutsk; he was to be given safe conduct to the Far East. On 4th January, Kolchak telegraphed Irkutsk that in these circumstances he surrendered his person to the Czechs, and at the same time announced his decision to abdicate in favour of Denikin; he appointed Semenov commander of all the Russian armed forces east of Lake Baikal and in the province of Irkutsk.[25]

Kolchak and his staff boarded a second-class coach attached to the train of the 6th Czechoslovak Regiment, and under Janin's instructions the car was somewhat ostentatiously decorated with the flags of America, Britain, Czechoslovakia, France and Japan. This act of Janin, unconscious in its irony, is symbolic of the grotesque tragedy of Kolchak and the course which Allied intervention had assumed; it is not difficult to imagine the feelings of this man as he passed in his decorated coach on his slow way through towns and villages so recently wrested from the enemy and saw them slipping into the hands of the Bolsheviks and breaking into flame. Only the final act remained to be played.

The Political Centre at Irkutsk demanded that Admiral Kolchak be handed over to them. General Janin, aware that the new government controlled the town through which the Czechs would have to pass on their way to Vladivostok and that failure to comply with their demands would undoubtedly involve his troops in bloodshed, discussed the matter with the Czech leader, Syrovy. By the time Kolchak's train pulled into a siding at Irkutsk on 15th January, a decision had been made. Armed workmen surrounded the slowing coach, and a Czech officer pulled open the door to announce that in accordance with the orders of General Janin, the Czech guard would be withdrawn. The Admiral listened calmly. 'This means', he said, 'that the Allies have betrayed me.'[26] He was taken to the jail at Irkutsk, and the Czech convoy passed on, leaving behind it, as well as Kolchak, the Imperial treasure consisting of gold bricks to the value of 650 million roubles (sixty-five million pounds or 325 million dollars at the time) and about 500 million roubles in valuables and securities, soon to be stored in Soviet coffers.[27] Gold and 'the head of Kolchak', it would appear, 'had to serve as the purchase price for free transit to the East'.[28]

Let us consider for a moment this Russian treasure. From the late summer of 1918 to September 1919, Britain, whose aid was always the most generous of all the Allies to the White Russian cause, contributed to the various Russian theatres during that year munitions and equipment valued at 100 million pounds.[29] France, over the same period, made a contribution of between thirty and forty millions.[30]

In Siberia alone, British ships carrying stores continued to arrive at Vladivostok after voyages halfway around the world until October 1919; and in all, seventy-nine vessels brought a hundred thousand tons of arms, ammunition, equipment and clothing for Kolchak's armies.[31] It will be seen that the value of the trainload of treasure handed over in one neat package by Janin to the Soviet government—indirectly, it is true—was not far short of the value of the total Anglo-French effort to the White armies for a year, and would undoubtedly sustain the impoverished Bolsheviks in their struggle for victory in the civil war, in spreading propaganda, and in attempting to promote revolutions on the Bolshevik pattern in other parts of Europe.

We may question the necessity for turning over either the gold or the person of Admiral Kolchak to the Political Centre at all. It cannot be supposed that the Czechs, if they had a mind to, could not have forced their way through Irkutsk with both the Admiral and the gold. If they had no inclination to do so—and relations between Kolchak and the Czechs had never been good—there was little reason to offer protection and safe conduct in the first place; when Kolchak accepted in all good faith, he left his own guards behind and was thereafter at the mercy of the Czechs. Surely it would have been better to leave him to his own devices—to give him a sporting chance. Part of the White Army under General Kappel, not far behind Kolchak, retained enough cohesion and discipline to fight through the partisan bands and to reach Semenov's territory east of Lake Baikal, and in company with these troops, his extrication was at least possible. Janin shrugged the matter off. He was responsible, he said, to the Government in Prague and the Inter-Allied Council for the safe evacuation of the Czechs. He had not set himself 'against the instructions I received so as to risk the destruction of the Czechoslovak Army for the sake of that man . . .'; for the Czar and his family, he went on, less fuss had been made.[32]

Again, Japanese forces in Irkutsk could have rescued the Admiral had a lead been given; as it was, they did not assume the responsibility. And the Americans? The nearest troops were those under Colonel Morrow guarding the Verkhne-Udinsk sector of the Trans-Siberian Railway to the east of Lake Baikal. They of course had no intention of getting mixed up in Kolchak's problem despite the United States' promised help in establishing the Admiral as head of an all-Russian government. Morrow permitted Semenov to send troops through his sector to put down the new authority at Irkutsk, and then, alarmed at the arbitrary acts of Semenov's subordinates in the area under his control, he applied restrictions. Fighting, which resulted in the death of two Americans and five Russians, broke out at the village of Posolskaya on the night of 10th January between the crew of one of Semenov's armoured trains and an American detachment.[33] In the end, fourteen hundred of Semenov's troops were disarmed by the Americans and the Czechs before it was felt safe to withdraw through the Ataman's territory on their way to the coast a fortnight later.[34] Semenov's proposed attack on Irkutsk came to nothing; his approach, in fact, had the opposite effect to that intended, as it merely precipitated the execution of Admiral Kolchak.

Six days after incarcerating Kolchak in the Irkutsk jail, the Political Centre, after a short life of only sixteen days and having achieved its main purpose of securing the Imperial gold and the person of the former Supreme Ruler, was replaced by a Soviet Military Revolutionary Committee,[35] which appointed an investigating commission to cross-examine the prisoner. The hearing was never finished. The threat posed by Semenov from the east combined with the approach of Kappel's last organized remnants of the White armies* from the west (demanding the immediate liberation of Kolchak) only hastened his inevitable death.[36] The Irkutsk Revolutionary Committee received authority from the Fifth Red Army to execute the former leader at its discretion.[37]

Kolchak had no illusions. He knew that the approach of his troops against Irkutsk would not avert his end. It was admitted by his captors that he carried himself with courage and dignity throughout his period of imprisonment. On 7th February, before dawn, he was executed by firing squad in the light of a truck's headlamps. His body was pushed through an ice hole in a tributary of the river Angara. The ordeal of this honest patriot was at last over.[38]

Kappel's force now swung away to bypass the town and reached Eastern Siberia unmolested. The fall of Kolchak marked the end of operations in Western Siberia; more than that, it was the end of Allied intervention, for twenty-four hours after the Czechs surrendered Kolchak to his enemies, the Supreme Council of the Allies in Paris decided to lift the blockade and trade with the Soviet Government.[39]

The question now arises, why did the White movement in Siberia fail? In the early summer of 1918, when the Czech Corps took up arms against the Bolsheviks in self-defence, they enjoyed the popular support of Siberians, irrespective of party. Anti-Bolshevik revolts flared up in town after town, rendering the task of the Czechs particularly easy; there was no large urban proletariat to be stirred by the Bolshevik leaders into effective resistance, and the peasant population remained largely apathetic. Social conditions, it would appear, favoured the ending of Communism to a much greater extent in Siberia than anywhere else, and from Siberia, with effective Allied aid, lay the best avenue for the overthrow of Communism in the rest

* General Kappel himself died from exposure on the way from Omsk.

of Russia. Why, then, should all this collapse in little more than a year?

A good many American students of the period, apparently anxious to justify the 'neutral' role adopted by General Graves, lay the blame on Kolchak; Stewart, for example, writes that the 'chief cause of failure' was the Admiral himself.[40] They point to the fact that he had little experience in the administrative fields and made no attempt to carry out social and political reforms. His government was a military régime, formed for the purpose of winning the war, which saw for itself no other function than raising armies and gathering funds to support them. 'The total absence of any radical land legislation to win the allegiance of the peasant and civil administration capable of assuring townsmen of a just and stable government estranged the common people.'[41]

While it is true that Kolchak had no political experience and his aim was 'the revival of the fighting power of the army, the triumph over Bolshevism, and the restoration of law and order so that the Russian people may without hindrance select its own form of government',[42] it can hardly be concluded that the personality of Kolchak or his programme were primarily responsible for White failure. We have noted his shortcomings. Yet as a man he was honest, loyal, and incorruptible. Kolchak was considered by Churchill to be 'the best man available' in Siberia, and as for his programme, there was 'no doubt that this . . . met the needs of the moment'.[43] The educated and middle classes, including the principal trading and industrial circles and the co-operatives, all supported Kolchak, as did the army. In addition, many thousands of persons who had sought refuge from Bolshevism in Siberia were all firmly behind him,[44] and the peasant, as previously noted, owned his land; the issue of landlordism, a burning question in European Russia, did not exist. Conditions in Russia under the Bolsheviks, with their insane programme, were worse during this period than at any time in Siberia under Kolchak, the strongest proof of this being the number of intelligent people who were willing to leave all that they had, to endure every deprivation, and even to risk death itself rather than live under Soviet rule. Yet the Bolsheviks won.

A review of the course which intervention followed forces one to the inescapable conclusion that the main reason for White failure in Siberia, far from being the personality of Kolchak or his programme, was the meddling of the Allied interveners. They brought with them little good; on the contrary, they did much harm. Without them, White forces would have had free access to the vast supplies at Vladivostok; the Trans-Siberian would have been in their hands for the circulation of the necessities of life as well as for the transportation of munitions and war supplies. Without Japan, it seems that economic chaos and civil unrest would have been unlikely; further, Semenov (whose cruelties and interference with the railway contributed largely to the collapse of the Kolchak Government) could have been cleared from the line without difficulty—though in the absence of Japan it is doubtful if he would have taken the stand he did. The Czechs, who quit the battle line largely because of Allied inactivity (thus depriving the Whites of their best troops), might have been induced to stay. And there would have been no discouragement caused through the Prinkipo proposals and piecemeal withdrawal. Nor can it be ignored that the invasion by foreigners (as intervention was undoubtedly regarded by the majority of Russians), themselves unable to agree in aim or action, contributed to the achievement of Russian unity under the Bolsheviks. As it was, intervention led almost at once to the throttling of Kolchak's supply line and to political disorder—and in assigning reasons for his failure, this must above all be accorded first place.

Siberia was the best theatre for effective intervention. Had the Americans and the Japanese been able to settle their differences, says Churchill, 'concerted efforts could quite easily have sustained Kolchak'.[45] But no central body was ever set up to study and concert Allied policy; the folly of an international intervention without an international command was not fully appreciated. Though events in the First World War had brought about the appointment of Foch as Commander-in-Chief, and though it had been deemed advisable to follow this precedent in Siberia, support for Otani was never more than half-hearted; the Americans found it very easy to circumvent the Japanese command, and the French and British ignored him later when Japanese disruptive tactics had become apparent. These mistakes were not repeated when, in 1950, Communism was at last effectively opposed in Korea; at that time it was realized that a united organization must be built.

Warnings were sounded but were ignored. In February 1919, Churchill pointed out the real cause of weakness to Lloyd George: 'military considerations', he wrote, 'are at every point intermingled with political decisions which have not been given'.[46] A fortnight later he termed the four months following the Armistice as 'disastrous almost without relief' for the anti-Bolsheviks, due not to any great increase in Bolshevik strength, but to 'lack of any policy on the part of the Allies, or of any genuine or effective support put into the operations'.[47] What would be the results of such lack of policy were quite clear to him. 'Whereas by taking the proper concerted measures we could, without any large additional employment of men or money, have established an anti-Bolshevik and modernized Russia . . . we are now within measurable distance of a Bolshevik Russia thoroughly militarized . . . bitterly hostile. . . .' 'It is a delusion', he continued, 'to suppose that all this year we have been fighting the battles of the anti-Bolshevik Russians. On the contrary, they have been fighting ours; and this truth will become painfully apparent from the moment that they are exterminated and the Bolshevik armies are supreme over the whole vast territories of the Russian Empire.'[48]

'Had harmony prevailed among the internationalists and between them and the counter-revolutionary elements,' MacNair and Lach conclude, '. . . it may be doubted that the Bolshevist government . . . would have survived';[49] but there was no harmony. The nearest approach to it came in June 1919 when the five plenipotentiaries at Versailles promised support for Kolchak. The nature of this support may be judged from the action of the French general Janin in turning Kolchak over to his executioners and in handing White Russian gold to the Bolsheviks, while Japan and the United States stood passively by. Without harmony, it would have been infinitely better for the Allies to have stayed out of Siberia and to have confined their help to the supply of surplus munitions to the White Russian forces.

The death of Kolchak marked the start of a general Allied withdrawal from Siberia. The Canadians and the British, as we have seen, had already gone, and as early as December 27, 1919, when Kolchak was in retreat from Omsk, General Graves advised his government that the 'safety of American troops demands concentration'.[50] The reply was not long delayed; he was to begin concentrating his force prior to a probable withdrawal.[51] The Americans indeed were serving no useful purpose; only in attempting to keep Japan from seizing eastern Siberia had they had some success, and even in that sphere the Japanese were more firmly established than they had been when the Americans arrived.[52] There was the constant danger that some isolated incident could spark open hostilities with Japan, as had been narrowly avoided at Posolskaya.[53]

On January 9, 1920, the State Department, in reply to a Japanese note of a month before, formally announced that American troops would be withdrawn; the objectives of the intervention as outlined in Wilson's *Aide Mémoire*, had been achieved as far as possible.[54] Graves, unfortunately, prior to the official announcement, issued a statement concerning the decision to withdraw, and Japan seized upon this as a pretext to remain in sole occupation; the sudden decision ('even without awaiting the complete departure of Czechoslovak troops') made without consultation, the Japanese Government claimed, rendered a simultaneous withdrawal impossible.[55] Thus, when the last of the American troops left Vladivostok on 1st April we find the Japanese still there and a Japanese band lining the docks and lustily playing 'Hard Times Come Again No More'![56]

The Czechs were given priority of shipping space over the other Allied forces—Poles, Serbs and Italians—and by May 24, 1920, all the Czechs had reached Vladivostok.[57] In June many of them crossed Canada en route to Europe[58] and by September the last of them had sailed from Vladivostok.[59]

The sequel can be told briefly. With the execution of Kolchak, the Socialist Revolutionaries and the militarists ceased to be significant west of Lake Baikal. The whole of western Siberia was incorporated into Soviet Russia. East of Lake Baikal, the Japanese and anti-Bolshevik groups still impeded the Bolsheviks. It might have been expected that the Soviet forces would have followed up their destruction of Kolchak's armies by advancing eastwards in an attempt to impose themselves on all the former territories of the Russian Empire, but such a policy would have brought them into direct conflict with Japan.[60] A fight against Japanese troops was out of the question for the newly created Red Army—'In the Far East the outstanding fact was the military weakness of the Soviet Government . . . it could not wage a war against Japan.'[61] 'Such a war', said Lenin, 'is beyond our strength.'[62]

Other courses were therefore necessary and were shortly to be improvised by the Soviets in the setting up of a buffer state—the Far Eastern Republic—which was nominally independent but in reality a satellite of the Soviet Union, and in promoting disagreement between America and Japan. It is interesting to note that Semenov,* who had been driven out of the Trans-Baikal in March, coolly

* Semenov lived until 1945, when he was captured and executed by the Red Army during operations on the Asiatic mainland against Japan.

offered his services as commander-in-chief of the armies of the new republic and 'protector' of the state.[63]

Not until October 25, 1922, did the last Japanese troops, under American pressure, finally quit Siberia. Until that date a conflict between America and Japan seemed not improbable. Naval construction in the United States and in Japan proceeded at high speed until 1922,[64] and the thread which led to Pearl Harbor can already be discerned. With the departure of Japanese troops the Far Eastern Republic removed the mask and dissolved itself. The whole of northern Eurasia, save Poland, the Baltic States, and Finland, had with this been brought under Moscow's rule.

SOUTH RUSSIA

The end of January 1919 saw Denikin firmly established in South Russia, his flanks protected by British flotillas on the Black and Caspian seas. This came about in accordance with the Anglo-French Convention of 1917, reaffirmed by the War Cabinet two days after the Armistice, whereby 'spheres of influence' were apportioned between the two countries. A British fleet entered the Black Sea as soon as the Dardanelles had been reopened, and a British military commission was sent to Novorossisk.[65] Troops, landed at Batum, occupied the 400 miles of Caucasian railway between that port and Baku and in addition a flotilla based at Baku on the Caspian soon secured effective command of that great inland sea.* Ships for the British Caspian Flotilla were found by arming Russian vessels, and by sending twelve coastal motor boats by rail. There were also forty seaplanes. The flotilla was turned over to Denikin on July 20, 1919. In all, a British force some 20,000 strong on the Batum–Baku line was by February protecting Turkey, Kurdistan, and Persia from Bolshevik incursions as well as safeguarding the independence of three new republics, Georgia, Azerbaidjan and Armenia; this it continued to do, without fighting, for about a year.† Of interest to Denikin, aside from British sea power on the two seas, was the decision taken by the War Cabinet on November 14, 1918, to assist him with arms and munitions.[67]

* A good account of British naval activities in Caspian waters during this period has been given by a Canadian who served there.[66]

† British troops left Baku and Tiflis in the summer of 1919. They did not leave Batum until July 1920, when the civil war had virtually ended in favour of the Soviets.

French entry into part of their sphere consisting of Bessarabia, the Ukraine, and the Crimea ended disastrously, and in order to understand it, some description of developments in the Ukraine must be given. The Germans, though a clause in the Armistice prescribed that German troops would remain on Russian soil until the Allies saw fit to recall them, had been obliged to evacuate the Ukraine immediately. It is now clear that such a condition was unwise without a force furnished by the Allies on the ground to replace them. No such force, however, had been arranged for, and the German withdrawal had the effect of removing the only authority which could prevent factional strife and preserve authority. On the departure of the Germans, the Bolsheviks quickly attempted to fill the vacuum.[68]

The three main contenders for power in the Ukraine were the Soviets, General Denikin, and a Ukrainian nationalist, Simon Petlura, who had been War Minister in the government of the Ukrainian Rada, and the rivalry between the various contending parties marked out the Ukraine for a period of desperate anarchy throughout 1919 and 1920.

The first round in the struggle for the Ukraine went to the nationalist Petlura. Bolshevik requisitioning detachments roused the general population against them, while Denikin—firm in his denial of the Ukraine's right to a national language and to political independence—was no more popular than the Reds.

In December 1918 the Bolsheviks moved against the Ukraine. Petlura's forces, which lacked arms and munitions, could do little to throw back the better-equipped Red troops. Against this background the French made the most ambitious attempt at direct military intervention of all the Allies during the course of the Russian Civil War. On 18th December French troops landed at Odessa, which they found in a state of chaos; Denikin's representatives, Petlurists, the local council, and Bolsheviks (who were emerging from the underground), all claimed power. The French recognized only the representatives of Denikin, and appointed one of his senior officers military governor of the city. Denikin himself hoped that the French would replace the Germans as an anti-Bolshevik force capable of maintaining order throughout the whole of the Ukraine.[69] It seemed that the French, with associated troops, had sufficient strength to do so.

Interventionist forces at first numbered 6000 French, 2000 Greeks and 4000 Poles. These were augmented until the French and Greeks had two divisions each, and in addition a Roumanian contingent was brought in; altogether some 45,000 foreign troops occupied the Odessa region, while a further force of 7500 French and Greeks entered the neighbouring Crimea. The proclaimed object of the French was to give 'the healthy and patriotic elements' the opportunity of restoring order, but these they found to be utterly confused. Few organized Russian troops existed—Denikin's Volunteer Army was fully occupied elsewhere, while the military forces of Petlura's Directory were extremely weak, made up largely of peasant levies, and without the trained officers and the munitions necessary for large-scale operations. If any real fighting was to be done, it was evident that the French would have to do it. Meanwhile, the Red advance into the Ukraine swept forward, meeting little opposition.[70]

The French pushed towards the north to meet the Bolshevik thrust, and by February had occupied the towns of Tiraspol, Kherson and Nikolaev, but already there were disturbing signs. French morale, understandable perhaps after a World War, was low, nor should it be forgotten that even during the life-or-death struggle on the Western Front, 'acts of collective indiscipline' had occurred in the French armies following the Nivelle offensive of 1917, when no less than eighty grave incidents took place between 25th May–10th June. These took the form of 'manifestations against the war, revolutionary songs'; 'refusal to go up to the trenches, especially to attack'; and the waving of red flags at the windows of trains.[71] Now a similar situation arose. French soldiers wore red rosettes; men refused to obey orders, and some even deserted to the Reds. The Communists seized on this opportunity to disorganize still further the hostile forces by means of propaganda, and a newspaper *Le Communiste* urged the French to remember their own revolution and not to interfere with this one. All of which had effect.

Having prepared the ground, the Soviet forces now moved south, using Ataman Grigoriev to spearhead their drive. This man, a Ukrainian nationalist, had sensed the forthcoming success of the Bolsheviks and had crossed over from the Petlurist to the Soviet side. His partisans led a spirited attack on Kherson and Nikolaev. Between 10th and 12th March, both towns fell, and French losses amounting to some 400 killed and wounded helped demoralize the troops in the field as well as their naval and military garrison at Odessa. Grigoriev pressed on towards the Black Sea port.[72]

The French authorities, shocked by the failure of their troops and

apprehensive that flagging morale could bring more disastrous results, decided to terminate the whole adventure. Little time was
wasted. Orders from Paris reached Odessa on 2nd April and by the
6th the last French ship steamed away. That day Grigoriev's partisans entered the city before sweeping on to occupy the Crimea.[73]

Denikin had put a small detachment of the Volunteer Army in
the Crimea, and this was insufficiently strong to hold the natural
defence line across the Isthmus of Perekop. That gone, the French
decided to evacuate the Crimea as well as the Ukraine. At the end
of April, Soviet troops were in full occupation of the Crimea with
the exception of the Kertch region at the eastern extremity of the
peninsula.[74]

The Soviets followed up Grigoriev's victories by some of their own
over Petlura in various Ukrainian towns. His forces were driven
from several centres west of the river Dnieper—Zhitomir, Kamenetz-
Podolsk and Tiraspol—and Petlura himself was forced into eastern
Galicia, a No Man's Land between the Polish and Soviet fronts.
Thus, at the end of April, the Soviet régime was again in power over
all the Ukraine with the exception of part of the Donetz Basin which
was held by Denikin.[75]

Meanwhile Denikin had become involved in the Don fighting
which followed an advance of the Reds on this front as well as in the
Ukraine at the end of 1918. Here the Red Army attacked in strength
—some 100,000 infantry and 17,000 cavalry massed against 76,000
Don Cossacks under Ataman Krasnov. Krasnov's long left flank
formed by the western frontier of the Don Territory had previously
been covered by the German occupation of the Ukraine and in these
favourable circumstances, during the summer, he had almost cleared
the Don Territory of Red forces; he had also launched attacks
against the Volga towns of Saratov and Tsaritsin. These, stubbornly
defended by the Reds, eluded him, Stalin being a prominent figure
at Tsaritsin* where resistance was especially important; its fall in
1918 would have made possible the junction of the White Russian
forces in the east and in the south which had been the dream of
Alexeiev. With the withdrawal of German forces from the Ukraine
after the Armistice, Krasnov was forced to cover his exposed left
flank in addition to opposing the main Bolshevik drive from the
north. Furthermore, he had owed much to German arms and supplies, of which he was now deprived. Cossack morale suffered in

* Later renamed Stalingrad.

consequence, and the ground gained during the summer outside the Don Territory soon fell to the Reds, as did the northern Don regions. The Red forces pushed on irresistibly during January, and in February Novo-Cherkassk, the Don capital, and Rostov were seriously threatened.[76]

At this critical stage of the Don fighting the uneasy relationship which had existed between Krasnov and Denikin came to an end. Krasnov, under British pressure, had recognized Denikin as the White commander in South Russia, but his support was never whole-hearted. In February, the Don Krug (Parliament) at Novo-Cherkassk passed a vote of non-confidence in Krasnov's military leaders, where-upon the Ataman also resigned. His successor, General Bogavesky, worked very closely with Denikin, now recognized as the undisputed leader of the White movement in South Russia.[77]

At the end of January, as we have seen, Denikin had cleared the North Caucasus of Red forces; thus he was free to support the Don Cossacks. The arrival of his troops, combined with a lull obtained through the spring flooding of the rivers which temporarily halted the Red advance, made possible the reorganization of the Don Army; both Rostov and Novo-Cherkassk were held. The strategy of the Reds in their campaign against the Don Territory is open to criticism. They had the choice of approaching Rostov and the Don capital through the Donetz Basin, the largest coal-producing region of Russia well served by railways, or through the Don steppes where road and rail facilities were much less favourable. It might have been supposed that the Bolsheviks would have concentrated on the strate-gically important Donetz Basin with its population made up largely of workers, likely to be sympathetic to their cause, but instead they advanced through the steppe country north and north-east of Rostov, inhabited by Cossacks, which lacked the strategic and economic sig-nificance of the basin.

Denikin was quick to appreciate the Soviet error. Hand-picked troops from the Volunteer Army under General Mai-Maevsky entered the southern part of the Donetz Basin, where they effectively barred the Red approach to Rostov and the important port of Tagan-rog, on the Sea of Azov. Attacks by greatly superior forces were repulsed by forming a considerable reserve which was thrown as quickly as the network of railway lines permitted against any threat-ened breakthrough. This skilful use of troops led the Soviets to believe that Mai-Maevsky had many more men than he actually possessed. The right wing of the Soviet armies was never able to break his resistance, and meanwhile the reorganized Don Army checked the Soviet centre on the line of the Donetz river. A sudden uprising of the Cossacks in the stanitsas of the upper Don against Bolshevik occupation by its stubbornness and success effectively ended the deadlock, and was in fact a prelude to Soviet defeat in the Don and Donetz regions. Red forces sent against the insurrectionists, whose numbers had swelled to 30,000, were defeated.[78]

Denikin's great opportunity was now to hand, and he grasped it firmly. Aided by British tanks, he turned swiftly to the offensive and smashed four Red armies in simultaneous attacks at the end of May and during the first few days of June. In the Donetz Basin, Cossack cavalry broke through the defences of the Eighth and Thirteenth Red Armies and put then to rout; the Thirteenth was so demoralized that it fell back 200 miles before it could again be formed into any sort of order. The Don Cossack Army, along the Donetz north and east of Rostov, crossed the river to hurl back the Ninth Red Army distracted by the Cossack uprising to its rear. These victories were rounded out when Wrangel broke up the Tenth Red Army, which had reached the river Manich in an attempt to take Rostov from the south-east, driving it back towards Tsaritsin. Sweeping advances followed during June : Kharkov fell on the 25th, and five days later Wrangel seized the elusive prize of Tsaritsin. Thus, by the end of the month, Denikin (now designated Commander of the Armed Forces of South Russia) was master of all the Don Territory, of part of the Eastern Ukraine including the Donetz Basin, and of the region north of the Sea of Azov including Ekaterinoslav on the river Dnieper.

It was now a question of exploiting success. Had Kolchak been advancing in June, instead of in April and May, Denikin's strategy would obviously have aimed at a link-up between the Siberian and southern theatres. Now, when an advance up the Volga was completely practicable with the capture of Tsaritsin, Kolchak was already retreating. Wrangel, however, still advocated a Volga thrust : the main effort, he said, should be made by his Caucasian Army on the right pushed forward on a narrow front with the goal of ultimate union with Kolchak. General Sidorin, whose Don Cossack Army was in the centre, favoured a cautious policy, the aim of which would be the consolidation of regions at present occupied before undertaking any further offensive.[79]

The plan finally adopted by Denikin on 3rd July called for the employment of all his armies on as wide a front as possible, having as their object the capture of Moscow and the heart of Russia. This was an ambitious programme, and was to become more so. On the left Mai-Maevsky, who now commanded the Volunteer Army since Denikin had assumed overall command, would advance with two objectives in view : first, a direct advance from Kharkov to Moscow along the railway; second, the capture of Kiev to the west, and of Nikolaev and Kherson in the South Ukraine. Sidorin and his Don Army would strike northwards in a direct thrust on Moscow, while on the right Wrangel's Caucasian Army would advance on the same objective by way of Saratov on the Volga. Not only were the White Russians dispersed over an extremely broad front by the terms of this order; subsequent embroilment in the Ukraine was to lead them as far west as the Dniester, a far wider dispersal than Denikin had ever contemplated in July. Under the circumstances prevailing in the Russian Civil War, to have stood still would in all probability have been fatal to the White cause, and in this can be found the reason for Denikin's employment of all his armies in simultaneous offensives. But concentration of force is a major principle of war, and better military results could have been expected from a shorter front, resting no further to the west than on the Dnieper, and on a concentration for one major drive on Moscow by the direct route Kursk–Orel–Tula. Incursions into the Ukraine soon led Denikin to conclude that he had incurred a military liability rather than an asset. Guerrilla activities there could have been relied upon to keep Soviet forces fully occupied without the diversion of White troops from the main objective.[80]

The balance of military success during July and August went to the Whites, but their gains were in the wrong direction. Both the eastern and central sectors of the front remained relatively static. Wrangel, on the right, pushed forward to Kamishin, a town on the Volga halfway between Tsaritsin and Saratov, but under the pressure of superior Red forces he was forced to abandon it and to fall back on Tsaritsin. This town he held firmly. In the centre Sidorin made little headway until 10th August, when a picked group of Cossack cavalry numbering about 8000 broke through the Soviet front near Novokhopersk, penetrated far to the Soviet rear, and finally returned to the White lines on 19th September after covering some 500 miles. This was no more than a large-scale raid, however, and though it helped break up a Red offensive launched during

August, it led to no spectacular advance of the main front towards Moscow. This deadlock on the right and in the centre was attributable to Denikin's lack of real strength at any given point coupled with a build-up of Soviet strength during July. The Bolshevik leaders had appreciated their critical position on the Southern Front, and had striven desperately to reinforce their armies and seize the initiative. Two offensives launched by them in August, however, failed. The first, aimed at Volchansk and Kupiansk with a view to exploiting in the direction of Kharkov and Belgorod, was turned back without difficulty, while the second, mounted against the northern Don and Tsaritsin, took the line of greatest resistance and was also repulsed.[81]

Meanwhile the White forces on the left had profited from Soviet preoccupation with guerrilla activities in the Ukraine. Mai-Maevsky, in sweeping advances, captured Poltava on 31st July, Kherson and Nikolaev on 18th August, Odessa on the 23rd, and Kiev on 31st August.[82]

The failure of the Soviet offensives during August enabled Denikin to recover the initiative, and this led to further gains in the Ukraine and, more important, to an advance of the centre of his front north of Kharkov in accordance with the original plan. Mai-Maevsky and his Volunteer Army captured Kursk, after bitter fighting, on 20th September. The Don town of Voronezh, east of Kursk, fell on 6th October, and six days later the Whites, pressing north from Kiev, captured Chernigov near the Ukraine's northern border. Denikin had now achieved a forward penetration of some 100 miles on a 300-mile front, and the high-water mark was soon to come when his troops, advancing rapidly from Kursk, covered a further hundred miles in seven days and, on 13th October, entered Orel on the direct road to Moscow. The Whites were now within 250 miles of the Soviet capital and only Tula, an important munitions centre, barred their way.

The spirits of the majority of the White troops would undoubtedly be high at this stage of the campaign. Fighting during 1919 had brought them from the rugged Caucasus well into the heart of Russia. They now controlled regions containing thirty millions of European Russians including the third, fourth and fifth largest cities of Russia. Between April and October they had taken a quarter of a million prisoners, 700 guns, 1700 machine guns and thirty-five armoured trains. Behind them, British munitions (no longer sent to

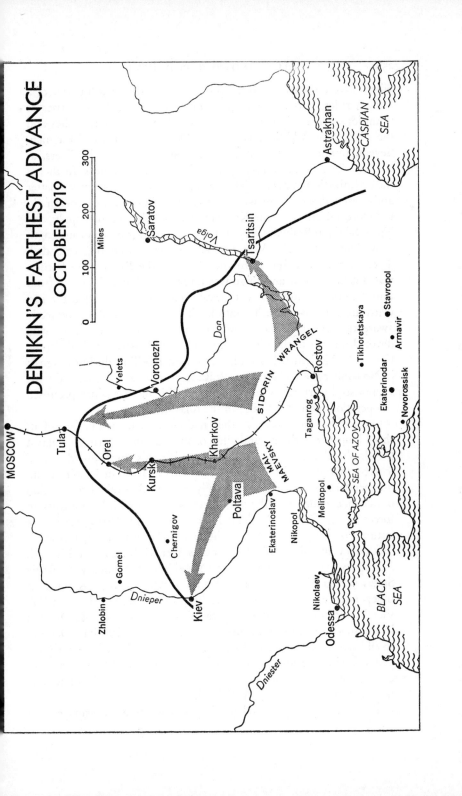

DENIKIN'S FARTHEST ADVANCE

OCTOBER 1919

Miles

0   100   200   300

MOSCOW

Tula

Orel

Kursk

Yelets

Voronezh

Chernigov

Poltava

Kharkov

MAI-MAEVSKY

SIDORIN

WRANGEL

Rostov

Taganrog

Ekaterinoslav

Nikopol

Melitopol

SEA OF AZOV

Ekaterinodar

Novorossisk

Tikhoretskaya

Armavir

Stavropol

Tsaritsin

Saratov

Astrakhan

CASPIAN SEA

Volga

Don

Dnieper

Kiev

Nikolaev

Odessa

Dniester

BLACK SEA

Gomel

Zhlobin

Siberia) were pouring into the port of Novorossisk : a 'quarter of a million rifles, two hundred guns, thirty tanks and large masses of munitions and equipment'[83] in all arrived via the Dardanelles and the Black Sea. Additionally, though Denikin never asked for men, 'several hundred British officers and non-commissioned officers, as advisers, instructors, store-keepers and even a few aviators, furthered the organization of his armies'.[84] Southern Russia was a much better anti-Bolshevik base than was Siberia. Denikin could use foreign aid far more effectively than Kolchak, whose sole line of supply, the Trans-Siberian Railway, was in hostile hands over much of its length as we have noted. The White armies, however, were over-extended. Their front, stretching from the Volga to the Roumanian border, was but thinly held and there was no reserve. And behind the front unrest caused Denikin to withdraw even more troops from the forward areas to re-establish control. Ukrainian nationalists, perfectly aware that independence would never be granted by a man who devoted himself to the ideal of an undivided Russia, revolted. In the Caucasus, Moslem tribes broke into open rebellion during August; in November the Kuban Cossack Rada, bent on autonomy, had to be suppressed by armed force and replaced with another which promised co-operation with the Whites in the final struggle.

Outside Russia's borders other nations which, on the face of it, should have been the natural allies of Denikin in his struggle against the Bolsheviks were obviously disturbed by his shortsighted refusal to recognize the right of any part of the old Russian Empire to an independent existence. Finland, fully mobilized, awaited recognition of her independence as the price of co-operation with White Russian forces under General Yudenitch in a march on Petrograd in the autumn of 1919. Kolchak, to whom the offer was made, refused it (his policy in this being the same as Denikin's), so that Finland, having received no encouragement, stood idly by. Similarly the Baltic States (Lithuania, Latvia, and Estonia), without any assurance of independence, had no incentive to keep up pressure against the Bolsheviks and thus prevent a withdrawal of Red forces to face Denikin in the south. The Roumanians, convinced that a victorious Denikin would never permit them to retain Bessarabia, hoped for an independent Ukraine and were sympathetic towards Petlura. Of most consequence to the fortunes of the Armed Forces of South Russia, however, was the attitude of Poland.

The Poles, who provided the largest and strongest army at war with the Soviets, had taken advantage of the Civil War and the confused conditions in the Ukraine to advance steadily, involving the Soviets in continuous expenditures in men and munitions, until, in August, the Polish line stood on Ukrainian soil. The White Russian offensive against Kiev at the end of August was undertaken solely to establish contact with the Poles with the object of future cooperation; without securing that goal, the dangerous lengthening of the White Russian front as far as Kiev would be futile. The least Denikin could expect was that the Poles would keep up the pressure, continuing to defeat the Bolsheviks on their borders, to prevent a transfer of Red troops opposite the main White Russian thrust; at best, he could hope for a Polish advance as far as the Dnieper to safeguard his western flank and enable him to bring troops forward for the drive on Moscow. A truce with the Ukrainian nationalists combined with steady pressure by the Poles might well have been decisive.

Polish aid, however, was not forthcoming. A meeting between the White general and a Polish mission at Taganrog in September arrived at no agreement. Neither of Denikin's expectations was ever fulfilled, both of them foundering on the rock of Poland's national aspirations. Though a victorious Denikin would recognize the Poles' independence, he would not countenance a Polish eastern frontier such as Poland's Marshal Pilsudski wished—fixed to include territory inhabited by millions of White Russians, Ukrainians, and Lithuanians. During the next two decisive months the Polish armies remained inactive, observing a *de facto* armistice with the Soviets, while Denikin's front was stretched to the utmost as a result of his abortive bid.

These antagonisms were beyond the powers of the White general to resolve. Furthermore, they were combined with administrative problems in the areas which Denikin occupied, brought about through the lack of any positive programme : White propaganda confined itself to a denunciation of the Communist régime without outlining what would replace it. Denikin was already fully occupied with military affairs and the conduct of the war, and had no resources with which to restore prosperity and the well-being of the general population. His one conviction, that Russia should not be dismembered, alienated all his potential allies in the war against Soviet Russia. This, then, was the position in October, when he stood poised for the attack on Moscow.

I

One thing was certain : Denikin's attack would have to be successful; the conditions behind his lines could only deteriorate in the face
of any major reverse.

A BID FOR PETROGRAD

Denikin's offensive on Moscow was co-ordinated with a lunge on
Petrograd from Estonia by the White general Yudenitch; before
returning to South Russia the fate of this will be examined.

As in the Ukraine, the Bolsheviks took advantage of the breakdown of German military power at the end of 1918 to bring the
formerly German occupied Baltic States—Lithuania, Latvia, and
Estonia—under their domination. That these countries declared their
independence of Russia in November 1918, that they were recognized by the All-Russian Soviet Executive Committee in December,
that the principal Allies soon afterwards accorded *de facto* recognition—all this meant little. The Bolsheviks paid lip service to the doctrine of self-determination, but in practice their policy was to use
this doctrine to reconstitute the former Russian Empire under the
Communist system by forcibly bringing seceding states together
again as a federation of Soviet Republics. This had become apparent
in Finland and in the Ukraine.

Soviet occupation of Latvia, Lithuania, eastern Poland and part of
Estonia, did not last long. Local forces, aided by German irregulars
and the British navy, succeeded in driving out the invaders—from
Estonia in February 1919, Latvia in May, and from Lithuania and
eastern Poland until, in the summer, a front was established east of
Minsk. By this time it had become evident to the Bolshevik leaders
that the threats presented by Kolchak in the east and Denikin in the
south demanded the concentration of all Soviet military strength in the
interior of Russia; nothing was left over for expansion to the west.

Meanwhile, a White Russian North-western force in Estonia was
growing, but Estonian support was never more than half-hearted. A
broad constructive policy by Kolchak towards Estonia would have
assured the willing co-operation of that country in the Baltic theatre.
In addition, in May 1919, Mannerheim pledged the support of Finland on the Baltic in exchange for recognition of Finnish independence, but it was not until the White Russian campaign against Petrograd had completely failed—Finland remaining aloof—that Kolchak
did at last accord his recognition. The stubborn unwillingness of the

Whites to make concessions which would have rallied Estonia and Finland to their support was a not inconsiderable factor in their ultimate failure as has been remarked in their attitude towards Poland and the Ukraine.

The American Relief Administration took in hand the provision of food both for White Russian troops and for the civil population of liberated districts. Through Churchill, the prime supporter of the North-western anti-Bolshevik movement, Britain promised to provide the war materials necessary for a White offensive. It is also possible that still more assistance might have been given had it not been for the head of the British Military Mission to the Baltic area, General Sir Hubert Gough (who had commanded an army in the Great War). Balfour's policy in the north following the Armistice, as we have seen, had been to protect the 'nascent nationalities' in the Baltic with the help of the fleet, and to supply the Baltic States with military material. Churchill extended this policy to include White Russian troops in the Baltic area, and expected Gough (as becomes clear from the latter's memoirs) to co-operate fully in an anti-Bolshevik campaign. Before the general proceeded to the Baltic, Lord Curzon, the new Foreign Secretary, saw him and warned against any encouragement of Mannerheim to march on Petrograd : the Foreign Office, he said, was against interference in Russian affairs in that area, and he had no wish for England to help install foreign troops in the Russian city. This policy was diametrically opposed to that of the British War Minister. As head of a Military Mission, Gough came directly under Churchill, and might have been expected to loyally carry out his master's policy, which was again made clear to him before his departure. But Gough neither implemented his final instructions nor did he ask for clarification : instead, he chose to treat his interview with the Foreign Secretary as 'confidential' and to act in strict accordance with Curzon's wishes while he remained chief of the Baltic Mission.[85]

At the end of September 1918 General Nicholas Yudenitch had a North-western force of about 20,000 men. American food had arrived in June; British munitions consisting of four tanks, six planes, 3000 rifles, 15,000,000 rounds of ammunition, as well as equipment for 10,000 men, in August; and more British supplies were arriving. The White general decided that the moment was propitious for a move on Petrograd. An offensive, if risked now, would have more chance of success than if left until later, and it could be co-ordinated with that of Denikin on Moscow. There was another consideration. The army might break up if left inactive. Desertions in the past few weeks had reduced its strength from 25,000 to its present number, whereas the Bolsheviks had managed to build up to 25,000 their Seventh Red Army standing between Yudenitch and Petrograd. At best, however, it was a risky venture. Another Red Army, the Fifteenth, lay further to the south, and this would threaten the flank and rear of the North-western Army as it hurled itself directly on the Seventh Army and the old capital. Petrograd itself, a Communist stronghold, contained tens of thousands of dedicated revolutionaries who could be counted on to resist the Whites to the end. But Yudenitch was close to the city and in Petrograd he had a limited objective; its loss might well stun the Bolsheviks and stir up general revolt against them. On balance, therefore, the gamble had to be taken.

The plan formulated by the White Russian commander had the merit of simplicity. The bulk of his force would attack in the north, seize Yamburg, and then strike directly against the old capital along the line of the Yamburg–Petrograd railway. Other troops would isolate Petrograd from reinforcements by cutting the railway lines which radiated south-west and south-east from the city. The Estonian role would be to interpose a force between the Red Seventh and Fifteenth Armies east of Pskov to prevent the intervention of the latter in the vital sector.

Other events made their influence felt. Another White force, operating in Latvia under Colonel Prince Avalov-Bermondt, had been expected to co-operate with Yudenitch, but instead it turned against Riga in an attempt to overthrow the existing Latvian Government. This had the unfortunate effect of diverting the Estonian army to Latvia to check the ambitious Bermondt instead of fulfilling the role which Yudenitch had envisaged; and in addition, British warships cruising in the Gulf of Finland, which might have been expected to co-operate with the North-western Army, also sailed for Riga. A flotilla of British motor boats, however, did break into Kronstadt harbour where it sank three Bolshevik warships. Bermondt's action had still another unfortunate result; it revived Estonian suspicions of White Russians as a whole and led them to question the intentions of the North-western Government towards an independent Estonia in particular should they be victorious at Petrograd.

Nevertheless, despite this poor beginning, Yudenitch attacked at the beginning of October. His move took the Soviet troops (whose vigilance had relaxed because of an expected truce with Estonia) completely by surprise. In any case, their military quality was low, and the appearance of a few British tanks demoralized them. Yamburg fell almost immediately on 11th October, the Seventh Red Army streamed back in disorderly retreat, and on the 16th the important railway junction of Gatchina, thirty miles south-west of Petrograd, had been entered. At Gatchina, Yudenitch despatched a force to cut the main Moscow–Petrograd railroad at Tosno, some twenty miles to the east, but the person to whom he entrusted the task was confident that Petrograd would soon be taken; and in his eagerness to be one of the first to enter the old capital, he disregarded Yudenitch's order. It was an omission which cost the Whites dearly, for though another attempt was made some days later, the Reds had by then gathered sufficient troops to defend the place. The main Moscow–Petrograd line therefore remained open to the Bolsheviks, who were not slow to bring forward troops and officers-in-training scraped together in Moscow to stiffen the Petrograd defences.

It might have been supposed that the Reds would also have brought in reinforcements from other fronts. The Southern Front opposite Denikin, however, was of such decisive importance that any weakening of it was out of the question. The other adjacent front, in the North, had been subjected some days previously to an offensive by the Allies to permit their safe withdrawal, and in the Murman area the White Russians were following up the Allied blow; no Red troops could be withdrawn from there. In this quandary, Lenin advocated that Petrograd should be abandoned. Trotsky disagreed. He insisted that the city could be successfully defended with what troops were immediately available and rushed there himself to take charge of operations. His plan was to bolster the strength of the Seventh Army both from the beleagured city and from Moscow, and he delivered personal exhortations for a stand to be made outside the city. Should that fail, all men who could bear arms were to be organized into bands for merciless street fighting.

From Gatchina Yudenitch continued to advance, pressing the Reds back in bitter and stubborn fighting. On 20th October the last defences of the Seventh Red Army were reached—the line of the Pulkovo heights in the suburbs of Petrograd. It is said that one White commander declined to survey the city through his field glasses—

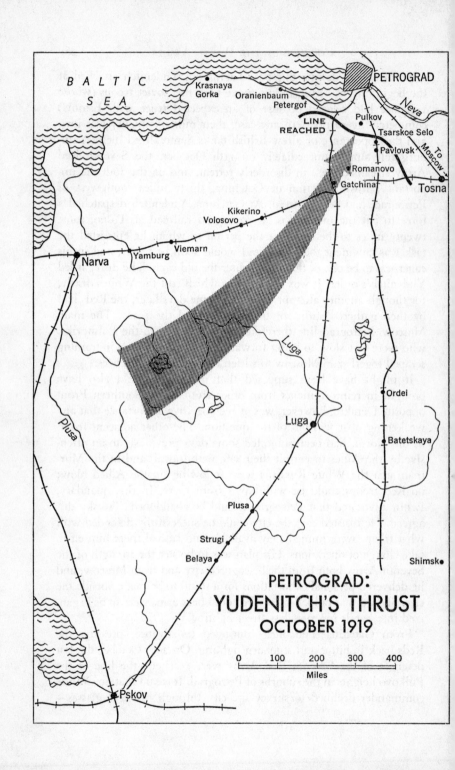

BALTIC
SEA

Krasnaya
Gorka

Oranienbaum
Petergof

PETROGRAD

Neva

Pulkov

LINE
REACHED

Tsarskoe Selo

To
Moscow

Pavlovsk

Romanovo

Gatchina

Tosna

Kikerino
Volosovo

Viemarn

Narva
Yamburg

Luga

Plusa

Luga

Ordei

Batetskaya

Plusa

Strugi

Belaya

Shimsk

PETROGRAD:
YUDENITCH'S THRUST
OCTOBER 1919

0   100   200   300   400
Miles

Pskov

next day, he said, he would be strolling along the familiar Nevsky Prospekt. But on the 21st, feverishly incited by Trotsky to stand firm, the Reds repulsed repeated and desperate attempts by the Whites to break through, and for the next two days the opposing forces grappled in swaying deadlock. On the evening of the 23rd, the exhausted Whites broke their hold, and were forced off the heights and out of the suburbs of Pavlovsk and Tsarskoe Syelo. They could do no more. Petrograd had to be carried in the first dash, or it could not be gained at all; for the Whites lacked the resources for sustained operations.

During the last days of October, Yudenitch held out at Gatchina, even launching counter-attacks, perhaps in the hope that his proximity to Petrograd might yet lead to a revolt in the city which would give him the final victory. But the contingency which he had feared and sought to guard against compelled his retreat; the Fifteenth Red Army now intervened from the south, occupying Luga and threatening his lines of retreat. He left Gatchina on 3rd November, and reached Yamburg, the starting-point of his drive, on the 14th. Here, on the Estonian border, the defeated Yudenitch came face to face with a hostile Estonia, a country which now considered itself released from all obligation to continue the anti-Bolshevik struggle and fully determined to negotiate with the Soviets. The White commander faced the alternatives of capture by the Bolsheviks or disarmament and internment in Estonia; choosing the latter, he crossed the border with his army, which was soon disbanded. The North-western Government, without purpose now that the North-western Army had collapsed, disappeared in turn.

Estonia discussed peace with the Soviets, and a treaty recognizing her independence was signed in February 1920. Thereafter, with Latvia and Lithuania, she enjoyed twenty years of freedom until in 1939 the Ribbentrop–Molotov Pact sealed her fate. In 1940 Soviet Russia realized her still lively ambitions by swallowing the Baltic States in their entirety to become an integral part of the Soviet Union.[86]

FAILURE IN THE SOUTH

Yudenitch's dash on Petrograd had no weakening effect on the Red forces facing the troops of Denikin. No troops had been withdrawn to meet it. The Bolsheviks appreciated quite correctly that the main threat to the Soviet régime now lay in the south, centred at Orel, and that the decisive battles of the Civil War would be fought in this sector.

Estimates of opposing strengths on the 700-mile front from Kiev to Tsaritsin, whether White or Red, give the advantage to the Reds. Soviet sources place 186,000 Reds against 112,600 Whites (the former having almost double the numbers of guns and machine guns), while Denikin himself claimed to have fielded 78,000 against between 140,000 and 160,000 of the enemy. Whatever the true figures are, it is clear that Denikin was heavily outnumbered.[87] In all, the White front was some twelve hundred miles long; much of it was intermittently patrolled by Cossacks, but its very extent meant that no depth could be given to defences over any appreciable distance. Furthermore the Whites had been compelled to detach some units to combat insurgent movements behind the lines, so that every available man at the front was committed to the existing forward defences; there was no mobile reserve which could be thrown into any threatened breach. The Reds, on the other hand, with superior numbers and far less line to man, were able to build up a shock group of 1500 cavalry and 10,000 infantry (with a reserve of one division) which might well be counted on to turn any closely contested action into a defeat for the enemy. This they concentrated west of Orel.

Seizing the initiative at the middle of October, the Reds attacked, forcing the Whites to commit their troops without being able to mass reinforcements at any vital place. The Whites, having some of the best divisions of the Volunteer Army at Orel, fought tenaciously, but the Red shock group turned the scale by thrusting hard from the south-west against the rearward rail communications. This, combined with the throwing in of a fresh division on the front and growing pressure of the Fourteenth Red Army on Denikin's left flank, forced the Whites to evacuate Orel on the 20th October, the same day Yudenitch penetrated to the last defences on the outskirts of Petrograd.

An hundred miles south of Orel lies Kursk, and a hundred miles to the east of Kursk is Voronezh. In the relatively small triangle formed by these three towns, the White Russian cause virtually ended.

From Orel, still fighting steadfastly, the Whites fell back to Kursk. Meanwhile, around Voronezh, the White cavalry, which had hitherto been responsible in no small measure for Denikin's victories, was decisively defeated by the Red cavalry corps of Simeon Mikhailovich Budenny. This man, a non-Cossack peasant of the Don and a former sergeant in the Imperial Army, now in his early forties, proved to be a cavalry commander of great skill.* His intervention at Voronezh came about through his own initiative—in definite contravention of specific orders to act against the Don Territory which Trotsky still mistakenly regarded as the key to Red victory on the Southern Front. Advised that the White cavalry under General Mamontov planned another raid behind the Red lines such as one the Don Cossack leader had successfully led during August and September, Budenny turned north instead, caught Mamontov unprepared, and routed his corps as well as his Kuban horsemen, seizing Voronezh on 24th October. Three weeks of stubborn fighting ensued in 'the triangle', finally broken by Budenny at Kastornaya.

Kastornaya, between Kursk and Vorenezh, was an important railway junction for the two towns. Around this place Mamontov had gathered the remnants of his cavalry and was attempting to reorganize them. On 15th November Budenny attacked, overwhelmed the White cavalry, and captured the town. With Kastornaya in enemy hands, a wedge had been driven between the Volunteer Army at Kursk and the Don Cossack front established south of Voronezh; communications between the two forces were effectively broken. The White cavalry, hitherto such a formidable instrument, was completely demoralized after this second defeat, and Budenny roamed at will behind the White lines, tearing up communications as he went; two days later, Kursk fell.

Denikin, who still hoped to restore the cavalry as a vital arm, ordered Wrangel to leave the Caucasian Army and to take over the Volunteer Army from Mai-Maievsky. The move was a wise one, for Wrangel had conspicuously demonstrated his ability to handle large masses of cavalry. Mai-Maievsky, on the other hand, had given way to pillage and orgies which had a demoralizing effect on the officers and men of the Volunteer Army. Undoubtedly courageous, this burly red-faced man still retained popularity with the rank and file, but his excesses called for his dismissal as an army leader. The change, however, had been left too late. Wrangel left Taganrog at the end of November, hoping to be in Kharkov shortly afterwards, but before he could get there Kharkov itself had fallen to the Reds.

---

* Budenny subsequently became a member of the Revolutionary Military Council, and Inspector of Red Cavalry. In the Second World War, Marshal Budenny commanded the Russian forces opposing von Runstedt's Army Group South.

Denikin's plan to re-form a powerful cavalry force east of Kharkov under Wrangel, which would not only check Budenny but drive him back, never materialized. The White cavalry units were far too broken. In a step towards this goal, Wrangel dismissed the unsuccessful general Mamontov, replacing him by a Kuban general, Ulagai, but this only served to alienate the Don Cossacks who resented the slight to Mamontov, their own best general of cavalry. Attempts by Wrangel to restore the morale of the infantry in the Volunteer Army by introducing stern disciplinary measures were equally abortive. What Voronezh and Kastornaya had done to the cavalry had been done at Kursk to the White infantry. At Orel and Kursk the Volunteer Army fought stubbornly and well—but after being defeated at Kursk it streamed back in disorderly rout, harassed repeatedly by Budenny's unchecked riders. There was no serious resistance whatsoever from Kursk to Rostov, more than 300 miles to the rear.

The defeat of the White forces in the Orel region during October and November is understandable in view of Red superiority. But the inability to make a further stand and their complete collapse during December only becomes comprehensible if one takes into account the condition of the rear. The Ukraine was aflame with anarchy; the Kuban, hostile to Denikin since his interference with the Kuban Rada, denied him help, while Kuban units in the White Army melted away; the Don Cossacks, temporarily alienated by Wrangel's dismissal of Mamontov, fought indifferently when they fought at all. In these circumstances the Red advance became as easy as a parade. After Kharkov on 12th December, Kiev fell on 16th December, and with this the third conquest of the Ukraine by the Bolsheviks was well under way. Denikin's troops in Kiev crossed over into Polish territory and were interned. Those which had been fighting Ukrainian guerrillas in the Ekaterinoslav area fell back to the Isthmus of Perekop where they managed to hold the gateway to the Crimea. The Donetz Basin, so hotly contested in the spring, was relinquished to the Reds without a struggle. Only at Rostov was an attempt made to halt the triumphal progress of the enemy, and here the line of the Don was held for two months.

Finally, the Reds infiltrated behind the White positions and threatened complete encirclement. The Whites abandoned the Don, then stumbled back towards the sea. There was no longer any thought of serious resistance, other than feeble rearguard actions to hold the Reds from the Black Sea port of Novorossisk. The Crimea alone offered protection, for Socialist Revolutionaries had sparked a peasant uprising in the Black Sea Province, south-east of Novorossisk, which had effectively ended Denikin's régime, and further south Georgia, bent on autonomy, had always remained aloof from White Russian aspirations. The Taman peninsula, as well as the port of Novorossisk, offered an escape route to the Crimea; but White apathy had permitted the Reds to seize the peninsula so that only the port remained.

Though by no means as long as the retreat in Siberia, the 200-mile journey equalled it in horror. Thousands of fugitives accompanied the troops, whole communities of Cossacks dragging with them children and whatever they could carry, choking the roads. Strangely oriental groups mounted on camels, such as the Kalmucks from Astrakhan, appeared silently like figures of doom out of the snow-covered steppes to join the pathetic throng. In addition to the severity of the Russian winter, the coastal *borah* wind piled ships in port with tons of ice and searched the bodies of emaciated stragglers through tattered uniforms and rags. Blue, frozen bodies, stripped of boots and coats, littered the roads, for the iron-hard ground precluded burial even had there been the will. Hunger, uncertainty, and finally raging typhus completed the suffering.

What remained of this human avalanche reached Novorossisk towards the end of March, swelling the population of the already overcrowded town. It would be gratifying to report that all the hardships had not been endured in vain, but evacuation proceeded amidst scenes of deepest tragedy. No estimate could possibly have been made of the scores of thousands who would seek to escape the Soviet advance, and plans to ship the troops had been based on many of them using the alternative escape route across the Taman peninsula. As it was, there were not enough ships to take off all the soldiers. People fought for a place on the waiting vessels. Families became separated, never to be reunited. Horses, camels, wagons, handcarts and other possessions which could not be taken, lined the water's edge. 'Many human tragedies', wrote Denikin later, 'were enacted on the streets of Novorossisk in those terrible days. Much brutality came to the fore in the case of imminent danger, when naked passions drowned the voice of conscience and man was enemy to man.'[88]

British and French warships appeared on the scene, bringing some

measure of order, and loaded to capacity with White troops. On the
night of 26th March, the last vessels left harbour. Many of the
abandoned refugees threw themselves into the sea rather than face
death at the hands of the Bolsheviks. Cries of entreaty mingled with
the thunder of guns as the naval vessels bombarded the approaches
to the town to hold the Red troops off. Fifty thousand persons, it is
estimated, left Novorossisk; twenty-two thousand troops and vast
quantities of stores were captured by the Red Army, while thousands
of others were massacred on the spot for resisting the new régime.
Kuban troops, who had broken all connection with Denikin, could
not protect the independence of their territory, and retreated south
along the Black Sea coast where they were joined by some units of
the Don Army which had been unable to embark. Georgia refused
to allow them to cross her frontier, and, short of food and supplies,
the force capitulated to the Reds.

Forty thousand White troops reached the Crimea, the Volunteers
fully armed and still equipped; the Don Cossacks, on the other hand,
had been forced to abandon their horses and few had weapons.
Military leaders and politicians placed the blame for the *débâcle*
firmly on Denikin. The White Russian leader, sick at heart at all he
had witnessed, aware that his cause was doomed, decided to withdraw from the struggle. His last order appointed General Baron
Peter Wrangel Commander-in-Chief of the Armed Forces of South
Russia and closed with the words: 'Lord, grant victory to the Army
and save Russia.'[89] He then left the Crimea for Constantinople.
From there, some time later, he sailed to England, taking the children of General Kornilov with him.

British aid, which had sustained Denikin throughout 1919 and the
first months of 1920, was now withheld. Denikin had never asked for
men, while supplies furnished by Britain, it could certainly be maintained, had been sufficient to carry his troops to Moscow had they
been used wisely. The White position was now considered hopeless.
In a letter dated April 2, 1920, from the British High Commissioner
in Constantinople to Denikin, and shown to Wrangel, the British
Government stated its absolute conviction that 'an arrangement with
the Soviet Government for an amnesty for the Crimean population
in general, and the Volunteer Army in particular, would be in the
best interest of all concerned'. It was prepared to make the arrangement with the Soviets, and offered a refuge for Denikin and his
principal supporters in Great Britain if they should consent. If not,

and if they decided to continue a 'manifestly hopeless struggle, the British Government will find itself obliged to renounce all responsibility for [their] actions, and to cease to furnish . . . any help or subvention of any kind from that time on.'[90] Wrangel therefore had no illusions, and at first he could see no possibility of resuming the struggle.

THE FINAL ACT

Wrangel's opportunity to continue the war came with the outbreak of Soviet–Polish hostilities on April 25, 1920. Responsibility for that war undoubtedly rested with the Poles. A strong Russia under Denikin would not have been in accordance with Polish aspirations; neither would a strong Russia under the Communists. For the first reason Poland had remained aloof from Denikin, and for the last Poland determined to attack the Soviets.

New states had already been created north of Poland, separate from Russia : Finland, Estonia, Latvia, and Lithuania shut the new Russia off from the Baltic Sea, pulling apart the work of Peter the Great. In the Caucasus, Georgia, Armenia, Azerbaidjan had all established republics outside the Soviet sphere. It needed only the Ukraine, to the south of Poland, to complete the arc of encircling states from the Baltic to the Caucasus, and to these might be added independent Cossack states in the Don and in the Kuban. A Russia barred from the Baltic and Black seas, deprived of the Ukrainian granary, shorn of the oil and minerals of the Caucasus, could never aspire to be more than a second-class power, incapable of threatening the independence of a Poland which, as the largest and strongest of them, would be able to influence the policies of the new surrounding states.

As might be expected, the Polish President, Marshal Pilsudsky, invaded the Ukraine, to meet with ready aid from the nationalist Petlura, who had already reached an understanding with Pilsudsky before the Poles attacked : the Ukraine was to be independent, under Poland's protection, while Eastern Galicia was to be ceded to Poland as the price of Polish help.

At first the Polish offensive was entirely and speedily successful, sweeping through Kiev to the Dnieper. But Bolshevik reaction was swift, and the Poles were harried back. At the beginning of July the Poles stood at the river Berezina, across the line of Napoleon's disastrous retreat from Moscow, and were defeated. Then, on 1st August,

Brest-Litovsk, and with it the line of the Bug, was lost; the victorious Red Army, vastly superior to the Polish Army, struck at Warsaw in the heart of Poland with no natural barriers left to impede its progress.

But Red grouping for the blow on Warsaw was defective, a fact which was not lost on General Weygand (Foch's chief of staff), who had been sent by France to oversee the Polish defence. The battle which developed at the middle of August in the vicinity of Warsaw has become known as the 'Miracle of the Vistula'. On 13th August the Poles stood and fought at Radimin, a few miles from Warsaw itself: four days later Red armies which had seemed irresistible were in full flight, leaving uncounted dead and 70,000 prisoners on Polish soil.

Overnight, Red triumph changed to catastrophe. The Poles surged forward from Warsaw and swept the Reds back. By now the Poles had the initiative and used it well. Brest-Litovsk was reoccupied on 19th August, Bialystok on the 23rd; Eastern Galicia followed, and during September the Poles contented themselves with grabbing as much territory as possible to ensure a favourable eastern border.

Both sides were now anxious for peace. Pilsudsky saw that his dream of an independent Ukraine could not be brought about by force of arms. Red ideas about a Soviet Poland had been rudely shattered on the Vistula; they wanted an end of hostilities so that they could deal with Wrangel. A peace signed on 12th October secured the independence of Poland for more than twenty years, when the Communists occupied half of Poland and after the Second World War at last saw a Polish–Soviet régime established.

A lesson which the Soviet–Polish War brings home is that the Red Army was by no means as strong as many apologists for the failure of the White forces and Allied interventionists would have us believe. On paper, at any rate, the Red Army in 1920 numbered more than five million officers and men, and yet Soviet Russia found itself unable to crush the newly formed and relatively small Polish forces. Instead, it suffered defeat at their hands. It seems incomprehensible therefore, in the light of the Red defeat at Warsaw, that properly organized Allied troops hand-in-hand with the White armies, if united under one command and committed to a common operational goal, could not have overthrown the Bolsheviks during 1918 when the Red Army was in its infancy.

Meanwhile Wrangel had taken advantage of Soviet preoccupation with the Polish war to carry out his own offensive. His army had been reorganized and was ready for action—indeed, inactivity might be dangerous. Another factor was that the mountainous and arid Crimea could not feed its own population let alone the White soldiers and refugees who had arrived there. These pressing reasons pointed to a breakout on to the Russian mainland. Wrangel struck on 6th June. The Volunteers smashed through the Soviet lines north of the Isthmus of Perekop while, hand in hand with the frontal attack, another force sent by sea descended on the Azov shoreline, taking the Reds completely by surprise. The detachment then consolidated its bridgehead and swept on to capture Melitopol, capital of the Northern Tauride, a province adjoining the Crimea. Within two weeks the whole of the Northern Tauride was in Wrangel's hands, giving him a rich grain region and doubling the area under his control. But, aware of the lessons which the White collapse in the winter of 1919–20 had taught, Wrangel did not go blindly on occupying territory which might have to be held down later; instead, he set to work to consolidate what he had got, to build up on 'a small bit of Russian soil . . . such order and such living conditions as would attract the people who are suffering under the Red yoke'.[91] Here was a figure, Churchill says, of 'unusual energy and quality, who thus too late reached the first place in White Russian counsels'.[92]

Not until August was Wrangel ready for the next step. The expulsion of the Poles from Kiev and the Western Ukraine eliminated any possibility of joining up with them, and in any case, the White leader had no wish to become further embroiled in the Ukraine as Denikin had done at great cost. He therefore looked elsewhere for a field for his activities, and concluded that the Cossack Territories would be most likely to offer him support. His June offensive had helped the Poles by holding large Soviet forces in the south; and the Poles had recognized the fact by returning some thousands of Denikin's troops (who had fled into Poland and been interned) to rejoin Wrangel's force in the Crimea.

Wrangel decided to send all his spare forces, not needed to guard the frontiers of the Tauride, to the Kuban and the Don; and on 13th August a mixed force of about 7000 infantry and cavalry under the Kuban general, Ulagai, landed on the Kuban coast of the sea of Azov. Subsidiary landings were also effected on Don territory near Norovossisk, on the Taman peninsula, and west of Taganrog. Though the invasions alarmed the Reds—Trotsky rushed to Taganrog to supervise operations against the White Baron who was trying to 'poke his head out of the Crimean bottle'—they were not successful. Ulagai pushed fifty miles inland to within thirty-five miles of Ekaterinodar, the Kuban capital, but then he hesitated, permitting the Reds through his delay to bring up large forces which eventually proved decisive. By 7th September the White forces had been forced out of the Kuban, and yet Ulagai brought out more troops than he had taken in. Minor operations in the Don area were a total failure. But, even so, 30,000 Red troops had been tied up in the Cossack territories at a time when they could have made the issue on the Warsaw front absolutely certain; and there was another consolation in that in August the French, filled with anxiety about the Polish situation, recognized Wrangel's régime as the *de facto* government of South Russia.

The October peace with Poland eliminated the western front, enabling the Soviet Government to throw overwhelming force against Wrangel in the south. The main decision facing the White leader was whether to face the Reds in the North Tauride, or to withdraw his forces behind the fortified lines of the Isthmus of Perekop. Withdrawal to the Crimea, he realized, would again expose his forces and the civilian population to hunger; and though he knew that he would face desperately uneven odds in both men and weapons if he remained on the mainland, he nevertheless determined to stay where he was and to fight in the Tauride. But it was a hopeless match. The Red attack, delivered in massive strength on 28th October, proved overwhelming, and badly shattered White forces were compelled to seek safety in the Crimea. Red plans to cut off their retreat and to annihilate them on the steppes of the North Tauride were frustrated; but even so the entrance to the Crimea could not hold out indefinitely, and Wrangel ordered evacuation plans prepared.

Meanwhile, on 7th November, the third anniversary of the 'October' Revolution, the Reds struck at the last White stronghold. There were three defensive lines across the Isthmus of Perekop: first, a line of barbed wire north of the town of Perekop; second, a barrier known as the Turkish Wall consisting largely of machine-gun emplacements, mutually supporting; and lastly, trenches and wire connecting several small lakes at the southern end. Frontal assaults, easily held at the first defensive line, were heavily repulsed throughout the day. On the night of the 7th, however, realizing the futility of a further bullheaded approach, the Reds despatched by sea across the Gulf of Sivash a picked force which landed centrally on the isthmus at a point behind the first two defensive lines. Here, aided by darkness, the Reds deployed behind the Turkish Wall. Grim fighting on the 8th failed to dislodge them, and that night the Whites, threatened in front and rear, pulled back from the first and second lines to the last defences to the south. Here the struggle contiued for two more days. Then, on the 11th, with conspicuous bravery in the face of heavy machine gun and artillery fire, the Reds penetrated one sector of the last defensive line regardless of losses, and began a slow move forward into the Crimean plain.

Wrangel knew that all was lost. He ordered a withdrawal to the ports while a cavalry screen covered the retreat. Every ship that could be sailed was pressed into service; British and French warships put in to the Crimean ports to assist in the evacuation, which, unlike Novorossisk, proceeded calmly and successfully. In all, 146,000 troops and civilians were taken off to Constantinople, the first stage of the long journey to emigré life in various parts of the world. Though the Reds still had to fight minor actions in the Caucasus and Central Asia, it was the end of the civil war.

At the Golden Horn, streets were crowded with Russian soldiers; the bazaars were loaded with Russian arms, furs, and jewellery. In the camp at Tchatldja, near Constantinople, the evening prayer, sung by thousands of Russian voices, surged out deep and sweet over the Bosphorus shore. It seemed that the ancient dream had in the end come true—that Constantinople had at last become a Russian city. And, indeed, it might have done had Russia not gone through a revolution and quit the Allied ranks. But in 1920 these singers were not masters in their own home; they were merely emigrants granted a temporary halting-place on foreign soil before scattering to the ends of the earth.

With the defeat of Kolchak, Yudenitch, Denikin, and Wrangel, the curtain fell on White Russian hopes. The Soviet Government was supreme in all the territories of the old empire save Poland, Eastern Siberia, parts of the Caucasus, and the Baltic States, each of which, sooner or later, would be swallowed up. But the land was exhausted, moving inevitably towards the great famine of 1921–22, its people groping through the ruins of the country motivated only by a blind and elemental will to survive.

Even in these early bare and hungry years, however, the Communists still preserved their faith in world revolution. Already the face of the new dictatorship could be vaguely discerned and its policy became more and more clear as the years went by. The aim of Soviet Russia, even then, was firm. Its methods, tactics, and its manoeuvres have altered to fit the circumstances, but the polar star of its policy—world domination—is a fixed star and has never changed. Amid the almost universal hatred and suspicion of the west, the Soviet Government began to move slowly towards its goal.

CHAPTER VIII

RETROSPECT

RETROSPECT

It is worth while to sum up this Russian story. Whatever the rights and wrongs of the Bolshevik Revolution, the fact remains that the rise and subsequent consolidation of Bolshevik power in Russia is the most significant event of the present century. All the ills which now beset the free world—the Berlin Wall, the missile race, space domination, and the expansion of Communism throughout the world—can be traced to the actions of a few desperate men who in 1917 seized power in Russia.

The fact that the Bolsheviks were able to overthrow the Provisional Government in 1917 is hardly surprising. In retrospect it seems logical and inevitable that the government of the day, middle-of-the-road as it was, unable to make either war or peace, backing neither the expropriation of the large estates or the property rights of land-lords, should fall. The Provisional Government of Kerensky satisfied nobody and had few defenders. But the holding of power, once seized by the Bolsheviks, can only be regarded as a great, almost miraculous, achievement.

What the new masters of Russia were faced with has been described: the Germans demanding the fruits of victory at Brest-Litovsk, their exploitation of the richest regions of Russia, and their occupation of the Ukraine; the outbreak of civil war, and growing White movements determined to destroy them; defeat in Finland; the loss of territory, stretching from the Urals to the Pacific, to the Czech Corps; the secession and proclaimed independence of minority Russian groups; Allied support of the Whites and Allied intervention; and finally, but by no means least important, the disillusionment of the Russian masses.

This last was always a serious problem. True, peasants acquired the land of the nobles and large farmers, but their new masters took away most of what was raised at the point of the bayonet. Workers had driven away the capitalists, but had less to eat than under the

Czar. Soldiers had been promised peace, but instead they were drafted to fight fellow Russians in a brutal civil war. And the insane internal policies of the Bolsheviks stirred up an almost universal hatred in all peoples and classes who suffered under them during the first two years of the new régime.

The Bolsheviks never were a majority party in Russia despite their name. The percentage of Bolsheviks in Siberia in 1918 was extremely small, while in the whole of Russia (and outside it) it is doubtful if there were more than 75,000* of them at the time of the March Revolution of 1917. And yet in spite of paucity in numbers, internal disruption and outside invasion, peasant uprisings, workers' strikes and Red Army mutinies, the gimcrack Bolshevik régime survived. The question remains, how could it possibly weather the opposition it aroused and emerge triumphant?

There is no simple answer. A good many factors, however, provide part of it, and chief among them is the attitude of the opposing parties themselves. On the one hand there was unity, dedication, and the unswerving purpose of the Bolsheviks; and on the other disunity brought about by self-interest and ignorance of what Bolshevism really meant. The latter of course generally applies to the Allied interventionists. And yet, though weakly opposed, there were times when the future existence of the Bolshevik régime 'trembled on a hair'. Had all the hatreds which the Bolsheviks inspired throughout Russia and in certain leaders of the West ever found outlet in co-ordinated expression under single leadership at any one time, the Soviet régime could not have survived and would have been swept away. But leadership was never forthcoming. The salvation of the Bolsheviks lay not so much in their own strength—though what they had was unified and strongly disciplined—but in the hopeless disunity of their opponents.

It is necessary to consider now this Bolshevik weakness, as well as the lack of co-ordination and leadership on the part of the Whites and their Allied supporters.

In 1918 Bolshevik strength was negligible. It could offer no resistance to the occupation of the Ukraine by the Germans. It could not prevent the liberation of Asiatic Russia from the Urals to the sea by a relatively small band of Czechs. It could not throw back the small but growing Volunteer Army from South Russia; nor could it even

* For Party strengths Chamberlin cites Sverdlov as follows : 80,000 members in April 1917 rising to 200,000 in August (*The Russian Revolution*, I, 186).

eject the insignificant numbers of Allied troops from their toehold in
North Russia. In Finland, Red troops suffered defeat. The Allies and
the anti-Bolsheviks possessed abundant strength to strangle the
Soviets at birth if they had been united in that purpose, and had their
strength been used in time.* The German occupation of the Ukraine
in the spring of 1918, which restored order in that area and served as
an incentive (and should have been a model) for intervention by the
Allies, required an initial occupation force of some 200,000 men.
Had the United States and Japan made any comparable effort (and
this might have been done with troops which could never have
reached the Western Front), decisive results would undoubtedly have
been gained before the Armistice in 1918. As it was, time favoured
the Reds. They seized Russia on November 7, 1917, but more than a
year elapsed before their opponents achieved any semblance of unity
under Kolchak in Siberia. It took Denikin even longer to assume
the stature of an all-Russian leader of the Whites. Meanwhile the
Soviets had been given a breathing space to build up under the fiery
Trotsky the striking power of the infant Red Army which in 1919
proved more than a match for what the Whites alone could hurl
against it.

The anti-Bolshevik factions could never co-ordinate their strength
at the moment when it would have been most decisive. First, Russia
was completely lacking in democratic experience—with the overthrow of Czarist autocracy bitter quarrels at once broke out as to
what should succeed it, and continued after the Bolsheviks had come
to power. Anti-Bolshevik circles deteriorated into a talking-shop;

* Bruce Lockhart, a British agent in Moscow at the time, at first opposed
intervention unless invited by the Bolsheviks. He later veered towards intervention even without Soviet consent. In June 1918, 'Believing that the Allies
would land in force, we were convinced that the Bolsheviks would be unable
to offer a serious resistance.' Then, 'On August 4th Moscow went wild with
excitement, the Allies had landed at Archangel', and, it was believed, in
strength. 'The Japanese were to send seven divisions through Siberia to help
the Czechs. Even the Bolsheviks lost their heads and, in despair, began to pack
their archives . . . with the adequate forces which I assumed we had at our
disposal, I had no doubt of our being able to reach the Russian capital.' Six
days later, Lockhart met Karachan (one of the three Bolshevik signatories of
the Brest-Litovsk peace), now a Commissar at the Foreign Office. 'His face was
wreathed in smiles. The dejection of the previous days had gone. . . . "The
situation is not serious," he said. "The Allies have landed only a few hundred
men." ' (R. H. Bruce Lockhart, *Memoirs of a British Agent* (Putnam, London,
1932), pp. 292, 308–9, 310.)

some reactionaries favoured a restoration of the monarchy; other groups preferred a constituent assembly to be followed by a parliament; still others wanted something more radical, even socialistic, in character. In these circumstances all attempts to create a democratic substitute for the Bolshevik régime failed. Although a leader of strong personality—the ardent champion of some positive programme which would be 'right' for Russia—might have reconciled and carried the warring factions with him, such a leader never appeared unless in the person of Wrangel, and he of course arrived far too late. Nevertheless, a man of lesser abilities, an honest patriot such as Kolchak, might have been enough, if disunity amongst the Allies in Siberia had not rendered his position absolutely untenable. Conducting an all-out struggle against the Bolsheviks in the teeth of active opposition by Japan, and the indifference of America he was bound to fail.

There was no programme, then, acceptable to all the warring anti-Bolshevik factions; neither was there an inspiring leader who might have made up for this deficiency. In the military field it was the same. When the Whites had mustered armies capable of advancing on the Bolshevik stronghold, there was no single, overall command to direct and co-ordinate their movements in any skilful pattern. Alexeiev had been slated for this role, but died before he could reach Siberia and was never replaced. And in the absence of a guiding hand, only two of the White offensives which took place in 1919— that of Yudenitch on Petrograd and Denikin on Moscow—were mutually supporting. Kolchak's furthest advance to within 500 miles of Moscow and almost to the Volga was achieved at the end of April —too early for co-ordination either with Denikin or Ironside—and even then he was of two minds whether to link up with Ironside in the north or Denikin in the south or to march on Moscow. He attempted to do all three, and, as might be expected, he failed. In June, when the Northern forces had been reinforced and could have co-operated in Kolchak's attack, the Siberian blow had petered out and was falling back—there was no point then in Ironside's pushing south to gain a few more miles of territory and little else. Again, in October, after Kolchak had been driven far beyond the Urals in full retreat and there was no longer any hope of co-operation from him, Denikin moved north on Moscow. How much better if the southern leader had kept out of the Ukraine and concentrated everything for an earlier drive on Moscow! As it was, the Reds, operating on in-

terior lines, were permitted by White ineptitude to strengthen each
critical front in turn at the expense of the others, and so defeat the
encircling White armies one by one, whether East, West or South,
and still to have sufficient strength to contain the North. Foch, the
architect of Allied victory on the Western Front (where closely related attacks at different points had been the mark of his strategy),
could only have been appalled when studying, as he must have done,
the piecemeal White offensives of 1919. That every one should end
in abject failure can hardly have surprised him.

There are fundamental principles (known as the 'principles of
war') on which the successful conduct of war is based. Though
weapons, organization, tactics and transportation change, the fundamental principles of war never change. They are so important that
all great nations recognize them and incorporate them in military
doctrine. The number of principles recognized by various nations
varies, depending on the interpretation, but almost all nations include these at least as fundamental truths: that the *objective*, or
aim, must not be lost sight of; and that *mass*, or maximum fighting
force, must be applied at the point of decision. To fulfil these principles there must be *unity of command*.

Let us first consider command. Unity of command brings about
the co-ordinated action of all forces towards a common goal, and
may be obtained by direction or by co-operation. It is best achieved,
however, by vesting in one man authority over all the forces. Can it
be said that either the White Russians or the Allied interventionists
gave this serious thought, or if they did, obeyed it? The Whites
appointed no overall commander to co-ordinate the actions of their
armies in the various Russian theatres, although Alexeiev might have
fulfilled that role had he lived. Without overall direction, armies
were frittered away in piecemeal offensives with neither co-ordination nor clear-cut goal. And in Siberia the Allies went their various
ways in the absence of a commander to direct their efforts towards
any common purpose.

The second principle mentioned above, which amounts to the
concentration of force at the critical time and place as far as the
situation permits, could also have been better achieved had there
been unity of command. The principle was flagrantly disregarded
in individual theatres, as it was at the time of Kolchak's spring
offensive in 1919, when the Siberian armies had the alternatives of
striking north to Archangel, directly west on Moscow, or south to

join forces with Denikin. A concentration of force for a thrust in any *one* direction held out good prospects for success, but all three were attempted simultaneously and, as a result, all three failed.

And, finally, what was the White aim? This is a 'master' principle. Undoubtedly it was the overthrow of Bolshevism, and to that end the defeat of the Bolshevik forces and a triumphant entry into Moscow. To achieve that aim, every military operation should have been directed towards the destruction of the enemy's armed forces and his will to fight. There would undoubtedly have been intermediate objectives, but the attainment of each of these should have contributed to the main aim or purpose. Can it be said that Denikin's invasion of the Ukraine in the summer of 1919 contributed towards the destruction of the Bolshevik enemy and the advance on Moscow? On the contrary, it embroiled his forces in bitter fighting with Ukrainian Nationalists. And that led to the contravention of another principle of war, *security*; his rear was never secure thereafter so that he could not retain the ability to employ his forces effectively and decisively. It extended his front to breaking-point, and left him unable to achieve a decisive concentration on the road to Moscow.

A further principle, *administration*, was consistently violated by all the White commanders, except perhaps Wrangel. Without efficient administrative arrangements no commander could obtain freedom of action in carrying out his plan. Gaida's thrust towards Archangel, for example, petered out through lack of supplies which were never sufficient to support three simultaneous offensives by the Siberian armies. Far better to have diverted all resources to back a single thrust in whatever direction was considered most likely to achieve decisive results over the Bolsheviks and to practise *economy of effort* —yet another principle—with perhaps only limited objectives in the other two.

At first glance, the principles of war may seem to be platitudinous; but they indicate a course of action that has brought success in the past, whereas disregard of them involves risk and has often brought disaster. The Whites not only disregarded them; they violated them, and this, in no small measure, contributed to their failure.

There is another factor in the defeat of the Whites which must be considered, and that is their failure to compromise on issues of vital importance to states and provinces which had broken away from Russia following the revolution. Unlike Lenin, whose attitude was governed by expediency, Kolchak and Denikin insisted on the integrity of the old Russian borders. States which had proclaimed their indepence would have to be taken back into the Russian fold, and this of course was contrary to their own national aspirations. In return for national recognition, they offered help, which was rejected when it would have been of value. Not one inch of the Russian motherland was to be allowed to secede; Finland, Estonia, Latvia, Lithuania, Poland, and the Ukraine, therefore, could hardly be expected to help the Whites to a power which would only permit them to carry out that policy. Thus the Whites alienated their natural allies in the struggle with the Bolsheviks, for no new nation would make common cause with White leaders who denied their right to independence. The refusal to accept Japan's offer of an army to crush the Bolsheviks in return for certain territories in Siberia can be understood; but rejection of the Finns, the Poles and other formerly Russian groups whose interests were the same as theirs (and to whom the Allies were sympathetic), when so much was at stake, showed the lack of foresight and statesmanship of the Whites.

As to the part played by the Allies in the affairs of Russia during this period, in both the military and the political fields, we have seen that intervention if aimed at unseating the Bolsheviks was unsuccessful; and unsuccessful intervention in another country's affairs seldom finds approval. Thus Allied action in Russia, whether after the revolution or following the Armistice, meets with general condemnation. But it should not be forgotten that intervention before the Armistice was directed against the Germans, as a necessary war measure. The early termination of hostilities had not been expected —indeed there were many who even looked upon the Armistice negotiations as a mere attempt to secure a truce, a German trick to secure a respite which would enable enemy troops to disengage and reach the Rhine. Plans for a 1919 campaign were advanced and ready, and it is against this background that the first intervention must always be seen and judged.

Following the Bolshevik Revolution, Russia had withdrawn from the war, with enormous consequences for the Allies. German troops from the east had been freed thereby for transfer to the west, giving numerical superiority to the Central Powers at a critical time. Brest-Litovsk and subsequent occupation of the Ukraine had handed over the vast resources of Russia to the enemy, nullifying the Allied blockade. It would have been criminal negligence to make no effort to reconstruct an eastern front and to deny, as far as possible, Russian resources in food and fuel to the Central Powers. These were the very cogent reasons which brought Allied troops at first to Russia, and once there they were anxious to co-operate with any group, whether White Russian or Czech, which professed a readiness to carry on the war with Germany and was struggling with the Bolsheviks. Support of the anti-Bolsheviks was a very definite part of Anglo-French policy, even if that meant embroilment with the Bolsheviks. To sweep away the régime which had taken Russia out of the war, though not stated, was implicit in their purpose of reconstructing an eastern front. Decisive results were not achieved, as they could have been even before the Armistice, because the British and French were unable to furnish sufficient troops. Both countries saw the policy as vital to the winning of the war and both were resolute in purpose. But they had been bled white on the Western Front, where they were still heavily committed, as well as in Salonika; and they had garrisons to maintain in various other parts of the world. Britain was also engaged in subsidiary campaigns in Mesopotamia and Syria. Britain and France sent to Russia enormous quantities of military supplies to aid the anti-Bolsheviks, and what manpower they could spare—troops unfit for the Western Front to the north, trifling numbers of garrison troops to Siberia, and a handful to South Russia—but the bulk of the intervention troops necessary for their aim had to be appealed for from elsewhere. The Americans and the Japanese, who had the men, responded by supplying contingents for very mixed motives. As a result, they never exploited the opportunities offered in the main theatre of intervention largely through ignorance of the nature of Bolshevism, rival policies, and mutual animosities. 'It seems certain', says Churchill, 'that a resolute effort by a comparatively small number of trustworthy American or Japanese troops would have enabled Moscow to be occupied by National Russian and Allied forces even before the German collapse took place.'*

Nevertheless, some measure of success was achieved with pitifully small resources. Dunsterville managed to withhold Caspian oil from the enemy while the war was on, and Maynard's operations immobilized German troops in Finland until it was too late for them to be of use on the Western Front.

Then came the Armistice which finally wrecked any hope there might have been of any concerted Allied action with regard to

* Churchill, *Aftermath*, 285.

Russia. Germany's occupation and exploitation of Russia and her new ability to fight a one-front war had provided the incentive for Allied military intervention; but that incentive was now removed. No policy as to war or peace with the Bolsheviks followed the cessation of hostilities on the Western Front, and each of the interventionist powers acted in accordance with its own lights. Even then, differences arose with regard to *national* policy, examples of which are the rival policies of Churchill and Curzon towards Finnish participation in the drive on Petrograd, and the split between Borden and his cabinet on continued Canadian presence in Siberia. Small wonder that military support for the Whites was hesitating and ineffectual.

Again, with the end of the war came demobilization. Troops returned to civil life, so that the irresistible power possessed by the Allies at the end of 1918 was allowed to slip away before anything had been decided about Russia. When, in the middle of 1919, a general policy of support for Kolchak was at last decided upon as being in the best interests of Russia, Kolchak's power, too, was on the wane; in any case, the promised support was much more verbal than real, and far too late to be of any value. Thus, when White failure to beat Bolshevism became apparent, the only remaining course was to protect as far as possible those Russians who had remained loyal to the Allied cause, and then to withdraw without delay from a conflict that could no longer be won. The means of winning it, which the Allies had always possessed, had been relinquished one by one and attempts to aid the anti-Bolsheviks had been largely unilateral or unconcerted. It should have been obvious, after experience in France had dictated the appointment of a supreme commander in 1918 and the setting up of a War Council to determine policy, that a similar arrangement would also be necessary to coordinate Russian action. It was done in the Second World War. It was done again in Korea, when, for the first time in history, Communism was effectively opposed by a coalition of powers. But it is obvious that the lesson, despite Churchill's clear warnings, had not been learned at the time of the Russian Civil War.

Nor, would it appear, were the lessons taught the Allies by intervention in Russia particularly noted. The Communists, on the other hand, took them to heart. They saw the results, and reaped the benefits, of divided counsels in Siberia, and have continued to foster dissensions between the partners of the West. They noticed how a weak military intervention enabled them to survive; their own interventions therefore, when deemed necessary, would be strong as was seen in Hungary in 1956. Contrast this with American action at the Bay of Pigs carried out so ineffectually that, far from crushing Castro in Cuba, it served only to drive him further along the road to Communism and even gave the Soviets a foothold for a time in the American hemisphere.

And yet Allied intervention in Russia, despite the fact that it was militarily unsuccessful and that its lessons were ignored, still cannot be written off as a complete loss. The presence of Allied troops in Russia, and the shipments of arms and supplies to the Whites, undoubtedly prolonged their struggle with the Communists. 'Had there been no intervention,' says Chamberlin, 'had Allied aid to the Whites stopped after the end of the War, the Russian civil war would almost certainly have ended much more quickly in a decisive victory of the Soviets. Then a triumphant revolutionary Russia would have faced a Europe that was fairly quivering with social unrest and upheaval.'* Bolshevism was like a stone cast into a pond, the disturbance spreading out in every direction, and when it is remembered that even on this side of the Atlantic it inspired the Winnipeg Strike of 1919 where seventy officers and more than a thousand troops were on call daily to suppress rioting, some effect of its impact nearer home can be judged. The Communists, who looked upon themselves as missionaries of a new world order, regarded their revolution as international in character, a commodity for export. But White resistance, sustained through outside help, kept the Soviets preoccupied; with a civil war on their hands, the Bolsheviks could not reap the harvest sowed by their agitation in other countries. 'It was lack of strength, not lack of will, that prevented them from supporting Bela Kun in Hungary and apostles of social revolution in other countries as energetically as Great Britain supported Kolchak and Denikin.'* And, as Churchill says, 'The Bolsheviks were absorbed during the whole of 1919. . . . Their energy was turned on the internal struggle. . . . Finland, Estonia, Latvia, Lithuania, and above all Poland, were able during 1919 to establish the structure of civilised States and to organise the strength of patriotic armies.'† So, although intervention did not bring about the destruction of the Soviet government, it helped confine the Soviet system within Russia's borders for some twenty years.

* Chamberlin, *The Russian Revolution*, II, 171.
† Churchill, *Aftermath*, 288.

The aim of Communism, it must be reiterated, has never wavered. As early as 1914 Trotsky had said : 'The time for fireside politics is over. We are now in the phase of permanent revolution. It will go on, without interruption, until one side or the other is lying on the ground.' And in 1959 Krushchev showed quite clearly that the same steadfast aim of world domination remained the guiding principle of Soviet policy : 'Communism will sooner or later rule the world. We live in the epoch of revolution.'

Here, then, is the secret of Communist strength. Communists know what they are fighting for and will stop at nothing to achieve it. They were willing to make peace with the Germans at Brest-Litovsk; they were quite prepared to plunge Russia into civil war; and later, with the Ribbentrop–Molotov Pact, they guaranteed Germany's eastern front in the full knowledge that this would enable Hitler to turn Europe into a battleground. As a reward for that, Soviet Russia gained the Baltic States, half of Poland, and part of Finland. These acts are to be judged by one standard and one motive only—did they help forward Communism at home, world revolution, and world domination? Lenin knew no other test for conduct. And *Radio Moscow*, thirty years later, voiced the same approach : 'From the view of Communist morality, only those acts are moral which contribute to the building up of a new Communist society.'

But during the period under review the aim and methods of Communism were insufficiently understood. Indeed, it was not until after the Second World War that American eyes were opened; and when they were, the determination to check the spread of Communism (demonstrated by the Marshall Plan, and resistance in South Korea) at last began to offer an effective barrier to Communist expansion.

REFERENCES

CHAPTER II

The abbreviation B.O.H. stands for the British Official History of the First World War; C.D.Q., the *Canadian Defence Quarterly*; N.R.E.F. denotes the Canadian North Russian Expeditionary Force, but where italicized it stands for the published War Diary of the 16th Brigade, Canadian Field Artillery; O.M.F.C. denotes the Overseas Military Forces of Canada unless italicized when it stands for the *Report of the Ministry, Overseas Military Forces of Canada*; P.A.C. indicates the Public Archives of Canada, and P.A.R.C. is for the Public Archives Records Centre, Ottawa.

1. R. W. Sellen, 'The British Intervention in Russia, 1917–1920', *The Dalhousie Review*, Fall, 1960.

2. Borden Papers, O.C. 515 (1), 55090–55097, Public Archives of Canada [P.A.C.].

3. British Official History [B.O.H.], *Operations in Persia 1914–1919*, 255–6.

4. B.O.H., *The Campaign in Mesopotamia 1914–1918*, Vol. 4, 105–6.

5. *Ibid.*, 102–3.

6. *Ibid.*, 104–5; *Report of the Ministry, Overseas Military Forces of Canada* [*O.M.F.C.*], *1918*, 20.

7. Borden Papers, 'Memoir Notes', V, 1917–1918, Kemp to Borden, Feb. 24, 1918.

8. File G.A.Q. 10-28. 'The Dunsterforce', Public Archives Records Centre [P.A.R.C.], Ottawa.

9. *Ibid.*.

10. *Ibid.*

11. B.O.H., *The Campaign in Mesopotamia*, Vol. 4, 106–7, 116, 119; Maj.-Gen. L. C. Dunsterville, *The Adventures of Dunsterforce* (London, 1920), 53–8, 103–4, 112.

12. John Buchan, *A History of The Great War* (London, 1922), Vol. 4, 298–9; George Stewart, *The White Armies of Russia* (New York, 1933), 73–4; W. H. Chamberlin, *The Russian Revolution* (New York, 1952), Vol. II, 406–11.

13. Captain W. W. Murray, 'Canadians in Dunsterforce', *Canadian Defence Quarterly* [C.D.Q.], January 1931, 215–16.

14. File G.A.Q. 10-28, 'The Dunsterforce', P.A.R.C.

15. 'Canadians in Dunsterforce', C.D.Q., April 1931, 380–1.

16. *Ibid.*, 385; B.O.H., *The Campaign in Mesopotamia*, Vol. 4, 183.

17. *The Campaign in Mesopotamia*, Vol. 4, 202–3; Dunsterville, 157–64, 186, 203, 207–8.

18. *Operations in Persia*, 332–3.

19. Lieut. H. Kingsley, R.C.N., 'The Baku Episode', C.D.Q., 1929–30, Vol. VII, 37.

20. B.O.H., *The Campaign in Mesopotamia*, Vol. 4, 204, 212, 215.

21. *Ibid.*, 215.

22. *Ibid.*, 223–4, 225–9, 232; Murray, C.D.Q., January 1932, 235.

23. *The Campaign in Mesopotamia*, Vol. 4, 238; Murray, C.D.Q., July 1931, 489–90, January 1932, 238.

24. *The Campaign in Mesopotamia*, Vol. 4, 242–8.

25. Dunsterville, 316–17.

26. *The Campaign in Mesopotamia*, Vol. 4, 249.

27. File G.A.Q. 10-28, 'The Dunsterforce', P.A.R.C.

28. *The Campaign in Mesopotamia*, Vol. 4, 208, 248, 323, 330.

29. *Ibid.*, 171–2, 174, 178–9, 186, 207; Murray, C.D.Q., January 1931, 210.

30. Edmund Ironside, *Archangel 1918–1919* (London, 1953), 17.

31. Maj.-Gen. Sir C. Maynard, *The Murmansk Venture* (London, 1927), 3.

32. Leonid I. Strakhovsky, *Intervention at Archangel* (Princeton, 1944), 2.

33. *Ibid.*, 2–3.

34. O.M.F.C. (G.S.) file A-77-33, 'Proceedings of Conference', n.d., P.A.R.C.

35. *Ibid.*, Minute initialled 'A.E.K.' from Brig.-Gen. H. F. McDonald to G.O.C., May 24, 1918; McDonald to C.G.S., O.M.F.C., May 31, 1918.

36. O.M.F.C. (G.S.) file 0-10-36, Vol. I, C.G.S., O.M.F.C., to Kemp, Feb. 24, 1919, P.A.R.C.

37. O.M.F.C. (G.S.) file A-77-33, Assistant Secretary, War Office, to Secretary O.M.F.C., July 12, 1918, and reply July 20, 1918, P.A.R.C.; Borden Papers, O.C. 518 (1), Kemp to Borden, Aug. 1, 1918, P.A.C.

38. O.M.F.C. (G.S.) file 0-10-36; War Office to O.M.F.C., July 30, 1918, P.A.R.C.; C.G.S., O.M.F.C., to Kemp, Feb. 24, 1919; Borden Papers, O.C. 518 (1), Borden to Kemp, Aug. 2, 1918, P.A.C.

39. O.M.F.C. (G.S.) file 0-10-36; War Office to O.M.F.C., Aug. 3, 1918; C.G.S., O.M.F.C., to Kemp, Feb. 24, 1919; *O.M.F.C.*, 21–2; P.A.R.C., 'Unofficial Diary, 16th Brigade C.F.A.', Sep. 21, 1918; Ironside, 26.

40. D.H.S. Folder 15, War Office to C.G.S., Ottawa, Dec. 9, 1918, P.A.R.C.

41. *War Memoirs of David Lloyd George*, Vol. VI (London, 1936), 156–7.

42. George F. Kennan, *Soviet-American Relations, 1917–1920*, Vol. II, 123–35.

43. [U.S.] *Foreign Relations, 1918, Russia*, Vol. I, 179–80, 473.

44. Maynard, 25–7.

45. A. W. Abbott, 'Lapland 1918–19. The British Army's Farthest North', *The Army Quarterly*, July 1962.

46. Captain J. E. Nesbitt, 'The Syren Party', P.A.R.C. file G.A.Q. 10-28.

47. John Hundevad, 'A Saga of the North', *The Legionary*, March 1937, 4 [Map].

48. Maynard, 23.

49. H.S. file 37-8-1B, folder 6, 'Report, Canadian SYREN Party', Dec. 13, 1918, P.A.R.C.

50. Maynard, 27.

51. *Ibid.*, 28.

52. *Ibid.*, 28–9.

53. *Ibid.*, 30–1.

54. *Ibid.*, 31.

55. *Ibid.*, 31–3, 55.

56. *Ibid.*, 39–51; File H.S. 37-8-1B, folder 6; 'N.R.E.F., General Staff, G.H.Q., SYREN' [Diary], June 1918.

57. Maynard, 51–3, 'N.R.E.F., SYREN' [Diary], June and July 1918.

58. Maynard, 52–3, 'N.R.E.F.' [Diary], June 29, 1918.

59. Maynard, 57, 'N.R.E.F.' [Diary], July 3 and 4, 1918.

60. Maynard, 58–63, 'N.R.E.F.' [Diary], July 4–14, 1918.

61. Maynard, 64.

62. *Ibid.*, 65.

63. *Ibid.*

64. 'N.R.E.F.' [Diary], July 22, 1918.

65. Abbott, 'Lapland 1918–19'.

66. *Ibid.*

67. Maynard, 67–8.

68. 'N.R.E.F.' [Diary], July 30, 1918.

69. Maynard, 88–90.

70. *Ibid.*, 89.

71. *Ibid.*, 90–1.

72. *Ibid.*, 94–6.

73. *Ibid.*, 96–7.

74. *Ibid.*, 98–9.

75. *Ibid.*, 101, 104–6.

76. Abbott.

77. Maynard, 110–12.

78. Captain E. Altham [Commanding H.M.S. *Attentive*], 'The Dvina Campaign', C.D.Q., 1923–4, Vol. I, 20.

79. *Ibid.*, 21–2.

80. Strakhovsky, 27–8.

81. Ironside, 37–8.

82. *Ibid.*, 38–47, 57, 68, 70–1; Strakhovsky, 132; Winston S. Churchill, *The Aftermath* (New York, 1929), 88.

83. Lt.-Col. H. F. Wood, 'The Farthest North Campaign', *The Legionary*, September 1962.

84. Ironside, 27–8, 31, 118; *N.R.E.F., 16th Brigade C.F.A.* (Toronto, n.d., a summary of 16th Brigade diaries), 6.

85. 'A Detailed Military Argument with regard to Allied Intervention in Siberia', War Office, June 19, 1918, P.A.R.C., A-88, file 2, folder 17.

86. E. M. Halliday, *The Ignorant Armies* (London, 1961), 13, 22, 28, 30, 36, 61.

87. *Ibid.*, 49, 53.

88. *Ibid.*, 56.

89. *Ibid.*, 56–61.

90. *Ibid.*, 60, 125.

91. Altham, 23–8.

92. Ironside, 29, 35–6.

93. *N.R.E.F.*, 49–50.

94. *Ibid.*, 6–8, 30.

95. *Ibid.*, 17.

96. *Ibid.*

97. *Ibid.*, 17, 19; Leonid I. Strakhovsky, 'The Canadian Artillery Brigade in North Russia, 1918–1919', *The Canadian Historical Review*, Vol. XXXIX, No. 2, June 1958, 135–6; War Diary, 16th Bde. C.F.A., Dec. 2, 1918; Halliday, 1–5.

98. Halliday, 30–1; Abbott, 237.

99. Halliday, 7–10.

100. *Ibid.*, 10–11.

CHAPTER III

1. George Stewart, *The White Armies of Russia*, 64.

2. W. H. Chamberlin, *The Russia Revolution*, Vol. II, 135.

3. *Ibid.*, 136.

4. *Ibid.*, 139.

5. *Ibid.*, 140–1.

6. *Ibid.*, 141–2.

7. *Ibid.*, 142–4.

8. *Ibid.*, 144–5.

9. Stewart, 68.

10. Chamberlin, II, 145–6.

11. Thomas Dadson, 'The Czechoslovak Armies in Russia', P.A.R.C., file EE 112, folder 5.

12. *Ibid.*

13. *Ibid.*

14. Winston S. Churchill, *The Aftermath*, 84.

15. Dadson, 'The Czechoslovak Armies'.

16. Churchill, 84.

17. Dadson.

18. *Ibid.*

19. *Ibid.*

20. General Ludendorff, *My War Memories* 1914–1918 (London, n.d.), II, 654.

21. Dadson.

22. *Ibid.*

23. Chamberlin, II, 5–6.

24. Dadson.

25. Chamberlin, II, 6–7.

26. Dadson; see also Chamberlin, II, 7.

27. Dadson.

28. *Ibid.*

29. Chamberlin, II, 7–8.

30. *Ibid.*, 8.

31. Churchill, 87.

32. Chamberlin, II, 10.
33. *Ibid.*
34. Dadson.
35. *Ibid.*
36. *Ibid.*
37. *Ibid.*; Chamberlin, II, 10.
38. Churchill, 87.
39. Chamberlin, II, 12–14.
40. Report by British Consul, Ekaterinburg, contained in telegram, Alston to Balfour, Sep. 16, 1918, *Collection of Reports on Bolshevism in Russia*, H.M. Stationery Office, April 1919.
41. Chamberlin, II, 15–16.
42. *Ibid.*, 20.
43. *Ibid.*
44. *Ibid.*, 21.
45. *Ibid.*, 176, 182.
46. *Ibid.*, 42.
47. *Ibid.*, 45.
48. *Ibid.*, 57–60.
49. *Ibid.*, 64.
50. *Ibid.*, 25–6.
51. *Ibid.*, 27–9.
52. John Erickson, *The Soviet High Command* (London, 1962), 41.
53. Chamberlin, II, 34–5.
54. *Ibid.*, II, 38.
55. Trotsky, cited Chamberlin, *The Russian Revolution*, II, 118.
56. Chamberlin, II, 118–19.
57. *Ibid.*, 119.
58. *Ibid.*, 120–1.

CHAPTER IV

1. Arnold J. Toynbee, *Survey of International Affairs, 1920–1923* (London, 1927), 433.
2. Clarence A. Manning, *The Siberian Fiasco* (New York, 1952), 18–19.
3. *Ibid.*, 20–1.
4. Prince A. Lobanov-Rostovsky, *Russia and Asia* (New York, 1933), 219–20.
5. John Albert White, *The Siberian Intervention* (Princeton, 1950), 49.
6. Toynbee, 433.
7. John H. Snodgrass, *Russia, A Handbook on Commercial and Industrial Conditions* (Washington, Department of Commerce, Special Consular Report No. 61, 1913), 215.
8. Manning, 23.
9. David J. Dallin, *The Rise of Russia in Asia* (New Haven, 1949), 158.
10. George F. Kennan, *Soviet-American Relations 1917–1920* (Princeton, 1956), I, 299–300; Lloyd George, *War Memoirs* VI, 161–2; [U.S.] *Foreign Relations, 1918, Russia*, II, 35–6, 49.

11. 'A Detailed Military Argument With Regard to Allied Intervention in Siberia', War Office, June 19, 1918, P.A.R.C., Siberian Records, A-88, file 2, folder 17.

12. *Ibid.*

13. *Ibid.*

14. *Ibid.*

15. *Ibid.*

16. *Ibid.*

17. *Ibid.*

18. 'Allied Intervention in Siberia and Russia', Supreme War Council Appreciation, July 2, 1918, contained in 'Reports and Information Military and Political', Siberian Records, P.A.R.C.

19. *Ibid.*

20. *Ibid.*

21. *Ibid.*

22. Dallin, 161.

23. H. F. MacNair and D. F. Lach, *Modern Far Eastern International Relations* (New York, 1950), 149, 151, 154.

24. *Ibid.*, 150.

25. *Ibid.*, 175.

26. *Ibid.*, 176.

27. [U.S.] *Foreign Relations, 1917*, 264–5.

28. Dallin, 162.

29. R. Lansing, *War Memoirs of Robert Lansing, Secretary of State* (New York, 1935), 306.

30. Manning, 31.

31. MacNair and Lach, 206.

32. Manning, 68.

33. Dallin, 157.

34. Macnair and Lach, 207; Dallin, 162; Manning, 72.

35. R. S. Baker, *Woodrow Wilson, Life and Letters* (New York, 1937), VI, 513.

36. *Russian-American Relations, March 1917–March 1920* (New York, 1920), 98.

37. Manning, 54.

38. *Russian-American Relations, March 1917–March 1920*, 219f.

39. *The Lansing Papers*, II, 343.

40. Charles F. Horne, *Source Records of the Great War*, V (U.S.A., 1923), 355–7.

41. Manning, 63.

42. White, 84–6.

43. *Russian-American Relations*, 205.

44. White, 315.

45. *Ibid.*, 327–8.

46. Manning, 62.

47. White, 230.

48. Manning, 80.

49. Winston S. Churchill, *The Aftermath*, 88.

50. *Foreign Relations, 1918*, II, 292 [Acting Secretary of State Polk to Ambassador Morris in Tokyo].

51. *Ibid.*, 301–2.

52. *Ibid.*, 306–7.

53. Horne, VI, 239.

54. Manning, 87.

55. *Ibid.*, 89–90.

56. William S. Graves, *America's Siberian Adventure* (New York, 1931), 55.

57. Dallin, 158.

58. MacNair and Lach, 209.

59. *Ibid.*, f. 119.

60. Director Military Operations, War Office, to the President of the Privy Council [Newton W. Rowell], July 9, 1918, Borden Papers, O.C. 518 (1), P.A.C.

61. Borden to Mewburn, Aug. 13, 1918, *ibid*.

62. Mewburn to C.G.S., July 12, 1918, *ibid.*; C.I.G.S. to Elmsley, Sep. 10, 1918, P.A.R.C.; 'Siberian E.F. 1919', Siberian Records.

63. Borden to White, July 25, 1918, Borden Papers, O.C. 518 (1); P.A.C.

64. Establishments, C.E.F. (Siberia), Siberian Records, D.A.A.G. 3 file.

65. *Ibid.*, 'Organization Rolls, C.E.F. Siberia', C.G.S. to G.O.C. Military District No. 11, Nov. 28, 1918; G.O.C. Military District No. 11 to Secretary Militia Council, Ottawa, Oct. 11, 1918; Minister of Militia to Prime Minister. Aug. 13, 1918, Borden Papers, O.C. 518 (1).

66. *Canadian Defence Quarterly*, Vol. VI, 419–20.

67. C.I.G.S. to Elmsley, Sep. 10, 1918; 'Siberian E.F. 1919', Siberian Records.

68. War Office to Mewburn, n.d., *ibid*.

69. War Diary, Force H.Q., C.E.F. (Siberia), Nov. 3, 1918.

70. *Ibid.*, Nov. 5, 8, 20, 1918.

71. *Ibid.*, Oct. 29, 31, 1918.

72. French Military Mission, Report No. 10, Sep. 27, 1918, Siberian Records, 'Reports and Information Military and Political', P.A.R.C.

73. *Ibid*.

74. *Ibid*.

75. *Ibid*.

76. *Ibid*.

77. *Ibid*.

78. *Ibid*.

79. *Ibid*.

80. *Ibid*.

81. *Ibid*.

82. 'General Summary of the Military Situation in Siberia', Oct. 31, 1918, Siberian Records; White, *Siberian Intervention*, 259.

83. Macnair and Lach, 211.

84. Colonel Robertson [acting as British Military Representative until the arrival of General Knox] to War Office, Aug. 19, 1918, P.A.R.C., Siberian Records.

85. Robertson to War Office, Aug. 14, 1918, *ibid*.

86. George Stewart, *The White Armies of Russia*, 140.

87. *Ibid.*, 140, 143.

88. White, 127.

89. *Ibid.*, 128–30, 155.

90. *Ibid.*, 134, 145, 147–8.

91. *Ibid.*, 154–60.

92. Manning, 95–7; MacNair and Lach, 207.

93. Robertson to War Office, Aug. 19, 1918, 'Movements and Composition of Forces', Siberian Records, Folder 17, file 3.

94. Stewart, 139.

95. *Ibid.*, 140–1.

96. White, 194–5.

97. *Ibid.*, 207.

98. Manning, 99.

99. White, 320–1.

100. *Ibid.*, 195–7, 266, 280; Stewart, 141–2.

101. White, 118.

102. *Ibid.*, 198–9; Stewart, 140–1.

103. White, 199–206.

104. *Ibid.*, 298.

105. *Ibid.*, 306.

106. *Ibid.*, 301; John Ward, *With the 'Die-Hards' in Siberia* (London, 1920), 66–7.

107. White, 302.

108. *Ibid.*, 297.

109. *Ibid.*, 109–10.

110. Stewart, 148–51.

111. Churchill, 181.

112. Knox to Elmsley, Nov. 6, 1918, Siberian Records.

113. White, 111.

114. 'General Summary of the Military Situation as on October 31st, 1918', Siberian Records, P.A.R.C.

115. 'Notes on the Railway Situation in Siberia as on October 31st, 1918', *ibid.*

116. Knox to Elmsley, 'Notes on the Present Military Situation in Siberia' Nov. 27, 1918, *ibid.*

CHAPTER V

1. War Diary, Force H.Q., C.E.F. (Siberia), Nov. 15, 16, 18, 1918, P.A.R.C.

2. Memorandum, Nov. 29, 1918, transmitted by Foreign Office to High Commissioner, Siberia, Dec. 7, 1918, P.A.R.C., Siberian Records.

3. Foreign Office to High Commissioner, Siberia, Nov. 30, 1918, *ibid.*

4. War Office to Elmsley, Dec. 18, 1918, *ibid.*

5. Winston S. Churchill, *The Aftermath*, 167.

6. John Albert White, *The Siberian Intervention*, 334.

7. Churchill, 168.

8. White, 323–4.

9. Foreign Office to High Commissioner, Siberia, Dec. 20, 1918, Siberian Records.

10. *Ibid.*

11. *Ibid.*

12. White, 166–7.

13. *Ibid.*

14. *Ibid.*, 170.

15. *Ibid.*, 173–4.

16. Elmsley to War Office, Feb. 6, 1919, P.A.R.C., Siberian Records.

17. White, 209, 383.

18. *Ibid.*, 209–10.

19. Labour Hall, Morricetown, B.C., to Department of Justice, Jan. 8. 1919, Siberian Records.

20. *Toronto Globe*, Dec. 28, 1918.

21. *Ibid.*

22. *Ibid.*, Dec. 31, 1918.

23. *Manitoba Free Press*, Dec. 6, 1918.

24. *Debates, House of Commons*, Mar. 10, 1919.

25. *Ibid.*, Feb. 25, 1919.

26. White to Kemp, Nov. 14, 1918, Borden Papers, O.C. 518 (1), P.A.C.

27. Borden to White, Nov. 20, 1918, *ibid.*

28. British General Staff Appreciation, Nov. 22, 1918, *ibid.*

29. Borden to White, Nov. 20, 1918, *ibid.*

30. War Office to Knox, Nov. 23, 1918, P.A.R.C., Siberian Records.

31. *Ibid.*

32. White to Borden, Nov. 22, 1918, Borden Papers, O.C. 518 (1).

33. Paraphrase of telegram, n.d., C.G.S. to War Office, *ibid.*

34. Borden to White, Nov. 22, 1918, *ibid.*

35. Borden to White, Nov. 24, 1918, *ibid.*

36. Borden to White, Nov. 27, 1918, *ibid.*

37. White to Borden, Nov. 29, 1918, *ibid.*

38. White, 115–16.

39. Knox to Elmsley, Nov. 27, 1918, P.A.R.C., Siberian Records.

40. George Stewart, *White Armies of Russia*, 241.

41. *Ibid.*

42. White, 114, 118.

43. *Ibid.*, 113–14, 117.

44. Stewart, 117, 124.

45. Elmsley to C.G.S., Nov. 12, 1918, Siberian Records.

46. British Consul, Ekaterinburg, to High Commissioner, Nov. 22, 1918, *ibid.*

47. Stewart, 246.

48. Knox to High Commissioner, Jan. 14, 1919, Siberian Records.

49. Elmsley to War Office, Nov. 28, 1918, *ibid.*

50. Knox to High Commissioner, Jan. 14, 1919, *ibid.*

51. Stewart, 254.

52. Knox to War Office, Nov. 24, 1918, Siberian Records.

53. Stewart, 253.

54. *Ibid.*, 254.
55. British Consul, Ekaterinburg, to High Commissioner, Jan. 3, 1919 [Report submitted after his visit to Perm], Siberian Records.
56. *Ibid.*
57. Chamberlin, *The Russian Revolution*, II, 188–9.
58. Stewart, 255.
59. Jack to Knox, Jan. 6, 1919, Siberian Records.
60. High Commissioner to Foreign Office, Feb. 5, 1919, *ibid.*
61. British Representative, Irkutsk, to High Commissioner, Dec. 18, 1918, *ibid.*
62. High Commissioner to Foreign Office, Feb. 5, 1919, *ibid.*
63. White, 137–8.
64. Clarence A. Manning, *Siberian Fiasco*, 111.
65. *Ibid.*
66. *Ibid.*, 154.
67. Stewart, 292.
68. War Office to Knox, Nov. 13, 1918, Siberian Records.
69. Elmsley to Department of Militia and Defence, Nov. 25, 1918, *ibid.*
70. Knox to High Commissioner, Jan. 14, 1919, *ibid.*
71. Report by Knox, Jan. 10, 1919, *ibid.*
72. Chamberlin, II, 187.
73. Knox to High Commissioner, Jan. 14, 1919, Siberian Records; High Commissioner [Omsk] to Acting High Commissioner [Vladivostok], Jan. 15, 1919, *ibid.*
74. British Military Mission, Siberia, to War Office [copy to Knox], Jan. 30, 1919, P.A.R.C., *ibid.*
75. Stewart, 274.
76. War Office to British Military Mission, Jan. 15, 1919; High Commissioner to Acting High Commissioner, Feb. 1, 1919. (Both in folder 17, file 2, of P.A.R.C., Siberian Records.)
77. Churchill, 165; White, 221.
78. High Commissioner to Acting High Commissioner, Feb. 1, 1919, Siberian Records.
79. *Ibid.*
80. High Commissioner to Acting High Commissioner, Feb. 3, 1919, *ibid.*
81. 'Agreement for Operating Siberian Railways', n.d. (initialled by Elmsley Jan. 19, 1919), *ibid.*
82. White, 149.
83. Manning, 117–18.
84. *Ibid.*, 118–19; White, 150–1.
85. White, 151.
86. William S. Graves, *America's Siberian Adventure*, 186.
87. Manning, 120.
88. White, 271–2.
89. *Ibid.*, 232.
90. Capt. W. E. Playfair [Canadian Press Correspondent], Report of Interview with Admiral Kolchak, April 27, 1919, Siberian Records, file 49.
91. Elmsley Papers, Siberian Records, folder 18.

92. Manning, 122.

93. *Ibid.*, 120.

94. Elmsley Papers, folder 18.

95. *Ibid.*

96. Knox to Elmsley, Dec. 26, 1918, Siberian Records.

97. Elmsley to War Office, Feb. 6, 1919, *ibid.*

98. Playfair, Interview with Kolchak, April 27, 1919.

99. Czech Intelligence Report, Feb. 20, 1919 (forwarded by Major Broz to Elmsley April 2, 1919, Siberian Records.

100. War Office to Knox, Nov. 26, 1918, *ibid.*

101. Elmsley to War Office, Nov. 28, 1918, *ibid.*

102. Elmsley to Lash, Nov. 4, 1918, *ibid.*

103. Elmsley to War Office, Nov. 2, 1918, *ibid.*

104. 'Instructions to Lieut.-Col. T. S. Morrisey', Dec. 7, 1918, *ibid.*

105. White to Borden, Dec. 6, 1918, Borden Papers, O.C. 518 (1), P.A.C.

106. Rowell to Borden, Aug. 9, 1918, *ibid.*

107. White to Borden, Dec. 6, 1918, *ibid.*

108. Borden to White, Dec. 9, 1918, *ibid.*

109. Robert Laird Borden, *His Memoirs*, II (Toronto, 1938), 875.

110. White to Mewburn, Dec. 10, 1918, Borden Papers, O.C. 518 (1).

111. C.G.S. to War Office, Dec. 23, 1918, Borden Papers, O.C. 518 (2).

112. War Office to C.G.S., Jan. 4, 1919, *ibid.*

113. C.G.S. to War Office, Jan. 10, 1919, *ibid.*

114. *Ibid.*

115. C.G.S. to War Office, Jan. 5, 1919, *ibid.*

116. High Commissioner to Foreign Office, Jan. 9, 1919, Siberian Records, P.A.R.C.

117. Elmsley to War Office, Jan. 8, 1919, *ibid.*

118. Lash to Elmsley, Jan. 13, 1919, *ibid.*

119. Morrisey to Elmsley, Feb. 14, 1919, *ibid.*

120. Elmsley to Acting High Commissioner, Nov. 4, 1918, *ibid.*

121. Knox to Elmsley, Dec. 27, 1918, *ibid.*

122. Reports by Capt. Playfair, Siberian Records, H.Q., C.E.F. (Siberia), file 49, P.A.R.C.

123. George F. Clingan, 'Account of the Canadian Expeditionary Force, Siberia', G.A.Q. file 10-29, P.A.R.C.

124. *Ibid.*

125. *Ibid.*

126. War Diary, 16th Infantry Brigade, Jan. 15, 1919, P.A.R.C.

127. *Ibid.,* Jan. 18, Feb. 4, 5, 7, 11, 21, 1919.

128. *Ibid.*, March and April 1919.

129. 'Notes on the Canadian Expeditionary Force, Siberia', G.A.Q. file 10-29; War Diary, 16th Infantry Brigade, April 1919, 'B' Company diary, appended. (Both at P.A.R.C.)

130. Siberian Records, Folder 17, file 2.

131. Debates, *House of Commons*, Mar. 11, 1919.

132. Elmsley to Department of Militia and Defence, Feb. 7, 1919, Siberian Records.

133. Minutes of Imperial War Cabinet, Dec. 30, 1918, Borden Papers, Box 333, P.A.C.

134. Leonid I. Strakhovsky, *Intervention at Archangel*, 139.

135. *Peace Conference Papers*, IV, 15-16.

136. Churchill, 171.

137. *Ibid.*, 170.

138. White, 332-3.

139. *Ibid.*, 333.

140. Churchill, 170.

141. Foreign Office to H.M. Embassy, Tokyo, Feb. 1, 1919, Siberian Records.

142. Borden, II, 904.

143. Chamberlin, II, 155-6.

144. White, 334-5.

145. Churchill, 175.

146. Chamberlin, II, 158.

147. Churchill, 172.

148. Chamberlin, II, 158.

149. *Debates, House of Commons*, Feb. 27, 1919.

150. High Commissioner to Foreign Office, Jan. 29, 1919, Siberian Records.

151. High Commissioner to Foreign Office, Feb. 3, 1919 (first message), *ibid*.

152. *Ibid*.

153. High Commissioner to Foreign Office, Feb. 3, 1919 (second message), *ibid*.

154. Borden to White, Jan. 28, 1919, Borden Papers, O.C. 518 (2), P.A.C.

155. Borden to Lloyd George, Feb. 7, 1919; Borden to White, Feb. 13, 1919. (Both *ibid*.)

156. Borden to White, Feb. 17, 1919, *ibid*.

157. Churchill to Borden, Mar. 17, 1919, *ibid*.

158. Stewart, 268.

159. *Ibid.*, 272.

160. Churchill, 182; Chamberlin, II, 189.

161. Stewart, 272-3.

162. Chamberlin, 191.

163. *Ibid.*, 189.

164. Stewart, 275.

165. Chamberlin, II, 190.

166. Churchill, 183-4.

167. *Ibid.*, 184-5.

168. *Ibid.*, 186.

169. Chamberlin, II, 262.

170. Churchill, 186.

171. Manning, 133.

172. Churchill, 244.

173. 'Canadian Expeditionary Force—Siberia', H.Q. file 4-18, P.A.R.C.

174. Churchill to Borden, May 1, 1919, Borden Papers, O.C. 518 (2), P.A.C.

175. Borden to White, Nov. 30, 1918; War Office to C.G.S., Dec. 9, 1918; both in Borden Papers, O.C. 518 (1).

176. C.G.S. to War Office, Dec. 11, 1918, *ibid*.

177. 'Applications for Transfer to British Military Mission', Siberian Records, P.A.R.C.
178. C.G.S. to War Office [repeated Elmsley], Mar. 24, 1919, Siberian Records.
179. Churchill, 256.

CHAPTER VI

1. 'A Detailed Military Argument with regard to Allied Intervention in Siberia', War Office, June 19, 1918, Siberian Records, Folder 17, file 2, P.A.R.C.
2. *Ibid.*
3. Maj.-Gen. Sir C. Maynard, *The Murmansk Venture*, 237–8.
4. *Ibid.*, 124, 143.
5. *Ibid.*, 143.
6. *Ibid.*
7. *Ibid.*, 143–6, 162–3.
8. 'The Syren Party', G.A.Q. file 10-28, P.A.R.C.
9. *Ibid.*; Maynard, 129.
10. 'The Syren Party.'
11. *Ibid.*
12. *Ibid.*; Maynard, 162; Letter, Lt.-Col. Leckie to Lt.-Gen. Sir R. E. W. Turner, Oct. 14, 1918, H.S. file 37-8-1B, folder 6, EE-112, P.A.R.C.
13. Maynard, 144–5.
14. John Hundevad, 'A Saga of the North', *The Legionary*, April 1936; Letter, Leckie to Turner, Dec. 13, 1918, H.S. File 37-8-1B, P.A.R.C.
15. Maynard, 164–5.
16. *Ibid.*, 165–6. Letter, Leckie to Turner, Mar. 10, 1919.
17. E. M. Halliday, *The Ignorant Armies* (London, 1961), 82–3.
18. *N.R.E.F., 16th Brigade C.F.A.* (Toronto, n.d.), 30.
19. Halliday, 82.
20. *N.R.E.F.*, 49.
21. Halliday, 83–4.
22. *Ibid.*, 84.
23. Edmund Ironside, *Archangel 1918–1919*, 107.
24. Halliday, 99–100.
25. Ironside, 90.
26. Halliday, 102–4.
27. *Ibid.*, 102–4.
28. *Ibid.*, 105–6; Ironside, 90–1.
29. *N.R.E.F.*, 49–50; Halliday, 120–1.
30. Halliday, 93.
31. Ironside, 73.
32. *Ibid.*, 72.
33. *Ibid.*, 73–4.
34. *N.R.E.F.*, 8.
35. *Ibid.*, 36; Ironside, 100–1; Halliday, 128–34.

36. Halliday, 134.
37. N.R.E.F., 38.
38. Ibid.; Halliday, 138.
39. Halliday, 138-9.
40. Ibid., 139; N.R.E.F., 38.
41. N.R.E.F., 38.
42. Ibid., 40; Halliday, 140-2.
43. Ibid.
44. N.R.E.F., 40.
45. Ibid.
46. Ibid., 42.
47. Halliday, 145.
48. Ironside, 102-3.
49. Ibid., 103.
50. Maynard, 168.
51. N.R.E.F., 42.
52. Maynard, 167-71; Report, Col. Leckie to Lt.-Gen. Turner, February 1919, H.S. file 37-8-1B, folder 6, P.A.R.C.
53. Maynard, 171; 'The Syren Party'.
54. Maynard, 172.
55. Hundevad, October 1936.
56. Maynard, 172.
57. Ibid., 172, 173-4.
58. Ibid., 173.
59. Ibid., 173-4; Hundevad, October 1936. Report, Leckie to Turner, February 1919.
60. Hundevad, ibid.; Maynard, 175.
61. Report, Col. Leckie to G.O.C. 237 Inf. Bde., Feb. 26, 1919, H.S. File 37-8-1B, folder 6, P.A.R.C.
62. Maynard, 174-8. Report, Leckie to Turner, February 1919.
63. Maynard, 179-83; War Diary [W.D.], N.R.E.F. [Murmansk], Mar. 11, 1919, P.A.R.C.
64. W.D., N.R.E.F., Mar. 7-9, 11, 24, 29-30, May 20, Aug. 29, Sep. 1, 1919; Maynard, 183-9, 206-13; Hundevad, March 1937.
65. N.R.E.F., 21.
66. Ibid.
67. Halliday, 161.
68. N.R.E.F., 21.
69. Ironside, 66, 86, 91.
70. Leonid I. Strakhovsky, Intervention at Archangel, 162-3; Letter, Col. Sharman to C.G.S.. Apr. 13, 1919, cited in 'Precis of Correspondence relative to North Russian Force' prepared for Sir Robert Borden, May 17, 1919, Borden Papers OC 518 (2), P.A.C.
71. Ironside, 114, 116.
72. Ibid., 66-7.
73. Ibid., 105.
74. Ibid., 86-7.
75. Strakhovsky, 132.

76. Ironside, 108.
77. *Ibid.*, 107, 114–15, 118.
78. Strakhovsky, 143, 152–64.
79. Maynard, 190–1.
80. 'The Syren Party.'
81. Maynard, 198–206, 214.
82. *Ibid.*, 216–17; Hundevad, December 1936.
83. Maynard, 217–18.
84. *Ibid.*, 219–22, 224; W.D., N.R.E.F. [Murmansk], Mar. 25, 1919, P.A.R.C.
85. 'The Syren Party'; Maynard, 227–8.
86. W.D., N.R.E.F. [Murmansk], May 15–21, 1919; Maynard, 228–30.
87. W.D., N.R.E.F. [Murmansk], June 4–8, 1919; Maynard, 230–5.
88. Maynard, 237–8.
89. *Ibid.*, 244.
90. *Ibid.*, 264, 266.
91. *Ibid.*, 261; W.D., N.R.E.F. [Murmansk], June 6, 1919.
92. Maynard, 251–8; W.D., N.R.E.F. [Murmansk], May 12, June 3, 10–11, 13, 20, 26 and 27, 1919.
93. Maynard, 258–9; W.D., N.R.E.F. [Murmansk], July 3, 9, 11–12, 1919.
94. Maynard, 259; W.D., N.R.E.F. [Murmansk], July 11, 1919.
95. Maynard, 256–7, 259; W.D., N.R.E.F. [Murmansk], May 1919, 'Instructions for the Reorganization of the Karelian Regiment', Appendix M.
96. Tel., Churchill to Borden, July 21, 1919, Borden Papers, OC 518 (2), P.A.C.
97. Tel., C.G.S. to Secretary of State for War [Churchill], July 22, 1919, *ibid.*
98. Maynard, 238, 264; W.D., N.R.E.F. [Murmansk], June 4 and 7, July 5, 8, and 11, 1919.
99. 'The Syren Party'; Maynard, 267–70.
100. Maynard, 271–2; W.D.. N.R.E.F. [Murmansk], June 3–4, 1919.
101. Maynard, 236–7; W.D., N.R.E.F. [Murmansk], June 11–13, 17, 20 and 28, 1919.
102. 'The Syren Party.'
103. Maynard, 276; W.D., N.R.E.F. [Murmansk]. July 6, 1919.
104. Maynard, 277–80.
105. *Ibid.*, 278, 284; W.D., N.R.E.F. [Murmansk], July 18, Aug. 3, 1919.
106. Maynard, 280–6; W.D., N.R.E.F. [Murmansk], June 18 and 30, July 1, 3, 5, 11 and 23, Aug. 3 and 5, Sep. 17, 1919.
107. Maynard, 272, 286.
108. *Ibid.*, 288–93, W.D., N.R.E.F. [Murmansk], July 22, 23 and 25, Aug. 3 and 8, Sep. 8 and 11, 1919.
109. *N.R.E.F.*, 43–4.
110. *Ibid.*, 44.
111. *Ibid.*
112. *Ibid.*; Ironside, 122.
113. *N.R.E.F.*, 10.
114. *Ibid.*, 44.
115. *Ibid.*, 46.

116. *Ibid.*
117. *Ibid.*, 23.
118. *Ibid.*; Ironside, 123.
119. *N.R.E.F.*, 23–5.
120. *Ibid.*, 12.
121. *Ibid.*, 25.
122. *Ibid.*, 27.
123. *Ibid.*
124. *Ibid.*
125. Letters. Borden to Churchill and Borden to Lloyd George, May 18, 1919, Borden Papers, OC 518 (2), P.A.C.
126. Ironside, 94, 127, 140–1, 147.
127. *Ibid.*, 152, 156, 158, 161, 164, 172.
128. *N.R.E.F.*, 12.
129. *Ibid.*
130. *Ibid.*, 12.
131. *Ibid.*, frontispiece.
132. Halliday, 169.
133. *Ibid.*, 170; Winston S. Churchill, *The Aftermath*, 174.
134. Churchill, 174.
135. [U.S.] *Foreign Relations, 1919*, 71–2.
136. Halliday, 136.
137. *Foreign Relations, 1919*, 619.
138. Halliday, 185; Ironside, 131.
139. *Ibid.*, 130.
140. Strakhovsky, 174.
141. *Ibid.*, 174–83.
142. Ironside, 132, 146.
143. *N.R.E.F.*, 48.
144. Ironside, 147.
145. Strakhovsky, 190–1.
146. Halliday, 200–1.
147. Ironside, 153.
148. *Ibid.*, 146.
149. *Ibid.*, 153.
150. *Ibid.*, 154–6.
151. *Ibid.*, 151.
152. Strakhovsky, 209–10.
153. *Ibid.*
154. *Ibid.*, 217–18; Ironside, 169.
155. Churchill, 251.
156. Ironside, 167.
157. *Ibid.*
158. *Ibid.*, 168; Strakhovsky, 218.
159. Churchill, 252–4.
160. Maynard, 294, 296; W.D., N.R.E.F. [Murmansk], Aug. 7–9, 17 and 27, 1919.
161. Maynard, 296–8.

162. *Ibid.*, 299–302; W.D., N.R.E.F. [Murmansk], Aug. 31, 1919.
163. Maynard, 302–9; W.D., N.R.E.F. [Murmansk], Sep. 14–18, 1919.
164. Maynard, 310.
165. *N.R.E.F.*, 30.
166. Halliday, 62–3.
167. Ironside, 123, 132.
168. Maynard, 258.
169. Halliday, 20, 165.

CHAPTER VII

1. W. H. Chamberlin, *The Russian Revolution*, II, 190.
2. *Ibid.*
3. George Stewart, *The White Armies of Russia*, 277.
4. Chamberlin, II, 191.
5. *Ibid.*
6. Stewart, 281–3.
7. Chamberlin. II, 191–2.
8. Stewart, 283.
9. Chamberlin, II, 192.
10. *Ibid.*; Stewart, 284.
11. Stewart, 288–9; Clarence A. Manning, *Siberian Fiasco*, 132.
12. Chamberlin, 192.
13. *Ibid.*, 192–4.
14. Stewart, 284.
15. Manning, 131.
16. *Ibid.*, 131–2.
17. *Ibid.*
18. Winston S. Churchill, *The Aftermath*, 241.
19. Manning, 134–5.
20. Chamberlin, II, 199.
21. *Ibid.*; Manning, 137.
22. Stewart, 294.
23. Chamberlin, II, 200; John Albert White, *The Siberian Intervention*, 343.
24. Manning, 138–9; Chamberlin, II, 201.
25. Chamberlin, II, 201; Churchill, 257; *Siberian Fiasco*, 139.
26. White, 346–7.
27. Churchill, 257.
28. Chamberlin, II, 202.
29. Churchill, 266.
30. *Ibid.*
31. *Ibid.*, 255–6; Stewart, 319.
32. Stewart, 318–19.
33. *Ibid.*, 312; Manning, 157.
34. Stewart, 311.
35. White, 347.
36. Chamberlin, II, 202.

37. *Ibid.*, 203.
38. Peter Fleming, *The Fate of Admiral Kolchak* (London, 1936), 216–17.
39. White, 347.
40. Stewart, 321.
41. *Ibid.*, 320.
42. Churchill, 181.
43. *Ibid.*
44. *Ibid.*; Chamberlin, II, 203.
45. Churchill, 268–9.
46. *Ibid.*, 179.
47. *Ibid.*, 180.
48. *Ibid.*, 270.
49. H. F. McNair and D. F. Lach, *Modern Far Eastern International Relations*, 210.
50. William S. Graves, *America's Siberian Adventure*, 302.
51. Manning, 171.
52. *Ibid.*, 170.
53. *Ibid.*
54. White, 352.
55. *Ibid.*, 357; McNair and Lach, 215.
56. White, 358.
57. *Ibid.*, 351.
58. Letter from Secretary, Immigration and Colonization to Prime Minister's Office, June 4, 1920, Borden Papers, O.C. 518 (2), P.A.C.
59. White, 352.
60. Arnold J. Toynbee, *Survey of International Affairs, 1920–1923*, 439.
61. David J. Dallin, *The Rise of Russia in Asia*, 164.
62. *Ibid.*
63. Dallin, 169; White. 371.
64. Dallin, 163–4.
65. Churchill, 165, 168.
66. Lieut. H. Kingsley, R.C.N., 'The Baku Episode', *Canadian Defence Quarterly*, Vol. VII, 36–44.
67. Churchill, 165–8.
68. Chamberlin, II, 128.
69. *Ibid.*, 165.
70. *Ibid.*, 165, 213.
71. British Official History, *France and Belgium, 1917*, II, 28–9.
72. Chamberlin, II, 166, 214.
73. *Ibid.*, 167.
74. *Ibid.*
75. *Ibid.*, 214.
76. *Ibid.*, 209.
77. *Ibid.*, 209–10.
78. *Ibid.*, 210–11.
79. *Ibid.*, 244.
80. *Ibid.*, 244–5.
81. *Ibid.*, 246–7.

82. *Ibid.*
83. Churchill, 260.
84. *Ibid.*
85. General Sir Hubert Gough, *Soldiering On*, 190–1.
86. J. A. Swettenham, *The Tragedy of the Baltic States* (London, 1952), 24–5, 43.
87. Chamberlin, II, 275–6.
88. Denikin, cited Stewart, 346.
89. Denikin, cited Chamberlin, II, 289.
90. Stewart, 356.
91. Chamberlin, II, 322.
92. Churchill, 271.

INDEX